Two Paths
to Women's Equality

*Temperance, Suffrage,
and the Origins of Modern Feminism*

SOCIAL MOVEMENTS PAST AND PRESENT

Irwin T. Sanders, Editor

Abolitionism: A Revolutionary Movement
by Herbert Aptheker

The American Communist Movement: Storming Heaven Itself
by Harvey Klehr and John Earl Haynes

The American Peace Movement: Ideals and Activism
by Charles Chatfield

American Temperance Movements: Cycles of Reform
by Jack S. Blocker, Jr.

The Animal Rights Movement in America: From Compassion to Respect
by Lawrence Finsen and Susan Finsen

The Anti-Abortion Movement and the Rise of the Religious Right: From Polite to Fiery Protest
by Dallas A. Blanchard

The Antinuclear Movement, Updated Edition
by Jerome Price

The Charismatic Movement: Is There a New Pentecost?
by Margaret Poloma

The Children's Rights Movement: A History of Advocacy and Protection
by Joseph M. Hawes

Civil Rights: The 1960s Freedom Struggle
by Rhoda Lois Blumberg

The Conservative Movement, Revised Edition
by Paul Gottfried

The Consumer Movement: Guardians of the Marketplace
by Robert N. Mayer

Controversy and Coalition: The New Feminist Movement
by Myra Marx Ferree and Beth B. Hess

The Creationist Movement in Modern America
by Raymond A. Eve and Francis B. Harrold

Family Planning and Population Control: The Challenges of a Successful Movement
by Kurt W. Back

Farmers' and Farm Workers' Movements: Social Protest in American Agriculture
by Patrick H. Mooney and Theo J. Majka

The Health Movement: Promoting Fitness in America
by Michael S. Goldstein

The Hospice Movement: Easing Death's Pains
by Cathy Siebold

Let the People Decide: Neighborhood Organizing in America
by Robert Fisher

Populism: The Humane Preference in America, 1890–1900
by Gene Clanton

The Prison Reform Movement: Forlorn Hope
by Larry E. Sullivan

The Rise of a Gay and Lesbian Movement
by Barry D. Adam

Self-Help in America: A Social Movement Perspective
by Alfred H. Katz

Social Movements of the 1960s: Searching for Democracy
by Stewart Burns

Two Paths
to Women's Equality

Temperance, Suffrage,
and the Origins of Modern Feminism

Janet Zollinger Giele

Twayne Publishers
An Imprint of Simon & Schuster Macmillan
New York
London   Mexico City   New Delhi   Singapore   Sydney   Toronto

8/97   # 30776997

Two Paths to Women's Equality
Janet Zollinger Giele

Copyright ©1995 by Twayne Publishers

Twayne Publishers
An Imprint of Simon & Schuster Macmillan
866 Third Avenue
New York, New York 10022

Library of Congress Cataloging-in-Publication Data

Giele, Janet Zollinger.
    Two paths to women's equality: temperance, suffrage, and the origins of modern feminism / Janet Zollinger Giele.
        p. cm.—(Social movements past and present)
    Includes bibliographical references and index.
    ISBN 0-8057-9700-9.—ISBN 0-8057-4523-8 (pbk.)
    1. Feminism—United States—History. 2. Temperance—United States. 3. Women—Suffrage—United States. I. Title. II. Series.
HQ1410.G54 1995
305.42'0973—dc20
                                                                94-26535
                                                                CIP

The paper used in this publication meets the minimum requirements of American National Standard for Information Sciences—Permanence of Paper for Printed Library Materials, ANSI Z39.48-1984.

10 9 8 7 6 5 4 3 2 1

Printed in the United States of America.

Contents

Preface   *ix*

1.   Where Do Women's Movements Come From?   1

2.   The Emergence of American Feminism, 1830–1870   27

3.   Temperance: The Extension of Woman's Power in
      the Home   63

4.   Suffrage: Women as Citizens   112

5.   Women's Rights and Feminist Caregiving since 1920   163

Appendix A: Content Analysis of Newspapers   205

*Appendix B: Biographical Comparison of Temperance and Suffrage
     Leaders   213*

Notes   225

References   261

Index   283

Preface

This book has undergone a total metamorphosis since it began in 1961 as a dissertation on social change in the feminine role. As the modern women's movement grew during the 1960s and 1970s, I shifted my focus to contemporary women's changing lives and the emergence of modern family policy. When I returned to the project in the 1980s, mere revision of the dissertation was impossible. What I saw instead was an opportunity to understand temperance and suffrage as two kinds of feminism, the first oriented to women's benevolent social concern for children and families, the second to equal rights for women. Instead of trying to prove that temperance advocates were obsolete relative to suffragists, I began to understand both kinds of feminism as equally valid and necessary. Moreover, rather than finding that both were finished in 1920, I discovered that their descendants live on today. I now believe that neither benevolent nor equal rights feminism alone could have accomplished the great emancipation of women that occurred at the beginning of this century. I also believe that both kinds of feminism are still needed today.[1]

I am grateful for three major influences that transformed this project over the past 30 years: vast changes in women's roles and the emergence of women's studies; the appearance of the civil rights, feminist, and anti-war activities that stimulated social movement research; and the lengthening of my own life history so that conclusions reached earlier were modified by later experience.

The grand flowering of women's studies since 1970 has given a new legitimacy to the sociological study of women's changing roles. In 1955, the British historian O. R. MacGregor wrote, "The emancipation of women is one of the most striking aspects of the industrialist phase of social development. Equally striking is its neglect in present-day writing."[2] At the time I chose my dissertation topic in the late 1950s, there was considerable feeling that the study of women's issues was of limited interest and value. A decade later the situation had begun to change. Where I had felt virtually alone before, there was now a company of scholars with whom I could share results and discuss findings. The new scholarship enriched my work. My 1961 comparison of 98 temperance and suffrage leaders was based on a couple of nineteenth-century collected biographies and penciled file cards generously lent to me by the editors of *Notable American Women*. Thirty years later these volumes had been published and my biographical analysis could be enriched and expanded. Similarly, I was able to supplement my early forays into describing the temperance and suffrage groups by placing them in the larger context of nineteenth-century women's associations. Other scholars had mapped that larger canvas of missionary societies, moral reform, temperance, suffrage, and the women's clubs.[3] As a sociologist, I was thus free to search for generalizations because historians had helpfully unearthed the particulars. The marvelous expansion of women's studies also helped me to lengthen my exploration of nineteenth-century feminism. I could reach further back to its roots. It became clear that the temperance and suffrage women stood on the shoulders of all those "Republican Mothers" of an earlier generation who gained an education to influence future citizens and who used their religious conversions to uphold a high moral standard for their families and children.[4]

The new scholarship on women also made it possible to trace forward the intertwining legacy of maternal and equal rights feminism right up to the present. Detailed histories of women's lives since 1920 provide a backdrop against which to sketch the ups and downs of modern women's fortunes. In addition, the project of understanding women's changing roles has become interdisciplinary. Psychologists and sociologists debate whether women more than men see moral issues from a slant that is concerned with the needs of others.[5] Economists and sociologists chart sex segregation and discrimination in the labor force. Political scientists measure women's voting behavior. Survey analysts record changing attitudes. Historians, political scientists, sociologists, psychologists, and philosophers have all begun to link the various interests of women to the broadening of the public sphere, social policy, and the welfare state.[6]

New research on social movements advanced my thinking about feminism. In the 1950s, with Nazism defeated, Eisenhower as president, the specter of McCarthyism still fresh, and the Cold War in full swing, social movements were portrayed as deviant.[7] But the civil rights movement, the protest against the Vietnam War, the second wave of feminism, and the environmental movement all brought new interest and respectability to the study of collective behavior. Where did the leaders come from? How did they find adherents? How did they succeed in social reform? Social scientists developed several ways of viewing these movements: as collective outbursts responding to social strain, as blueprints for the institutionalization of alternative values, as rational strategies for serving the leaders' interests, as definitions of the situation that represented various perspectives on reality.[8] In addition, feminist scholars were charting the modern women's movement and reported a range of women's activities, from intimate consciousness-raising groups to more formal equal rights organizations.[9]

These studies of feminism and other social movements validated the research strategy I had used from the beginning—a comparison of two similar but distinct groups through a sampling of the leaders and a content analysis of their newspapers. The social movement literature helped me to state and affirm my theoretical framework—that the leadership, ideology, organizational structure, and protest strategy of temperance and of suffrage were connected to the particular type of personal and social conflict felt by each movement's members. Temperance women were primarily concerned about women's equality in the home and with care for the weaker persons in the community. Suffrage women worked for women's access to the public sphere and equal opportunities with men.

My own experience as a wife, professor, and mother also affected the shape of this book. Younger women find it hard to believe what the world was like in the late 1950s and how ambiguous were a professional woman's choices about her future life pattern. Being married and taking the major responsibility for parenting after children were born were still the normative ideals even among highly educated women. College instructors like me who were teaching in the early 1960s and nevertheless having babies were still pioneers, and some of us found our innovations resisted. Our intellectual work on the changing roles of women also fell outside the scholarly canon. Nevertheless, forging a multiple role as worker, wife, and mother was one of those instances of what Joyce Antler termed "feminism as life process," which advanced my insight into the lives of my subjects.[10] Rather than live a life apart from men or separate the home from the public sphere, it now seems to me that the temperance and suffrage pioneers were also trying to create a bridge between the worlds of women and men.

When I began the dissertation I considered the temperance women narrow-minded and out-of-date. I came to a fuller appreciation of them as I read new research on the Woman's Christian Temperance Union showing the wide and prescient range of their concern with alcoholism—poverty, white slavery, violence against women and children—and myself taught in a school of social welfare where I could see the continuing importance of these issues. Although at the beginning I was on the side of the suffragists, I was like everyone else inclined to think that they had solved the problem of equality by getting the vote in 1920. The rise of the new feminist movement was an eye opener. Equal pay, sex-blind college admissions, abortion, maternity leave, sexual harassment, election of more women to public office—here were a host of issues that the suffragists had not addressed, some of which they had not even envisioned.

This book is entitled *Two Paths to Women's Equality* because I now believe that both the maternal feminism of the temperance women and the equal rights feminism of the suffragists were needed to emancipate women from the confines of their traditional roles. Neither one was more old-fashioned or up-to-date; neither one was more or less important. One of my aims has been to demonstrate that the nineteenth-century women had both "masculine" and "feminine" qualities, both "instrumental" and "expressive" capacities.[11] The temperance women tended to focus on the feminine, the expressive, and the domestic while the suffragists focused on the masculine, the instrumental, and the public. In so doing, the early feminists displayed not only the wide range of interests within the ranks of women but also the overlap between the worlds of women and men. As modern women continue to press for family-friendly communities, greater recognition of women in the workplace, and greater presence of men in the home, they will perhaps rediscover how to gain equality not only by reaching for the same goals as men but also by getting men to adopt the goals of women.

Since my focus is analytic—to show the roots and characteristic features of women's movements—this book does not attempt to provide a complete history of the whole spectrum of American feminist activity in the nineteenth or twentieth century. The book opens with a consideration of why women's movements arise and finds the primary cause to be the strain between traditional expectations and the changing reality of women's lives. Chapter 2 shows how temperance and suffrage emerged from the missionary work, moral reform, and antislavery activity of the period between the Revolutionary War and the Civil War. An intensive case study of the Woman's Christian Temperance Union follows in chapter 3 and of the two main suffrage organizations in chapter 4. Each study covers the leaders, ideology, organizational development, and tactical strategies of these two principal branches of the first large women's movement. The closing chapter brings the analysis up to the present by identifying the social and equal rights strands of feminist thought in late twentieth-century U.S. legislation and social policy.

The reader who is looking for a more general history of American feminism will find here a theoretical armature around which the histories of smaller and more specialized branches of the women's movement can be arranged. Those who wish to pursue these other strands will find a rich history in the Twayne Publishers series American Women in the Twentieth Century edited by Barbara Haber.[12] In *Controversy and Coalition, Revised Edition: The New Feminist Movement across Three Decades of Change,* Myra Marx Ferree and Beth Hess have analyzed modern feminism as a social movement; their book appears in the Twayne's series Social Movements Past and Present edited by Irwin T. Sanders.[13]

As this project comes to a close after so many years I express my appreciation to the many organizations who have given their support. Wellesley College awarded me a junior faculty leave in 1967–68. I was a fellow at the Bunting Institute during 1970–72. From the time when it was still named the Radcliffe Woman's Archives, the Schlesinger Library has made me welcome to use the materials in its care. Widener Library of Harvard University, Clapp Library of Wellesley College, and the Goldfarb Library at Brandeis University made it possible to consult the many volumes of the *Woman's Journal* and the *Union Signal.* During 1975–79 I was privileged to serve on the Social Science Research Council's Committee on Work and Personality in the Middle Years; that experience opened to me the field of life course studies and made me theorize about social change in women's lives.

One semester as Center for Education of Women Scholar at the University of Michigan in 1986 and another as Visiting Scholar at the Murray Research Center on the Study of Lives at Radcliffe College in 1987 helped me to combine my interests in the life course with my historical studies of nineteenth-century women. I owe thanks to many other sources for sustaining my work on other projects over the past several decades that ultimately enriched this one: the Ford Foundation, the Lilly Endowment, the National Institute on Aging, the Rockefeller Gender Roles Project, and the German Marshall Fund of the United States. The Family and Children's Policy Center of the Heller School at Brandeis University has provided facilities and general research support. A splendid finale to the project came in August 1993 when I was able to complete chapter 2 as a resident fellow at the Rockefeller Study and Conference Center in Bellagio, Italy.

There are many individuals to thank for their help and encouragement, which have reached over a span of many years. On the day in 1960 when I visited the Sophia Smith Collection in Northampton, Massachusetts, Eleanor Flexner, the first modern scholar of the woman suffrage movement, generously invited me to her home for lunch and offered her encouragement. Edward T. James, lead editor of *Notable American Women,* lent me his lists of prominent women for my comparison of suffrage and temperance leaders. Talcott Parsons, my thesis advisor in the Harvard Social Relations Department, asked penetrating questions and let me know that he thought my topic important and my findings original, exciting, and worthy of a book. In the late 1960s at a time when I was working very hard but making little progress toward publication, Anne Firor Scott, whom I had never met, wrote me out of the blue a message that inspired me for years to come—that she had just read my dissertation, that it was good, and that I "SHOULD GET IT OUT!"

But the problem in "getting it out" was that I didn't know how to justify a focus on temperance and suffrage compared with all the other changes in women's roles that were going on at the same time. In 1980 Irwin Sanders proposed that I publish my book in a new series by Twayne Publishers on social movements. By accepting this invitation I was at last able to see that my particular contribution was not as a historian of women but as a sociologist of the historical women's movement. In so conceiving my role, I have learned much from my colleagues in women's history and women's studies, especially Ruth Bordin, Suzanne Marilley, Anne Firor Scott, and several members of the women's studies community at Brandeis: Joyce Antler, Susan Okin, and Shulamit Reinharz. Anne Colby, Rose Coser, Glen Elder, and Matilda White Riley have been mentors, friends, and colleagues in the field of life course studies, and Neil J. Smelser a guide to sociological theory and the challenge of combining history and sociology, especially as related to social change, the family, and collective behavior. Thanks to David Riesman for continuing as a mentor and teacher over the years, even in ways that he did not know at the time.

Many others have lent their help to the research process. I am proud to claim Mary Gilfus, Louise Kaplan, and Connie Williams as my former doctoral students at the Heller School of Brandeis University, whose work on their dissertations forwarded my thinking about women's roles and social movements. I also thank my research assistants: Helen Lefkowitz Horowitz long ago at Wellesley College, who coded the newspaper stories for reliability; more recently at Brandeis, Dorene Shulman, who extended the comparison of leaders; Dan Mazur, who produced the maps; and Jillian Dickert, who searched for illustrations. Diane Hines put the entire original draft into the computer, Berne Webb printed recent versions, and Randee Fuhrman brought out the final draft. At Twayne Publishers, Carol Chin was a supportive and intelligent senior editor with excellent substantive suggestions for improvement of the manuscript; India Koopman, a meticulous and sympathetic manuscript editor. Pembroke Herbert and Sandi Rygiel were superb consultants in locating the photographs and prints that illustrate the book.

Finally, I thank friends and family who helped me through moments of discouragement to reach the joy of completion: my late parents, Albert and Ellen Zollinger, who nurtured my earliest intellectual striving; my sisters, Margaret and Alberta, who were in Ohio in the late 1980s to help my parents when I could not be; my long-time friend and coauthor Hilda Kahne; and the three main loves of my life—David, Elizabeth, and Ben.

Chapter 1

Where Do Women's Movements Come From?

Feminist movements, though they have existed for well over a century in different parts of the world, were virtually unknown before 1840. Women had long been oppressed by unequal laws and opportunities for education and employment, and by and large they bore their lot without public protest. But in the summer of 1848, in Seneca Falls, New York, a small band of women and men met in a Wesleyan chapel and read a "Declaration of Sentiments" that boldly paralleled the Declaration of Independence. It cited the many wrongs done by men against women: denial of the franchise (the right to vote); government without representation; civil disability, loss of property and loss of guardianship as a result of marriage; unequal employment, remuneration, and education; and preemption of moral authority and exclusion from the ministry in the church. The declaration concluded with a ringing appeal for women's right as citizens to vote as men: "Now, in view of this entire disfranchisement of one-half the people of this country, their social and religious degradation—in view of the unjust laws above mentioned, and because women do feel themselves aggrieved, oppressed, and fraudulently deprived of their most sacred rights, we insist that they have immediate admission to all the rights and privileges which belong to them as citizens of the United States."[1]

Why did feminism emerge where and when it did, in the 1830s and 1840s in upstate New York? Why did this new movement start among a small band of women active in a number of reform causes? Who later

1

joined it? And why did the movement take so long to accomplish one of its central goals, the vote for women, which was not granted until 1920 in the United States and even later in other countries such as France and Japan? Few studies have analyzed why some women questioned the status quo and developed an alternative vision. Nor has there been much detailed sociological or political analysis of the key organizations that helped to bring about emancipation.[2] Women's movements are continuing group efforts *by women* to change some aspect of their own or others' lives. *Feminist* movements involve women's efforts on their own behalf, especially for political, economic, and social equality. This study observes two key American women's movements in the nineteenth century—temperance and suffrage—in order to trace the principal strands of early feminism. The similarities and differences in their membership and style help to illuminate why feminism emerged when it did.

Feminism appeared in women's church groups and missionary societies, and after the Civil War in women's clubs, the College Women's Alumnae Association, and the coalition of consumers and working women that resulted in the Women's Trade Union League. In that whole array temperance and suffrage were probably the two single most important groups to challenge women's traditional subordinate status both at home and in public life. They were also two of the longest lived women's reform groups of the nineteenth century. Temperance and suffrage, while similar in trying to change women's roles, were noticeably different in their strategies and ideological appeal. Temperance advocates were especially concerned with prohibition and suffragists ostensibly sought the vote for women. Although both movements began with a strong link to Protestant values and democratic individualism, they differed in their ideology, basic structure, leadership, rank and file, and long-term success. The temperance women more often worked through churches and enjoyed earlier popular acceptance at the local level. Suffragists relied primarily on secular organizations and in their early years operated through informal networks of leaders and through annual national conventions.

Temperance and suffrage are now better remembered for their contribution to women's liberation, although both were thought at the time to have had a role in winning prohibition.[3] Each represents a prototype of feminism. Temperance was more oriented to the enhancement and upgrading of the traditional feminine role of wife and mother. Suffrage focused on winning the same rights for women as those enjoyed by men. Temperance women were the earliest and largest single constituency to support the ballot for women; they wished to establish restrictions on the licensing of saloons, but later they supported the broad feminist goal of giving women full rights to citizenship. Temperance women popularized interest in women's exercise and women's health. The Woman's Christian Temperance Union (WCTU) introduced health education into the public schools along with scientific temperance instruction. Their campaign for social purity was aimed at removing some of the chief causes of prostitution: addiction to alcohol, inadequate housing and poor training for working girls, and permissive laws that set the age of consent as low as 12 to 14 years in some states. The WCTU also tried to improve the general position of women abroad. Through missionary activity they carried their suffrage and temperance concerns to other Western societies, such as Australia and New Zealand. In parts of Africa and Asia, where women lived in even more restricted situations than in the West, they sought to bring new ideas of liberation and equality.

Suffrage women, more than helping the unfortunate, focused on helping women themselves. By oratory and example they articulated woman's rights, sought access to higher education, and argued for women's ability to serve in such professions as medicine, the law, and the clergy. Their key goal was the vote, the ultimate sign to them of women's full citizenship and equality with men in the public sphere.

Although most of the women behind both movements were middle class, they reached out to working women and the trade union movement; the WCTU during the 1890s to the Knights of Labor through its leader Frances Willard, and the suffragists at the turn of the century to the Women's Trade Union League. Temperance and suffrage sought many of the same ends: equality for women in both private and public spheres, the vote to exercise their rights in each, and improvement of public life, which in the minds of many suffragists as well as temperance women was impossible without strict curbs on alcohol production, sale, and use.

But the movements were also subtly yet unmistakably different. The temperance cause spoke to those who defined women as particularly responsible for personal and domestic concerns. Through prayer, personal suasion, and later the vote, the temperance movement gave women a vehicle for the exercise and extension of power in the domestic realm. Temperance provided a critical bridge to another, more uncompromisingly public and "masculine" role for women that

was represented by suffrage. Unlike temperance, suffrage at first alien-
ated the great majority of American womanhood; it stood in their
minds for unfeminine behavior, questionable innovations such as
wearing bloomers and speaking in public, and rebellion against established authority, especially the church. Gradually, however, more
women completed school or entered the newly opened colleges. As
the idea of women's voting on local option (whether sale of alcoholic
beverages would be allowed in their towns) and in school board elections became increasingly familiar and as western states permitted
women to vote in national elections, the strangeness of woman suffrage began to fade and the right of women to extend their responsibility into public life took hold.

This is not a story of how the temperance movement turned into
the suffrage movement, or of how the two movements were all along
really one and the same. Instead my analysis traces both the separate
courses and the interweaving of two voices, each speaking to a somewhat different range of feminist concerns, at times almost in unison, at
other times in harmony or in dissonance. My purpose is to identify the
two different themes, to show how their origins were slightly different
and how they appealed to somewhat different audiences. In the end,
however, I want to demonstrate not only that temperance and suffrage
were closely related but that each was necessary for the feminist
enterprise to become established.

Feminism around the World

The origin and course of American feminism parallels that in other
countries. There is no historical record before 1800 of any women's
group specifically organized to change women's rights or status. Yet
after 1800, women all around the world began to protest their status
by founding women's societies and launching women's movements.
They eventually won concessions extending from the right of custody
for their children to the right to vote.

Why did feminist protest begin when it did? The Renaissance and
Reformation encouraged education of both women and men, and radical branches of Protestantism supported the priesthood of all believers.
The ideas of the Enlightenment—liberty, freedom, justice, and individualism—also played an important role. In addition, the emergence of
universal manhood suffrage in Britain set a precedent in the new right
of all male citizens to vote. Even more basic were the transformations

in women's everyday lives that no longer made them unquestioningly accept a role of dependency and subordination. A profound structural transformation was at work. Every women's movement was in one way or another the product of economic or political change in the country where it occurred.

British women formed their first suffrage group when they presented a petition to Parliament in 1866. By 1910 the British suffrage movement was one of the largest in the world, and in 1918 it was finally successful. Australia and New Zealand launched women's movements in 1885, after the visit of an American organizer from the Woman's Christian Temperance Union. In 1894 New Zealand became the first country to enfranchise women, followed by Western Australia in 1899 and the whole Australian nation in 1901.[4] Sweden and other Nordic countries (Norway, Denmark, Finland, Iceland) made the most rapid progress of all. Swedish feminists organized in the 1870s, Norwegian and Finnish women in the 1880s, and Icelandic women in the 1890s. By the time of World War I, women could vote in Finland and Norway.[5]

Feminist activity also appeared in the Far East. With the opening of Japanese society to Western influence, suffrage for Japanese women was proposed in 1867 at the prefectural level, and five Japanese women were sent abroad for a Western education in 1871. But soon after, sentiments on behalf of women's emancipation receded, and only a tiny suffrage group maintained the pressure for woman's rights during the first half of the twentieth century. Not until 1945, with the ending of World War II and the institution of a democratic regime, did woman suffrage come to Japan. Japan was not alone in its delay of equal rights for women. A number of other countries had fledgling women's movements, but only a handful had suffrage by 1920. More than 40 countries had instituted woman suffrage by 1945, more than 100 by the 1970s.[6]

What accounts for this remarkable emergence of women's movements in a relatively brief span of time during the nineteenth century? *Every single women's movement appears to have been a collective effort by women to gain freedom to act autonomously as responsible individuals rather than as dependent wives or daughters.* Women's traditional roles did not allow such freedom. Women were subordinate to men in the family, in religious matters, and legal and business affairs. Nor did women seem to question their condition in traditional society. Women's inferior status could be rationalized in a premodern economy and kinship system, where management and control of the family

Sophia G. Hayden, architect, who designed the Woman's Building at the World's Fair Exposition of 1893 in Chicago. From *The Book of the Fair* by Hubert Bancroft, 1895.

Woman's Building, World's Fair Exposition of 1893 in Chicago, which popularized the women's movement in the United States. From *The Book of the Fair* by Hubert Bancroft, 1895.

were identical with the unit of economic production, the peasant farm, cottage industry, or small family business. Control of women's economic activities in both Eastern and Western societies was embedded in a larger kinship system typically headed by males.[7]

The nuclear family structure of industrial and urban society, however, could not effectively operate within an extended kinship structure dominated by a patriarchal head. The splitting of the household from the workplace that typically occurred during modernization placed new demands on men and women.[8] Men needed to be able to operate as free agents in competitive and individualistic labor markets. Women also needed to be able to act on their own behalf and as representatives of their families. Their former roles as minors or dependents subordinate to a husband's or a father's ultimate authority were no longer compatible with the larger social and political structure.

It is impossible to test these hypotheses today by asking nineteenth-century women what they actually felt about the emerging new family structure, economy, and government that surrounded them. But the historical record suggests how women felt in cultures that were industrialized.

Urbanization and American feminism.   Nancy Cott analyzed the diaries and letters of 100 women who lived in the early part of the nineteenth century. Women's dual feeling of sisterhood and oppression was expressed in Sarah Grimké's phrase "the bonds of womanhood." Cott discovered a profound change in women's lives between 1780 and 1830. In 1830 women had all the disabilities they experienced at the time of the Revolution, but they felt much more at odds with their condition. Women's lack of the right to make contracts, to retain custody of children, and to vote was the more galling when all white men had these rights and could vote regardless of their property holdings. Female economic dependency became more of a problem once the farm economy was displaced by an urban economy, and women's independent production and earnings from textile making and other crafts became less important. Women were also gradually gaining more education and were badly needed as teachers in the schools, yet they were paid only a fraction of what men could earn. The urbanization and industrialization of society thus heightened women's frustration with their lot. Even though changing economic and political conditions demanded greater autonomy and gave women less security, their legal and economic rights were more in keeping with the restricted opportunities of an earlier era.[9]

Cott clearly attributes the dramatic change to the process of historical modernization, noting that

the period between 1780 and 1830 was a time of wide- and deep-ranging transformation, including the beginning of rapid intensive economic growth, especially in foreign commerce, agricultural productivity, and the fiscal and banking system; the start of sustained urbanization; demographic transition toward modern fertility patterns; marked change toward social stratification by wealth and growing inequality in the distribution of wealth; rapid pragmatic adaptation in the law; shifts from unitary to pluralistic networks in personal association; unprecedented expansion in primary education; democratization in the political process; invention of a new language of political and social thought; and—not least—with respect to family life, the appearance of "domesticity."[10]

Parallels in modern Japanese feminism. Although similar aspects of modernization came to Japan almost a century later, after World War II there are striking parallels in the impact on women, and for them we do have information from surveys on women's attitudes and feelings. These surveys reveal some of the strains that became evident as Japanese women saw their traditional roles give way to a modern urban and industrial order. A 1941–42 survey by the Japanese broadcasting corporation compared the daily time use of persons aged 16 and over in families of farmers, small businessmen, clerks, and factory workers. Women in farm families spent 9 hours a day in productive labor, almost as much as men's 10.5 hours; in addition they worked far more hours on household tasks.

The time use of urban women, however, was dramatically different: wives of small businessmen spent only five hours a day in productive work and six hours a day in housework. The wives of clerical employees and factory workers spent virtually no time in the labor force but between 10 and 11 hours a day in managing the household.[11] In 1955 in the region of Nagoya, 63 percent of the farmers' wives managed household expenses, but 82 percent of the urban wives had this responsibility. Thus a wife evidently had greater responsibility for autonomous management of the household in the modern nuclear family than she did in the farm family. Yet she did not yet have full legal rights to such management. In 1956 less than half of young women and young men believed in primogeniture (inheritance by the eldest son), compared with four-fifths of older people aged 60 and over.[12]

Japanese women in the postwar period also expressed a desire for liberation. In 1956, 30 percent of urban and 27 percent of rural women said they were not happy to be women because they were not free. No man, however, gave a comparable response. Instead well over half of the urban and rural men said they were happy to be men because they were free.[13]

A feminist movement emerged in Japan as the country became more urban and modern. By 1945 secondary education had become almost equally available to Japanese girls and boys, and nearly 40 percent of young women found their way into the labor force. The ancient inheritance, marriage and divorce laws, and exclusion of women from public life became increasingly intolerable to women in contemporary society. In 1971, political scientist Susan Pharr interviewed young Japanese women who had become involved in politics and concluded that they did so primarily because they were challenging the traditional domestic definition of women's roles that was still dominant at that time.[14]

Origins of feminist thought. These examples of nineteenth-century Western women's movements and twentieth-century Japanese feminism suggest that *women create feminist movements as their principal means to expand the feminine role from the private domestic sphere to the public sphere.* Few commentators, however, have traced the cause of women's liberation movements to the single powerful structural contradiction between traditional dependency and the new need for autonomy that is produced by economic and political modernization. Instead, they attribute each feminist movement to a particular set of cultural, historical, and political influences and to the accumulation of specific chronological events. I believe, however, that women's movements stem from the tension between traditional expectations that females in their roles as wives and mothers will be dependent on men and the new expectations that they must be able to act as autonomous individuals. Feminist movements help to bring about the independence that women's new roles require, whether in the family, the community, or the workplace.

Yet in order to mobilize, these movements must be able to draw on cultural precedents that legitimate women's autonomy. Where these precedents are weak or absent, feminism is either slow to develop or absent altogether. Olive Banks in *Faces of Feminism* attributes both British and American feminism to three major strands of modern intellectual history: evangelical Christianity, the ideas of the Enlightenment, and socialism.[15] Each of these traditions was a tool for enhancing women's independence and extending their influence and responsibility into the community.

Evangelical Christianity, which spread with the Second Great Awakening in America in the 1830s and 1840s, emphasized the *moral and religious* autonomy of women. Three out of five of the converts during the wave of revivals that swept New England and New York were women.[16] Women's moral authority having thus been established within the Protestant tradition of the priesthood of all believers, women established missionary societies, then maternal associations, and then temperance groups. A few claimed the right, even the moral duty, to speak in public. Significantly, this pattern of new behavior was not confined to America. Moral reform, especially as it was expressed in temperance and prohibition campaigns, also appeared along with woman's rights and the suffrage movement in Scandinavia, Australia, and New Zealand.[17]

Enlightenment ideas, which fueled the American and French Revolutions and Norwegian and Finnish nationalism, focused on the *political or civil* autonomy of individuals. These ideas provided a philosophical basis for rejection of all kinds of legal dependency, from slavery to undemocratic relations between the ruling class and the workers and between men and women. Middle-class liberals were particularly drawn to the liberal and individualistic beliefs of the Enlightenment. Thus women's movements in many countries, such as Great Britain and the United States, were led primarily by middle-class educated women. They at first envisioned their autonomy in terms of domestic roles that would give women primary charge for the home. John Stuart Mill in *The Subjection of Women* (1869) presented an argument well understood and widely accepted among the middle classes:

When the support of the family depends not on property, but on earnings, the common arrangement, by which the man earns the income and the wife superintends the domestic expenditure, seems to me in general the most suitable division of labour between the two persons. If, in addition to the physical suffering of bearing children, and the whole responsibility of their care and education in early years, the wife undertakes the careful and economical application of the husband's earnings to the general comfort of the family; she takes not only her fair share, but usually the larger share, of the bodily and mental exertion required by their joint existence. If she undertakes any additional portion [i.e., paid employment], it seldom relieves her from this, but only prevents her from performing it properly. The care which she is herself disabled from taking of the children and the household, nobody else takes; those of the children who do not die grow up as they best can, and the management of the household is likely to be so bad as even in point of economy to be a great drawback from the value of the wife's earnings. In an otherwise just state of things, it is not, therefore, I think, a desirable custom that the wife should contribute by her labour to the income of the family.[18]

Not surprisingly then, middle-class secular women's reform at first focused on giving women more autonomy in matters relating primarily to the household: women's property rights, child custody, judicious use of alcohol, and extension of education.

A third tradition, socialist and communist in origin, appealed to the working-class segment of the population and addressed questions of *economic equality and autonomy* for women. Ideas of communal living with shared household and child-rearing tasks that were first proposed by Claude Henri Saint-Simon and Charles Fourier in France did not catch on widely in America except in community experiments like New Harmony, Indiana, and Oneida, New York. But in other countries, where the middle-class reform movements were weak and a large working class or peasantry confronted authoritarian regimes, the appeal of socialist ideas was enormous, and women's movements became allied with them. Socialist ideas were an inevitable touchstone for equality of the sexes in the Soviet Union, the Eastern bloc, and China. In Russia, by the October Revolution of 1917, feminist leaders building on the ideas of Friedrich Engels and August Bebel had allied orthodox Marxism with feminism by labeling women-as-property a capitalistic notion and holding out the prospect that socialism would liberate women by allowing them a role in production and political life as well the chance to share with the larger community such household duties as cooking or child care. After the Russian Revolution these feminists impressed on the Bolshevik leaders the need to educate women, to liberate them from the patriarchal grip of the traditional Russian family, and to bring them into the labor force if the revolution was to succeed.[19] In China, as early as 1927, Mao Tse Tung wrote that women were especially oppressed. He too called for the overthrow of feudalistic political, clan, religious, and male authority in order to liberate women and involve them in productive labor to support the revolution.[20]

As in the case of evangelical or Enlightenment ideas, these socialist philosophies were used to promote women's autonomy and to expand their public responsibilities. By arguing that the private bourgeois family enslaved women and that their liberation would come about through community sharing of housework and child care, socialist feminists promoted women's autonomy in the private sphere. By declaring women's equal rights to join the production line, to participate in community affairs, and to vote and stand for office, they extended women's responsibility into the public sphere.

Feminist movements came to different countries earlier or later depending on how soon women were faced with the contradictions of political or economic development. The first wave of suffrage reforms occurred between 1893 and 1922 in the non-Catholic, Western democracies with a long history of individualism, the most Europeanized colonies, and the United States and the Soviet Union. Second were late-developing societies—Catholic Europe, Eastern Europe, and the most developed countries of the Third World—who between 1923 and 1949 granted the vote to women. An excellent example is France, where women did not vote until Charles de Gaulle's provisional government established woman suffrage by decree in 1944. French feminists, although well organized and energetic as early as 1900, were caught between revolutionary socialism and church authority and failed to win suffrage before 1920, as had other nations of comparable urban and industrial development.[21] The third wave of suffrage reforms came in 1950–71 in newly independent Third World countries such as Pakistan (1950), Indonesia (1950), a number of African countries, and a late advanced country, Switzerland (1971). Finally, a fourth group of countries, primarily Muslim, began to debate the rights of women only recently. Only since 1972 has woman suffrage been granted in Saudi Arabia, Jordan, Yemen, and Kuwait.[22]

This historical pattern suggests that whatever the time or place, feminist movements originate for roughly the same structural reasons. Increasing economic and political complexity and the need for women's greater autonomy and independence are the precipitating causes. Women, having gained expanded opportunities for education and enlightenment, see the contradictions in their cramped and subordinate status and strive for emancipation. But whether a feminist movement succeeds or is delayed is another story. Acceptance and legitimation depend on the specific nation, its religious, political, and cultural traditions. In Scandinavia, the United States, and Great Britain these traditions worked together to produce fairly early acceptance of women in the public sphere. In countries such as France and Germany, however, where women's emancipation seemed opposed to rather than allied with religion and where women's voluntarism was neither nurtured nor welcomed by the state, feminism existed but failed to thrive.[23]

This study of the American woman's temperance and suffrage movements necessarily takes the American cultural heritage as given and develops the story without further reference to comparable developments in other nations. The comparative method that produces insights from contrasts between nations can, however, be adapted to comparisons within the United States.[24] Analogous questions are possible: Which branches of feminism were earliest to emerge and thrive? In what regions and states was the greatest support to be found? What were the religious, political, and class origins of the adherents? And what combination of tactics, strategy, and alliances was most likely to produce success? To answer these questions requires a theory of social movement formation and development. From it one can chart the key features of feminism that we now credit with accomplishing change.

Structural Features of Women's Rights Movements

A social movement theory for explaining and interpreting the nature and significance of American feminism does not come ready-made.[25] Eleanor Flexner's classic and comprehensive study *Century of Struggle* provided the first modern historical description of the nineteenth-century American women's movement. Recent historians have generally asked how the temperance and suffrage movements managed to transform radical and far-reaching reforms into much narrower and less daring struggles. They found especially interesting the radical arm of the suffrage movement and thus generally gave less notice to moderate women's groups that included women's clubs and missionary societies. Aileen Kraditor documented a shift in the ideas of the suffrage movement from an emphasis on justice and equality between women and men to emphasis on expediency in order to win the vote. In a similar vein Andrew Sinclair, after demonstrating the association of woman

International Women's Year, Mexico City, 1975. Bettye-Lane Studio.

suffrage with white supremacy in order to win the southern vote, suggests that the woman's ballot when it was finally won had "been reduced to a mere 'convenient symbol' in their minds, by the slow and politic method of its getting."[26] William O'Neill was even more emphatic about the limited significance of feminism:

> It took seventy-two years for women to get the vote. Generations wore out their lives in pursuit of it. . . . Yet when the vote was gained it made little difference to the feminine condition. . . . The position of women did improve over time, yet this seems mainly to have been the result of broad socio-economic changes which affected the entire population. No one has been able to demonstrate that feminism was directly responsible for the tangible gains that were secured. . . . When I began studying the history of women it was with the usual assumption that the feminist movement had been at least moderately successful. I now think otherwise.[27]

Sociological research, influenced by recent theories of social movements, also documented the transformation of the early women's movement and the narrowing of reform to single issues such as prohibition and the vote. Steven Buechler, in the only major sociological study of the suffrage movement, focuses on the transformation of the movement in Illinois from broad-based to narrow and from radical to moderate. Brenda Phillips has applied the resource mobilization framework to the national suffrage movement to show how a formal social movement organization eventually emerged from the informal networks and sporadic annual meetings that were typical of the early woman's rights movement.[28] McCarthy and Zald, after observing late twentieth-century social movements working for civil rights, peace, and environmental protection, suggest a more general rule: that professional and sophisticated organizations often manipulate grass-roots protest for their own ends and are shaped by external considerations of expediency as well as internal ideals.[29]

These sociological interpretations have been influenced by two types of social movement theory. Collective behavior theory emphasizes the importance of the internal worldviews of the participants and their grievances. Resource mobilization theory focuses on the external social context, the nature of the opposition, and the role of the social movement organization in accomplishing change.[30] The few existing sociological studies of early feminism have developed insightful analyses along both lines. Gusfield, in his account of the WCTU, examined the characteristics of constituents and linked the narrowing of movement goals to a gradual decline in their social status and an accompanying concern for maintaining the society of an earlier era. Rosenthal and coworkers, by noting the number of links among women's organizations created by the overlapping memberships of leading feminists, suggest that the feminist cause prevailed because of a vast network of weak ties. Keith Lance compared the success of suffrage campaigns in various states and concluded that the social and political contexts, particularly party control and socioeconomic characteristics of the broader population, were the key determinants of success. Buechler explains the narrowing of the Illinois suffrage movement as the result of a combination of internal change in the membership and its grievances and of external change in the political and social context.[31]

Yet neither the historical nor the sociological studies of early feminism conducted recently answer the questions that I find sociologically most interesting. Why did the woman's movement appear at that precise moment in history when women's status and roles were beginning to change drastically? And what was the relationship of feminism to the emancipation of women and to equality between the sexes? The predominant theme of many suffrage historians—that the suffrage movement did not make much difference because it forgot its radical origins and settled for the limited goal of the franchise—loses sight of the larger picture of the changes in women's roles and almost certainly underrates the feminist contribution. In her 1992 book *Protecting Soldiers and Mothers,* Theda Skocpol shows the amazing contribution made by the women's clubs and other women's organizations to such social reforms as lowering the infant mortality rate and establishing the Children's Bureau.[32] Yet Rosenthal and coworkers give no attention at all to the substantive content surrounding women's roles that made the various women's organizations and the networks among them appear. Buechler reveals little empathy with the participants; like Kraditor, Sinclair, and O'Neill before him, he subtly denigrates the efforts and accomplishments of the suffragists after 1900. They are depicted as middle- and upper-class moderates who have lost the founders' visionary critique of the larger social order and have settled for enfranchisement of women as the minor adjustment that will solve the world's major problems without a threat to their own class interests.

In all such accounts the voices of the women who are actually laboring for the vote, exerting their energies, and suffering defeats in successive state referenda are somehow lost. I believe it is now time to pursue a different type of investigation of the first feminist movement, one that gives greater place to the perspectives of its grass-roots adherents and to the emergence of a popular base of support for feminism. My effort is parallel to that of Aldon Morris, who in his research on the origins of the 1950s civil rights movement discovered a vast army of indigenous supporters in southern black churches and local communities and demonstrated that their efforts had been obscured by an emphasis on the role of outside organizers and sympathizers.[33] Past research on the transformation and narrowing of feminist organizations has similarly left the ordinary supporters in the shadow. Now more attention should be given the diversity of adherents, the proliferation of local temperance and suffrage clubs, and the mechanisms by which feminism reached such a rapid crescendo before 1920. This program requires attention to the movement as a whole, not just to the fortunes of an important segment.

Such a research program also requires a set of categories different from those that have dominated social movement theory in recent years. Rather than using feminism to illuminate the natural history of social movements by focusing on the evolution of suffrage organizations over time, social movement theory should now be used as a tool to explicate the connection between feminism and the changing roles of women. A whole new set of questions then emerges. How did the membership and leadership of the temperance and suffrage groups differ from other women's organizations, such as the women's missionary societies or women's clubs? What themes distinguished their organizational goals and purposes? How did their strategy for winning their objectives differ from that of other women's groups with different constituencies and different goals?

Four aspects of social movement development.   Research of such a comparative and cross-sectional nature requires seeing each major segment of the feminist movement as a collectivity or a social system oriented toward bringing about some aspect of change in women's roles. As a social system each social movement organization had to meet certain common functional prerequisites that enabled it to operate effectively. First, formation of a lasting identity and means for creating a culture (*pattern maintenance*): the movement had to develop a coherent thought structure that linked its activity to the values and culture of the larger society. Second, recruitment of leaders and replenishment of membership for continuity of goals over time (*goal attainment*): the movement resulted from coalescence of a loyal band of like-minded leaders and members who articulated grievances, envisioned goals, and set in motion the processes that would give direction to the movement over time. Third, development of a stable organizational structure (*integration*): to achieve its purposes the movement needed an organization to mediate among many different interest groups. Fourth, resource mobilization, tactics, and strategy (*adaptation*): the movement had to find the means to accomplish its goals by mounting materials, money, and personnel to win majority support for the social change that it sought. The four dimensions of social movements are outlined in figure 1.1.[34]

If one examines only one major branch of the feminist movement, such as suffrage, there is no baseline for characterizing these major dimensions of social movement activity. But by the comparison of at least two feminist groups it is possible to see how all these factors are intertwined in the creation of each distinctive stream of feminism. A particular ideology shaped by the founders led to a particular set of goals and strategies for realizing change in women's roles. If one could compare the ideology, leadership and membership, organization, and tactics of a whole spectrum of feminist organizations, the division of labor might become clear. I here confine my comparison, however, to only two key groups, temperance and suffrage. I will argue that each of these branches of the larger feminist movement had a slightly different ideology, fed on different grievances, appealed to a somewhat different membership, and proceeded by use of different tools.

In following this line of investigation, I take guidance from a number of previous studies of historical and modern women's groups. Marilley, in her description of the successful Colorado suffrage campaign of 1893, demonstrates the vital importance of cooperation between the suffragists and the WCTU to create a winning majority.[35] Carden and Ferree and Hess, in their accounts of contemporary feminism, note the range of feminist organizations, from radical to moderate, and the distinctive ideologies, constituencies, goals, and strategies that are characteristic of each.[36] Yet if one compares how both temperance and suffrage met the challenges of creating and maintaining a viable movement, it becomes clear that the two branches of feminism were similar in some ways and different in others, as illustrated in a description of the ways that their systems functioned.

Formation of a belief system—pattern maintenance. Social movements generally begin as the result of precipitating contradictions

Figure 1.1
Four Aspects of Social Movement Development

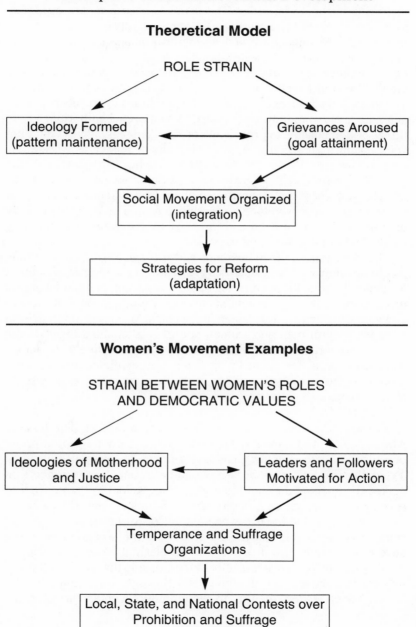

Theoretical Model

ROLE STRAIN

Ideology Formed
(pattern maintenance)

Grievances Aroused
(goal attainment)

Social Movement Organized
(integration)

Strategies for Reform
(adaptation)

Women's Movement Examples

STRAIN BETWEEN WOMEN'S ROLES
AND DEMOCRATIC VALUES

Ideologies of Motherhood
and Justice

Leaders and Followers
Motivated for Action

Temperance and Suffrage
Organizations

Local, State, and National Contests over
Prohibition and Suffrage

or strains in the social order. The people whose lives are especially affected by such strains are those most likely to launch the movement.[37] Pioneers have to devise an explanation for what is wrong in their social world and create a program for social change. In the case of temperance and suffrage, changes in social structure made less viable the traditional rules governing women's roles and status. Technological advances and modern economic arrangements rewarded autonomy, yet women were shackled by patriarchal authority and the threat of a husband's improvidence or drunkenness. Wives could not vote, obtain higher education, or enjoy independence as workers or property owners. Those women who were anchored in alternative religious traditions (such as Quakers) or regional subcultures (such as upstate New York) that accorded women relatively more authority and respect were those who took leadership in formulating a new ideology of responsible womanhood and in envisioning a future with property rights, higher education, and the vote.

The ideologies of the temperance and suffrage movements are difficult to distinguish. The similarities are evident in both groups' support for general humanitarian reforms such as cessation of child labor and urban reform. But my content analysis of the newspapers of the two movements after 1870 (explained in appendix A) reveals differences in their imagery of men and women and of relationships between the sexes. Temperance women were somewhat more likely to picture women as the active agent lifting fallen man, while suffragists were more likely to focus on the rights of men that women should also be able to enjoy.

Emergence of a successful leadership—goal attainment. The leaders who articulate the movement's ideology generally develop a proto-organization with specific goals and a fledgling group of followers. Typically, the first members have some unusual experience that makes the goals of the movement especially salient to them. Modern sociological research on Mothers against Drunk Driving (MADD), for example, shows that the overwhelming majority of members have had some direct personal experience with the death of a child or other relative at the hands of a drunk driver. Similarly, Blocker found in his study of the 1873 Woman's Temperance Crusade that some of the key leaders had experience of alcoholism through a husband, son, or father.[38] Such leaders then try to recruit others with similar interests.

Whether such an organization experiences success in the long run depends on loyal members who pay their dues, come to meetings, organize campaigns to influence the electorate, and sustain the capacity of their leaders to speak for a constituency of significant size. The roster of members usually reveals meaningful patterns in the types of people who join.

To compare the suffrage and temperance leadership it is necessary to examine the lives of the pioneers as well as their beliefs about what was wrong with women's roles and how they should be changed. One might well expect that leaders and members of both reform groups would be similar in such demographic characteristics as education and social status, which imply greater responsibility and power for women. To the extent that the ideology and goals of temperance and suffrage really diverged, however, one would expect to find in the lives of the temperance women experiences that gave alcohol special significance and of the suffragists experiences that gave political action and the vote particular meaning. Moreover, since both movements lasted so long, their character—as well as the characteristics of their leaders—probably changed over time, leading possibly from greater similarity in the beginning to greater difference in the end.

My comparison of about 50 leaders from each group (described in appendix B) in fact reveals that they were similar in higher education and socioeconomic background, but different in their life stories. The temperance women were more likely to have suffered some trauma connected with home and family, and the suffrage women were more likely to have been frustrated by barriers to their education, careers, and other achievement outside the home.

Social movement organization—integration. Every sustained social reform movement eventually develops an organization to work systematically for change in the social order.[39] Owing to its bureaucratic nature, the organization designates specific officers to cover different functions and hold power and authority. Effective social movement organizations also usually develop a regular way of collecting dues, recruiting members, and communicating with their constituency through a newspaper or periodic meetings. The organization exists to promote change in the laws, rules, and norms of society, but it must also constantly define its purpose to continue its appeal to members and win additional outsiders. If heterogeneity of the membership becomes great enough, the organization sometimes splits into distinct branches with slightly different goals and methods.

The temperance and suffrage movements each developed distinctive organizational structures, with somewhat different techniques for diffusion of ideology and goals. Temperance women had many more clubs and groups at the local level and were more closely tied to the churches, whereas suffragists had a looser organizational structure. These somewhat distinctive organizational styles resulted from the slightly different origins of the movements and gave rise to somewhat different outcomes. The differentiation between temperance and suffrage in fact constituted a division of labor within the feminist movement in which the temperance groups were responsible for contact with the rank and file while suffragists focused on lobbying and state and national pronouncements. Together the two organizations probably furthered the goals of feminism more than either could have done alone.

Strategies for reform—adaptation. After a movement has emerged, developed its ideology and organization, and enlarged its membership, it tries to change the rules that it set out to protest. Rarely does the movement win on its first try. Leaders repeatedly state their goals and revise their strategy to accomplish social change. The opposition protests and resists change. Success results when the movement has sufficiently adapted to existing political and social conditions so that it mobilizes broad popular support and the help of sympathetic lawmakers.[40] Defeated issues sometimes reappear and are later won because the movement's adherents have learned by trial and error how to gain adherents and use political pressure effectively.

Contests about temperance and suffrage differed in the nature of the reformers' agendas and the timing and outcome of major strategies. Temperance forces fought for bringing "scientific" temperance instruction to the schools, raising the age of consent, and introducing prohibition amendments to state constitutions. Suffragists focused on broadening women's educational and employment opportunities and on introducing suffrage amendments to state constitutions. After 1900, woman's temperance was ever more closely tied to prohibition, and temperance forces did not hesitate to portray the vote for women as a tool for making a town or a territory dry. Suffragists, on the other hand, were wary about having too close an alliance with the prohibition forces, for they were in constant danger of arousing powerful anti-suffrage sentiment among brewers and among the many ethnic groups that had no interest in teetotaling.

Two Paths to Women's Equality

This book examines the similarities and differences in the temperance and suffrage movements by examining the origin, development, and legacy of each. Following chapter 2, which traces the origins of the maternal and equal rights streams of feminist thought before the Civil War, chapters 3 and 4 describe, respectively, the woman's temperance movement and the woman suffrage movement as distinct entities, each with its own ideology, leadership, organizational structure, and tactical history of defeats and victories. The final chapter traces the continuation of these two streams of feminism into our own time. To what degree did each movement accomplish its purpose? Why did success come when it did; and in what ways did the insights and contributions of each live on?

Over and above the significance of these two large and important feminist organizations for the understanding of social movements, each may have a lesson to teach about women's moral and political concerns today. This book's title reflects the historical fact that temperance and suffrage were two of the principal arenas for reform through which women sought political equality in the nineteenth century. The title also refers to the two types of feminist outlook that characterize social and political discourse about sex roles even now.

The first of these perspectives, which predominated among temperance women, looks on women as being different from—even superior to—men in ability to care for others and to help those in need. According to this outlook, women improve government by bringing their compassion and care into politics and statecraft. Women provide a model for human behavior that men find worthy of emulation. In 1900 in a speech in Northampton, Massachusetts, to a group of college presidents, the Honorable William T. Harris, U.S. Commissioner of Education, nicely summarized the special contributions women could make to government. Saying that "Man has a tendency to use the principle of justice, not only in dealing with his fellow men in their full maturity, but with children and the weaklings of society, who have not the full normal endowment of responsibility," Harris claimed that Woman has the characteristic of graciousness and kindness, perhaps I should say tenderness. Justice and grace or graciousness are thus the two characteristics appertaining to sex, and the admission of women into all spheres of social influence will bring the principle of nurture into those provinces where the principle of justice has been found not sufficient for the best development of certain classes of society. . . . Just as the tenderness of the mother nurtures the child into a responsible will power . . . so this feminine element added to the State will make it able to provide for that very larger population which fills the slums of our cities and constantly menaces life and property.[41]

The second perspective, more common in the suffrage movement, regards men and their worlds as holding the keys to enlightenment, freedom, and justice. For women to share in these benefits, and in the full rights of citizenship, women and men are to be seen as more similar than different. Women, according to this view, should give up their parochialism, become educated in science and law just as men are, and improve their world by application of rational and scientific thought and the principles of justice. In 1900 Ellen H. Richards, a member of the faculty at the Massachusetts Institute of Technology and principal founder of the field of home economics, expressed parts of this view in an article for the suffrage newspaper, the *Woman's Journal:*

One of the most disheartening things of the day is to see the waste of time and energy in the occupations of nine-tenths of American women. . . . They still cling to tradition. They defy natural law. . . . To take one of the most frequent exhibitions of this contempt for law—a woman's behavior in a crowded street car. Fully three-quarters of the sex do not know how to stand erect in a swaying car, and are not able to keep their balance when the car starts. Yet it is a mere matter of simple laws in relation to bodies in motion and at rest, laws which every school girl should know, and which every school boy does know practically, if not theoretically.

The secret of success in housekeeping, as well as in manufacturing, lies in the right use of *methods* and *machinery*. . . . It is not a profound knowledge of any one or a dozen sciences which women need, so much as an attitude of mind . . . which impels them to ask, "Can I do better than I am doing?" "Is there any device which I might use?" . . . "Am I making the best use of my time?"[42]

Many contemporary readers will recognize the parallels between these views and the two types of moral language described in Carol

Gilligan's *In a Different Voice:* a language of compassion and care that is especially characteristic of women, and an impersonal language of rules and laws more usual to men that is based on an ethic of rights and justice.[43] In historic examples from the women's movement, however, the two ethics defy simple classification by gender. The ethic of compassion attributed to women is here spoken by Harris, a male educator. The importance of rules and laws, scientific as well as legal, is claimed by a woman scientist, Ellen Richards. What I should like to illustrate in these examples is that feminists based their arguments for emancipation on difference or sameness and related ethical traditions: women's special capacity for care with its concern for the particular individual; and women's equal right to justice with its emphasis on universal rules that disregard individual characteristics such as age, sex, or race. The two themes intertwined as they mobilized not only advocates but outsiders. Each ethical tradition drew on the personal outlooks of some participants and fit in with the complex and contradictory expectations surrounding women's roles.

The need for women's compassionate contribution to the state was a message that rang true especially for home-oriented women living outside the big cities and for those people who espoused temperance as the central reform issue of the day. Temperance used women's domestic roles as the primary arena from which to launch efforts for social change.

In the suffrage organizations, however, equal rights and justice arguments predominated. This ethic appealed to those who had fought for the abolition of slavery, who had argued for women's right to enter higher education, and who recognized the need for diversity in a fast-changing society where only the state could resolve conflicts among narrow interests. Rather than emphasizing the redeeming virtues of women and the model of the family as the way to help those in need, the suffragists focused primarily on the impersonal public order as the vehicle for social justice. To claim that women should be admitted to full rights of citizenship, they used men's public roles as a model and argued that women were just as intelligent and competent as men.

Viewed from a broad historical and sociological perspective, I believe that both types of group were necessary to the ultimate realization of women's rights as citizens. For centuries woman's primary role had been linked to the private rather than the public sphere. To legitimate the women's movement in the public realm of responsibility, there had to be an immense social and cultural reorganization of woman's actual roles as well as the symbolic representation of them. Accordingly, one stream of collective effort was directed toward broadening domestic concerns to encompass community and nation, where women in public life would be able to find roles analogous to that of wife and mother. This argument relied on demonstration that women were different from men, more sensitive, more compassionate, and therefore needed in statecraft. The other major stream of collective effort was directed at the barriers that kept women out of public life. Arguments for removal of those barriers emphasized how women were similar to men—just as intelligent, just as competent, just as worthy of the rights of citizenship. Temperance and suffrage, to the extent that they respectively specialized in the arguments of difference and sameness, were thus a complement to each other. Together they brought about the momentous shift toward equality of the sexes more surely than either could have done alone.

Chapter 2

The Emergence of American Feminism, 1830–1870

The women's organizations and activities that appeared in America in the 1830s were the first in the world to lead to a large, persistent women's movement during the succeeding century. During the seventeenth and eighteenth centuries women intellectuals had influenced cultural and political thought in France, England, and Germany. Women had formed their own revolutionary networks during the French Revolution. In the mid-1800s British women also began protesting exclusion from the universities and discrimination under the law; some, like Florence Nightingale, became known for their patriotic service and charitable work. But American women were distinguished by their widespread participation in benevolent associations and their early call for suffrage, which was widely debated as early as the 1880s and eventually drew the support of a broad coalition of women's groups.[1]

When reduced to its essentials, the American feminist movement comprised two major branches, one oriented to upgrading women's domestic role, the other to assuring their voice in the public sphere. Since a parallel dichotomy appears in the feminist movements of Scandinavia, England, Australia, and Canada, it is instructive to examine the origins of these two branches and their modes of operation. In the United States both groups originated in the ideals of American democracy and Protestant individualism. But these ideals when applied to women were everywhere met with contradictory economic

27

and social institutions that subjected women to traditional male authority or questioned their capacity for independence and initiative.

Women responded by forming groups of their own to work for change. The female charitable societies showed that women could make an important contribution to social reform and social improvement. Women's benevolent associations dealt with all types of human ills, from poor mothers and children needing food and clothes to drunken men and prostitutes needing shelter. The woman's rights groups, on the other hand, focused primarily on women's dependency and oppression; they discovered how to use the rights of free association and free speech to press for women's official equality under the law.

Together these two types of early women's organizations constructed a new feminist subculture that would give rise to a much larger and more sustained women's movement after the Civil War. According to this culture, women were capable of acting on their own behalf as well as for the good of society. They also produced new social and political tactics that would later be used to advance the feminist cause. These inventions included the special-purpose prayer group, the charitable association dedicated to a particular benevolent cause, the annual regional or national meeting convened for the purposes of making speeches and of gathering far-flung supporters, the signature-petition aimed at reforming specific state laws, and the special-interest lobbying effort organized to enact state constitutional amendments and statutes. These early organizational discoveries were used by most activist women's associations that emerged after the Civil War.

This chapter will show how two paths to women's equality began to diverge during the antebellum period: one, more closely allied with family and religion, was to be followed by the post–Civil War woman's temperance movement; the other, more secular and oriented to government and the law, was to be taken by the woman suffrage movement. Common to both was a fundamental belief in the strength and power of women that was drawn from everyday civil, domestic, and religious experience.

Republican Motherhood: Foundation for Citizenship

Between 1750 and 1800 the experience of the American Revolution caused a reorientation of thinking about the place of women. Up to that time, women had been expected to manage the household in clear subordination to the male head and in a manner that was private and uncoordinated with the actions of other women. During the Revolution, however, wives and mothers were asked to support embargoes on foreign imports by banning tea from their tables and substituting homespun for the manufactured fabrics from abroad. Their lives became more obviously intertwined with the larger political fortunes of the country. Their contribution was as much to the nation as to their own households. The result was a new sense of their own self-worth and of their importance to the nation. Abigail Adams's famous plea to her husband John, to "Remember the Ladies" at the Continental Congress, conveyed this new spirit of self-confidence and entitlement to citizenship.[2]

Once the Revolution had passed, however, and the Constitution was ratified without formal recognition of their rights, women knew their status to be ambiguous. They were presumably included in those stirring words of the Declaration of Independence, "All men are created equal and endowed by their Creator with certain inalienable rights among which are life, liberty, and the pursuit of happiness." But they were expected to continue their deference to husband or father at home and be satisfied that their civil interests were better represented by men than by themselves. Out of the tension between egalitarian and patriarchal ideologies and a rapidly changing domestic economy came a new culture in which women were able to challenge the old regime and propose new rights for themselves.

Equality as a democratic principle.   Although the American Revolution had prepared the ground for women's representation of their own interests in government, the Constitution was silent on the subject of woman's rights. Women had made unusual strides during the Revolution by raising money and making sacrifices for the war effort. The Daughters of Liberty in the 1760s had substituted herbs for foreign teas and held massive spinning bees to reduce importation of textiles. They knitted stockings and sewed clothing for the soldiers. Sparked by a broadside, "The Sentiments of an American Woman," the first large-scale woman's association was formed in Philadelphia in 1780 to raise money to further compensate the soldiers. Considering it an honor, leading women of the city canvassed all the wards as well as other cities such as Bethlehem and Lancaster to ask women to give up little luxuries for themselves and their families in order to contribute to the added comfort and well-being of the Continental Army. The wife of Pennsylvania's governor was the "treasuress." Similar campaigns were mounted in New Jersey, Maryland, and Virginia, and the collection was ultimately sent to Martha Washington and then to General Washington himself. The donors had hoped that the sum they collected ($300,000 in continental money, which converted into about $7,500 in specie) would be used for something beyond basic necessities. But Washington resisted their idea because thousands of shirts were badly needed. The women finally relented and to save money actually helped to sew the shirts themselves. Sadly, however, their monumental efforts were trivialized by some, who referred to them merely as "General Washington's Sewing Circle."[3]

Women did vote in New Jersey from the 1780s until 1807, when the right was revoked. The New Jersey Constitution was broadly worded in a way that was interpreted as allowing the right of franchise to all citizens who had met the property and tax qualifications. In 1790, a New Jersey election law even referred to voters as "he or she," and by 1800 woman suffrage was so well established that a special constitutional amendment was thought unnecessary. A vote-packing scheme in 1807, however, was unfairly attributed to election abuse by women and blacks and immediately resulted in their disenfranchisement. Opponents of women's right to vote claimed that women were weak, subject to influence of husbands or fathers, and therefore not to be trusted with the vote.[4]

In the face of such reverses, thoughtful women could do little more than read and discuss the works of writers who in the 1790s put forth the major arguments for women's equality—the radical English philosopher Mary Wollstonecraft, the New England poet and author Judith Sargent Murray, or historian Mercy Otis Warren.[5] Ordinary women could also express their beliefs in domestic equality and independence by adapting their patriotism and democratic instincts to the confines of the feminine role. This is precisely what they accomplished through a focus on the education of patriotic sons and dutiful daughters that has been termed "Republican Motherhood." As "Republican Mothers" they educated their children to become the responsible future citizens of the new nation, thus justifying their own participation in the civic culture. Historian Linda Kerber regards Republican Motherhood as an important cultural invention that spared ordinary women the ridicule unleashed on a radical like

Wollstonecraft while at the same time allowing them to join mothering and family life with service to the nation.[6]

The duties of Republican Motherhood required that future mothers themselves be educated. Mary Beth Norton has analyzed the educational background of 79 of the early women leaders described in *Notable American Women* born before 1810. Of those born between 1700 and 1770 only one-fifth had any kind of schooling beyond a simple primary education. But this ratio had risen dramatically by the end of the century to three-fifths of those women born during the 1770s and 1780s and three-fourths of those born between 1800 and 1810.[7]

Before the Revolution girls had been schooled somewhat haphazardly in dame schools and adventure schools set up in private homes. After 1790 middle-class and well-to-do families began to see it as their duty to educate their daughters in a boarding school or nearby academy. The result was a marked improvement in women's literacy and capacity to teach their children. At the same time the graduates of the academies raised the standard of teaching and created the first real profession for women. Some of the most famous of the early academy graduates later founded schools of their own. Emma Willard in 1819 appealed to the New York state legislature to support her female seminary at Troy. Hundreds of graduates of the Troy Female Seminary later became teachers on the expanding frontier.[8] Catherine Beecher established a female seminary in Hartford, Connecticut, in 1823, the Western Female Institute near Cincinnati, and a normal school in Milwaukee. Mary Lyon helped to plan the Wheaton Female Seminary (now Wheaton College in Norton, Massachusetts), which opened in 1835; she also founded Mt. Holyoke Female Seminary in 1837, which later became Mt. Holyoke College.[9]

Education would turn out to be the key that unlocked the door of women's domestic confinement. The earliest statement of feminist sentiment came out of a female academy, Miss Sarah Pierce's famous school in Litchfield, Connecticut. On 4 July 1839, in words that both echoed the Declaration of Independence of 1775 and foreshadowed the July Fourth Declaration of Sentiments at Seneca Falls in 1848, the "Humble Address of a Thousand Federal Maids" stated the nature of the injustices done to women in their exclusion from the public weal:

When in the Course of Human Events it becomes necessary for the Ladies to dissolve those bonds by which they have been subjected to others, and to assume among the self styled Lords of Creation that separate and equal station to which the laws of nature and their *own talents* entitle them, a decent respect to the opinions of mankind requires, that they should declare the causes which impel them to the separation.

We hold these truths to be self evident. That all *mankind* are created equal; that they are endowed with certain unalienable rights, that among these are life liberty and the pursuit of happiness.[10]

Here was truly a manifestation of "role strain." Women who were more educated than many of their fellow male citizens were protesting their exclusion from governing their own lives as well as the larger society. Mary Beth Norton has described their expression of a new sense of citizenship through their womanhood:

The domestic realm, which had hitherto been regarded as peripheral to public welfare, now acquired major importance. With the new stress on the household as the source of virtue and stability in government, attention necessarily focused on women, the traditional directors of household activities. . . . Before the war, females had been viewed as having little concern with the public sphere. [But it was becoming evident that] the nation would not survive unless its citizens were virtuous. [Thus] feminine influence would play a special role in the United States.[11]

In this manner the political and patriotic elements of American culture justified women's growing desire to broaden their roles.

Equality as a religious principle.   Religion also helped to legitimate women's quest for equality. Of the five women who planned the Seneca Falls convention in the summer of 1848, four were Quakers. Historian Margaret Bacon has asked why the tiny Religious Society of Friends contributed such a disproportionate number of leaders to the feminist cause.[12] It turns out that Quakerism was a veritable seedbed for the new feminism. As early as the seventeenth and eighteenth centuries, Quaker women had served as traveling ministers, on occasion leaving behind husbands and children, so strongly did they feel called to do the Lord's work. Well before the Revolution the American Friends had also established a tradition of women's business meetings separate from the monthly community meeting. In addition, Quaker women who felt moved by the Holy Spirit to speak in meetings were expected to do so. Finally, the Quakers believed in education for all— rich and poor, girls and boys. Thus the four Quaker women who planned the Seneca Falls convention were building on more than a century of precedent within Quaker communities for women's independent organization and initiative in causes which they felt to be morally right.

More broadly, one might ask why religion was so intimately involved in the activities of the early feminists—visible both in the religious affiliations of the early leaders and the religious coloration of their work. They met in churches; they opened their meetings with prayer; they received support from certain members of the clergy and from larger bodies of church people. In terms of the collective behavior theory put forward in chapter 1, religion was important to American women's early involvement in feminism because it provided a partial solution to the problem of role strain. The one outlet for independent thought and action open to early-nineteenth-century American women was religious expression. While St. Paul had said that wives should be subject to their husbands, it was also written in the Book of Galatians that "There is neither Jew nor Greek, there is neither bond nor free, there is neither male nor female: for ye are all one in Christ Jesus."[13] This ideal of equality of all God's children, coupled with the Protestant tradition of individualism and the priesthood of all believers, rejected ecclesiastical hierarchy and infused feminists with the courage to challenge prevailing beliefs.

During the same period American religion became "feminized," not in the sense of becoming weak or effeminate but open to women's experience and influenced by their moral and social perspectives. This remarkable reorientation of culture is detailed by Mary Ryan in her account of women's religious activity during the Second Great Awakening in Utica, New York, in the 1830s and 1840s. Women and youths were the great majority of converts when evangelists like the renowned Charles Finney preached to camp meetings and revivals calling for repentance and commitment to a godly life.[14]

Why should women have been so responsive to this religious ferment? Ryan follows the lead of Whitney Cross, who showed in the *Burned Over District* (1950) that the great social movements that swept across upstate New York prior to the Civil War (the anti-Masonic movement, temperance, Mormonism, suffrage, and the utopian Oneida Community) found a fertile field along the Erie Canal. The growing towns that bordered the canal had experienced rapid social change, in-migration, and consequent ferment in their community life.[15] The women who responded to the evangelists, according to Ryan, were especially likely to be wives of entrepreneurs, not the poorest of the community, but members of families who had some leisure.

These women were relieved from assisting in the farming, artisan production, or sales that once took place within the household workplace. Many of them were wealthy enough to purchase household supplies in the shops on Genesee Street and to employ servants to meet the domestic needs of husbands and children. It would follow that involvement in the benevolent activities filled a vacuum recently opened in the everyday lives of urban upper-class women as the work of men was removed to the shops, stores, and offices of Genesee Street.[16]

Nancy Cott discovered a similar preoccupation with religious matters in the letters and diaries of 100 women who lived in the first half of the nineteenth century. She quotes the English traveler Harriet Martineau, who had observed that women "pursue religion as an occupation" because they were constrained from exercising their full range of moral, intellectual, and physical powers in other ways.[17] Religious activity thus seems to have served a function parallel to an occupation for men: it helped women to define their identity at the same time that it helped them to overcome isolation and form bonds with others in the community.

Religion in nineteenth-century America thus offered women a solution to the conflict in their daily lives between having heavy responsibility and little power. The revivals helped to bridge the gap between independence and submission by emphasizing the importance of women's self-reflection and self-improvement and their influence over their families and the life of the community around them. Transcendentalism, a radical movement among New England Congregationalists and Unitarians, called for just this sort of inner reflection and social reform. Prominent among the Transcendentalists were Bronson Alcott (father of Louisa May), who educated both boys and girls in his progressive child-oriented school, and Margaret Fuller, a leading feminist thinker who in her writings and living room "conversations" in 1840s Boston projected new attitudes that assumed the equality of women in matters of intellect and morality. Outside Boston at Brook Farm, Ralph Waldo Emerson, the Alcotts, and other leading Transcendentalists briefly experimented with a means to live out their ideals through a communal life.

But the most important and lasting legacy of women's religious activity, as well as of Transcendentalism, was a reorientation of popular culture that began to give a larger place to the values and influence of women. Women's intuition and emotional insight were especially valued by the new religious leaders of the era. No longer were people expected to prostrate themselves before an angry God. They valued instead the capacity to understand the universe and the Creator. In *Women of the Nineteenth Century* (1843), Margaret Fuller links women's strength to their inner sense of truth and right: "Women who speak in public, if they have a moral power . . . , that is, if they speak for conscience' sake, . . . invariably subdue the prejudices of their hearers." At the same time, each sex is the better if it shares the strengths of the other: "There is no wholly masculine man, no purely feminine woman. [As Goethe said,] 'The excellent woman is she, who, if the husband dies, can be a father to the children.'"[18]

Thus Quakerism, the new Evangelism, and Transcendentalism equipped women in the early nineteenth century for challenging the existing social order. Women from these religious traditions especially would question their confined and subordinate roles with a confidence and fervor born of inner conviction.

The need for women's equality in the home.   After the Revolution American women also saw a possibility for equality in domestic affairs. As grown persons, sometimes with more wealth or intellectual ability than a husband or guardian, they were supposed to submit to the rule of men and to a traditional patriarchal code of behavior that was rapidly becoming outmoded and dysfunctional. Demographic and economic changes in family life were making possible greater choice in marriage, fertility, and employment, yet women's domestic rights were not expanding at the same pace. Women could live with inequality by accepting the ideology of submissiveness and domesticity, or they could reject it and attempt to change the status quo through protests and legal action. In actuality, both types of adaptation occurred.

The new demographic and economic realities. The net effect of a falling birth rate and a rising life expectancy was to put more time at women's disposal. Advances in technology were also taking many productive tasks, such as spinning, out of the home to small mills and factories where teenagers and young people of both sexes were employed as workers. The effect showed in the statistics. Between 1800 and 1860 the birth rate dropped by nearly a third from 278 to 184 per thousand women of childbearing age. At the same time life expectancy was improving from around 35 years before the American Revolution to more than 50 years for persons born in the 1780s.[19] Urban occupations were also increasing, and more women had paid employment. Between 1820 and 1860 the proportion of nonfarm workers grew from 28 percent to 41 percent, and by 1870 urban workers constituted half of all the employed.[20]

Families changed as a result of greater longevity, lower fertility, and the gradual process of industrialization. Marriages were now much more likely to be based on the young couple's own desires than on parents' wishes and property considerations. The opening of the frontier and the rise of individual enterprise made women's independence more important. A two-sphere theory of sex differences developed in which men's world was understood to be business affairs and women's world that of the household. Families became more child-centered, and women focused much of their energy on motherhood. Some married later, and others remained single.[21]

The cult of domesticity. These new developments brought elaboration and extension of women's domestic roles. Barbara Welter has described four qualities that were celebrated in the "cult of domesticity" or "true womanhood": piety, purity, submissiveness, and domesticity.[22] Women between 1830 and 1850 were especially praised if they accepted their separate sphere in the home and were religious, somewhat asexual, but morally pure and submitted to parental or spousal authority. Their homes were to be havens of rest from the busy world where they sheltered men and children and upheld the noble virtues and higher motives which they as women were particularly qualified to represent.

Catherine Beecher, the leading exponent of practical domesticity, described the rational and ordered running of a household but also conveyed a larger moral vision that charged women with the principal responsibility for influencing children's character as well as the character of the whole nation.[23] In the 1820s she developed a moral philosophy that transcended the evangelistic piety of the era and encouraged her students to rely on individual conscience. In the *Treatise on Domestic Economy* (1841), Beecher gave advice on health, diet, domestic architecture, and household management for the competent housewife and mother; included were tips on cooking, infant care, laundry, and candle-making.[24] She continually sought teachers to fill a pressing need in the West; the schools she founded in Ohio and Wisconsin during the 1840s and 1850s were largely devoted to training future teachers. Because teachers in new towns frequently preceded the minister, they were often chiefly responsible for setting the tone of the community. Beecher envisioned a community that would coalesce around its women, if not the church.[25]

Thus, despite the submissiveness called for by the cult of domesticity, women were applying the ideal of Republican Motherhood to society itself and the governance of their families, thereby living out Beecher's moral philosophy of teaching and serving others.

[A]s women are more and more educated to understand and value the importance of their influence in society, and their peculiar duties, more young females will pursue their education with the expectation that unless paramount private duties forbid, they are to employ their time and talents in the duties of a teacher, until they assume the responsibilities of domestic life. Females will cease to feel that they are educated just to enjoy themselves in future life, and realize the obligations imposed by Heaven to live to do good.[26]

This ideal of service would combine with Republican Motherhood to provide one of the strong motives behind the many women's benevolent and charitable associations that blossomed in the 1830s and 1840s.

Domestic Feminism and Charitable Work

Just as the Enlightenment brought a rational critique of monarchy and helped to spawn the American Revolution and Republican Motherhood, so it caused a critical reappraisal of religion that resulted in spiritual revivals and widespread conversions in both England and America. Religious feelings, infused with new and immediate meaning, inspired personal change and individual perfectionism. For women of the early nineteenth century, whose domain was the home, the personal meaning of conversion was worked out in their care for family and friends. Their world was not yet so much divided between private and public as between earthly and eternal. For most women, all life this side of death was bound up with family life. Yet families might be torn by internal differences. In addition, death removed individuals irretrievably from the embrace of the family. What was not family life was therefore associated with God and the afterlife. In this worldview friendship took on great emotional and intellectual importance because it could transcend the religious, political, and economic differences that sometimes divided family members. For these reasons, historian Irene Brown suggests that friendship became one of the key preoccupations of eighteenth- and nineteenth-century men and women. And in the tension between earthly and eternal, friendship could even transcend death.[27]

The possibility of friendship allowed women to extend their emotional relationships and domestic skills beyond the family without having to take up the uncertain and risky entrepreneurial activities of men. Following the American Revolution, women began organizing themselves to help other women, most often widows and poor children. Soon various other benevolent and missionary associations were formed to assist and educate a wide range of people, including "heathen" women and children both at home and abroad.

As commerce and travel increased during the 1820s and 1830s and as cities grew, women withdrew from farm work and became more specialized in child rearing and family care.[28] Alongside various charitable and benevolent associations there sprang up a great number of maternal associations and moral reform societies to address new threats of sexual temptation and drunkenness that appeared along with rapid population growth and migration in the burgeoning cities and towns. Moral reform societies to end prostitution and temperance societies to end drunkenness gained enormous popularity after 1830. Both, however, introduced a new element into women's activism: new demands on men.

When men began to accuse women of ranging beyond their proper sphere, reform-minded women responded by asserting their moral and spiritual equality with men. This confrontation between men and women coincided with a nascent structural change that by 1850 had begun to distinguish the private world of the family from the public world of business and government. Male leaders in foreign missions, moral reform, and temperance all asserted that women should work for these good causes but not vote or take leadership roles because their place was in the home. Thus for women to be able to cross the divide into public life a new argument was required: that women were at least the equals of men in the home, and that their abilities as homemakers were also needed in public life, a stance that has since been termed "domestic feminism."[29]

Women's arguments that their mothering should extend outside the home took a number of different forms—benevolence, foreign missions, moral reform, and temperance. While some women belonged to several such organizations, it seems clear that there was no simple progression by which the earlier benevolent or missionary groups evolved into later moral reform or temperance societies.[30] Instead these many different causes taken together had the effect of pushing out the walls of women's traditional roles in a way that helped lay the foundation for educational and political emancipation. Domestic feminism not only led to equal rights feminism, it also paved the first major path to women's participation and equality in public life.

Benevolent associations.   From 1800 to 1830, simple charity, along with religious work, was the main activity of organized women's groups. One of the earliest and best-known examples was the New York Society for Aid to Widows and Poor Children, founded in 1796 by Isabella Marshall Graham. An educated woman, Graham grew up in Scotland, but when widowed, endured poverty and supported herself by running a school for children in her home. After immigrating to New York City in 1789 and opening a successful school for girls, Graham sought ways to help other women who were faced with sudden poverty. The New York Society provided material help, work, and a temporary home for the "worthy poor"—respectable women in reduced circumstances.[31] Its work caught the imagination of others and by 1820 there were branches or followers in Portland, Boston, Providence, Philadelphia, and other smaller cities. Historians have discovered scores of similar women's charitable organizations arising between 1800 and 1830: for example, the Newburyport Orphan Association founded in 1803, the Female Benevolent Society of New York City to help abandoned females in 1813, and the Boston Female Refuge Society in 1821.[32]

These charitable associations of the early 1800s seem distinctive in their generosity devoid of moralistic judgment. Rather than condescension, they offered help in a way that implied equality of spirit if not of wealth. Historian Anne Firor Scott notes that the clientele were the "worthy poor," who in background were similar to the members of the philanthropic societies but were simply thought to have fallen on hard times.[33] Such friendly and sympathetic efforts, which extended women's nurturing activities beyond the home, showed women capable of wider pursuits. In addition, by stretching the boundaries of "woman's sphere," these benevolent associations prepared the ground for the rise of feminism. In the words of Anne Boylan, "They justified women's organizational activity as the extension of the mothering role and succeeded in making legitimate women's desire for public roles."[34]

Missionary societies.   Home and foreign missions provided fields where women might live out their religious hopes and ideals. Missionaries and their wives traveled to India, China, Africa, and the American West, not so much to convert a "heathen" society as to serve as living examples of Christian life. Missionary couples introduced the Bible, taught reading and writing, and showed foreign women a model much nearer to equality of husband and wife than permitted in Hindu, Mohammedan, or Buddhist custom. The Reverend Jonathan Allen, when preaching his farewell sermon for Adoniram and Ann Hazeltine Judson before they left for Burma in 1812, expressed such hopes: "It will be your business, my dear children, to teach these women, to whom your husbands can have but little or no access. Go then, and do all in your power, to enlighten their minds, and bring them to the knowledge of truth. Go, and if possible, raise their character to the dignity of rational beings, and to the rank of Christians in a Christian land. Teach them to realize that they are not an inferior race of creatures; but stand upon a par with men."[35]

Missionary societies were set up to provide material support, Bibles, and tracts for the home and foreign mission field. The concept of cent and tract societies was inaugurated around 1800 when someone hit upon the idea of making some small daily sacrifice as a means of contribution to the purchase and distribution of Bibles and other religious literature. By 1818 several thousand women in New England alone were contributing 52 cents a year to organizations with such worthy goals as distributing Bibles or contributing funds for missionary efforts at home or abroad. By 1820 these tract societies were supplemented and partly eclipsed by the burgeoning foreign missionary societies, which were based on a similar philosophy of asking women to make small domestic sacrifices for the further spread of Christianity. While missionary societies had both male and female members, women predominated, comprising roughly three-fifths of the membership

"'Take her too,' said the officer," a depiction of missionary Ann Hazeltine Judson at the time of her husband's capture and imprisonment in Burma, 1824. From *Lady Missionaries in Foreign Lands* by Mrs. E[mma] R[aymond] Pitman, 1889.

and contributing as much as two-thirds of the moneys raised—a remarkable feat given most women's lack of independent income.[36]

Between 1800 and 1850 women's missionary societies were the single most common form of female voluntary association. Why were they so popular? Most important, perhaps, they were a natural extension of church membership and required no radical departure from traditional expectations of women in connection with Christian duties. But the immense popularity of the biographies of missionary heroines suggests that women were inspired by the challenge of the missionary's task as well as the example of the missionary wife. Ordinary women could identify with both the heathen woman being educated and the missionary who was educating her.[37]

Knowledge of the inferior position of women in other lands made American women thankful for their own good fortune. They particularly deplored the harems, seclusion, and cruel treatment Muslim women were said to endure in India and other Asian countries. Women missionaries represented the hope that American women could surmount these barriers and reach their pagan sisters through education, teaching them to read and to follow what was felt to be the superior and more civilized marriage and community practices of the Christian world.[38] Women living isolated or monotonous lives in rural America appeared to identify with missionary wives and vicariously participate in their success and sacrifice.

The life of the missionary wife was embodied in the thrilling story of Ann Hazeltine Judson. She struggled to get her missionary husband released from prison in Burma, safeguarded his translation of the Bible, smuggled gifts into the prison, pleaded with the viceroy for his freedom, bore a child during this ordeal, and ultimately succeeded in obtaining her husband's release only to die shortly after in 1826. This stirring account, written by her husband and distributed widely across the country, told of a remarkably shrewd and intelligent woman able to act independently through adversity yet also imbued with a Christian vision. The story not only lifted women out of their daily round; Ann Judson symbolized an independence and nobility of character that bespoke women's spirited and intellectual equality rather than their inferiority and subordination. Historian Joan Jacobs Brumberg has aptly termed this quality "religious feminism."[39]

Maternal associations and moral reform.   While women's charities and missions extended Christian friendship to the less fortunate and expressed American women's implicit belief in their own spiritual equality with men, a new kind of organization emerged around 1820 that recognized and tried to control a new and threatening element in women's experience—isolation and loneliness in the burgeoning cities and new towns that sometimes led to economic and sexual exploitation. Between 1810 and 1830 there appeared maternal associations, designed to prepare children to resist sexual and other forms of moral temptation. Then, beginning in the 1830s, came moral reform societies, which tried to help prostitutes and to stamp out the economic and sexual exploitation of women.

One of the first accounts of maternal associations describes one in 1815 in Portland, Maine, where mothers every few weeks would bring their children to their women's meetings, using these occasions for religious instruction and cautionary examples to warn against unbridled sexuality and drunkenness. In Utica and Whitestown, New York, where many such groups appeared during the 1820s and 1830s, it appears that parents were anxious about the uncertainties of the new commercial culture and that mothers were trying to instill inner controls in their children that would substitute for the family controls of an earlier era.[40]

Maternal associations sprang up in many cities and towns alongside the charitable and benevolent associations, the cent and tract, and missionary societies. Many women had memberships in more than one such women's group. Where the maternal associations went beyond the earlier charitable and religious groups was in drawing moral lessons to protect and improve the lives of children in their own families and friendship circles. Not surprisingly perhaps, Ryan's analysis of these groups' membership in upstate New York shows them to be of the small business and artisan class, a segment of the population in a rapidly growing commercial culture who were especially sensitive to the individualizing effects of urbanization and loss of extended family ties.[41] At the same time in New England, similar associations sprang up that also seemed to be responding to major social change in the larger society: girls coming off the farms to work in the textile mills of Lowell; young people moving to Boston unattached and alone; or single young people living in boardinghouses in the industrializing towns of western Massachusetts.[42]

Moral reform societies focused the diffuse anxieties of the maternal association about sexual temptation on prostitution, the economic conditions that gave rise to it, and the men who supported it. In the 1820s, the Boston Seamen's Society and the Providence Association for Employment of Women added an element of activism to their help: they tried to raise women's wages, "the profit of the needle," so that indigents could survive on sewing or other available domestic occupations.[43] The New York Moral Reform Society, founded in 1834, had within a few years 445 auxiliaries in other cities and rural areas. The Boston Moral Reform Society, founded in 1835, could likewise count 131 rural auxiliaries by 1839.[44] The Boston Society for Employing the Poor in 1836 noted some husbands' improvidence and abuse.[45] These associations sought out prostitutes, provided them with shelter, and tried to help them find respectable employment. Some of the societies also briefly published the names of men who visited brothels, but for this they were told they were "out of their sphere," and soon desisted. By the 1840s, however, the Boston group campaigned for antiseduction laws and got them passed.[46]

Historians have noted the hostility to men that permeated much of women's early activity in moral reform as well as their feelings of sisterhood as they identified with one another as women. Their purpose was to be rid of sexual license and the double standard by prodding the conscience of American males with respect to chastity and adultery.[47] At the same time they wanted to train sons and daughters to a standard of premarital celibacy and virginity. By 1837 the *Advocate of Moral Reform,* the newspaper of the movement, had a national circulation of 16,500; it published the names of men who patronized prostitutes.[48] Women, by challenging the double standard of male prerogatives, brought their own standard into public view and in the process learned to organize and to articulate an agenda for change. These activities seem to represent the first example of women trying to accomplish change through governmental action and thus set an important precedent for women's action in the political realm.

Women's temperance groups. As in the case of women's charities and missionary societies, women had long been connected to temperance work. The Society of Friends in 1760, the Conference of the Methodist Church in 1780, and the Universalists in 1800 had all declared themselves opposed to the use of alcoholic spirits.[49] The Finney revivals of 1814 to 1838 had linked conversion to signing a pledge never to drink wine or spirits. In Utica in the 1840s, for example, 8,000 people signed the pledge.[50] As a result, temperance work was as much a natural extension of the Christian life as training children through the maternal associations or trying to stamp out sexual license and moral corruption through the moral reform societies. In the 1840s and 1850s, however, women's temperance activities outstripped the earlier forms of women's benevolence as women's auxiliaries sprouted from the Washingtonian Society, the Sons of Temperance, and the Independent Order of Good Templars. In Cincinnati the Daughters of Temperance, founded in 1846, had 200 members by 1848 and a total national membership of 30,000. The Independent Order of Good Templars in Ohio had 3 lodges by 1854 and 176 lodges by 1856. By 1857, the organization counted 80,000 members nationwide.[51] At the same time, sporadic incidents of women's collective action against saloons began to appear.[52]

Of all the women's groups that flourished before 1850, temperance associations created the most direct path to women's organized political activity. Like moral reform, temperance concerned men's behavior—drunkenness, abuse, and failure to support wives and children. The movement also evolved from an emphasis on individual moral change (such as signing the pledge or cooking without alcohol) to a recognition that legislative change (such as the Maine prohibition law of 1851) was needed. But unlike moral reform, temperance addressed a more widespread problem and produced a broader-based movement. Alcohol was the third most important industrial product in 1810, accounting for nearly 10 percent of total national manufacturing output. Per capita consumption in 1840 was approximately three times what it was in 1940.[53] On her travels across America one observer, Harriet Martineau, noted intemperance even among women: "It is no secret on the spot, that the habit of intemperance is not infrequent among women of station and education in the most enlightened parts of the country. I witnessed some instances and heard of more. It does not seem to me to be regarded with all the dismay which such a symptom ought to excite."[54]

In the early 1840s Martha Washingtonians (women's groups devoted to temperance) established more than 40 chapters in New York City alone. The group trained and gave domestic employment to women alcoholics and their children and collected and donated clothing to victims of drunkenness and their needy families.[55] As the Washingtonian groups waned, fraternal orders and temperance sisterhoods took their place. Reformers of the 1850s, expressing concern for family and the home, advised against the use of alcohol in cooking and medicine. At the same time they translated the effects of drunkenness

into the cash terms of the marketplace: inebriates could neither
work productively and save money nor support those dependent on
them.[56]

Thus, like a catalyst in a chemical solution, the introduction of the
temperance cause into the unsettled rural and increasingly urban society of the 1830s to the 1850s suddenly shifted the discourse of
women's benevolence from one of friendship and of reconciliation
between earthly and eternal to one of equal rights and of bridging the
gap between private and public. The Sons of Temperance Convention
in Syracuse in 1852 and the World's Temperance Convention in New
York City in 1853 brought these issues to a head. On both occasions
women delegates were not seated on the convention floor and were
not allowed to speak. At the New York Women's Temperance
Convention held in Rochester in April 1852 and at the WHOLE World's
Temperance Convention in New York that followed the convention in
1853, women spoke their minds. They attacked the unfair system that
gladly accepted their money and their work but refused their right to
speak or to vote. At the 1852 convention in Rochester, Elizabeth Cady
Stanton promised, "We shall do much when the pulpit, the forum, the
professor's chair, and the ballot-box are ours." She then outlined the
list of claims to come:

1. Let no woman remain in the relation of wife with the confirmed drunkard.
Let no drunkard be the father of her children. Let no woman form an alliance
with any man who has been suspected even of the vice of intemperance; for
the taste once acquired can never, never be eradicated. . . .
2. Let us petition our State governments so to modify the laws affecting marriage, and the custody of children, that the drunkard shall have no claims on
either wife or child.
3. Let us touch not, taste not, handle not, the unclean thing in any combination. Let us eschew it in all culinary purposes, and refuse it in all its tempting
and refined forms.
4. With an efficient organization, lectures, tracts, newspapers, and discussion, we shall accomplish much.[57]

Here then was the agenda that emerged from the religious and
domestic feminism that took hold between the American Revolution
and the Civil War. Whether in benevolence, missions, moral reform,
or temperance, women were trying to raise responsibility for higher
levels of self-control on the part of children and men at the same time
that they sought greater autonomy for themselves in the domestic and

the public sphere. The combination led inexorably to equal rights feminism and a demand for the woman's vote.

Equal Rights Feminism and Admission to Citizenship

Stemming from Republican Motherhood and the evangelical tradition of the Protestant enlightenment came another stream of feminism. More than the women's benevolent and charitable associations, it sought improvements in the lives of women themselves. This "equal rights" feminism documented women's exclusion from higher education and the professions, the public platform, the courts of law and legislatures, and the right to vote.

In contrast to the rich fabric of local associations that characterized domestic feminism, the equal rights strain appeared in life stories of illustrious individuals: the Grimké sisters, who were pioneers in public speaking; Ernestine Rose and Fanny Wright, who lectured on woman's property rights; Lucretia Mott and Lucy Stone, who like many others worked for the abolition of slavery; and perhaps best known of all, Elizabeth Cady Stanton and Susan B. Anthony, who focused on the female right to the ballot. Unlike the anonymous members of benevolent and missionary societies, woman's rights advocates were known by name. They faced much greater opposition than the respectable women's groups that grew out of the church. They were self-aware and conscious of being at odds with established custom.

Woman's rights leaders also traveled between towns to visit friends, attend conventions, or gather petitions to the state legislature. As a result they built up networks of support that linked them to other leaders in the woman's cause or to temperance and abolition. In the way that a priest or trader in a peasant society might bridge city and hinterland and in the process transcend parochial customs, these woman's rights leaders transcended the thinking of their day and were thus able to persevere in the face of opposition.

In comparison with the domestic feminists, the equal rights feminists also had more of a sense of their own history and self-consciously recorded and published their proceedings in biographical accounts and in the six-volume *History of Woman Suffrage*. These deliberate records provided continuity and public recognition despite relatively small membership and periodic reverses. The older generation wrote down their lectures, conferred with one another at conventions, and gradually developed a coherent ideology of woman's equality. Some overcame initial exclusion from higher education or the professions; others carried petitions to the legislature on behalf of woman's property rights or the abolition of slavery; still others protested paying their taxes and tried to vote. Eventually these streams of individual belief and effort coalesced into a collective movement that changed public sentiment and finally the law.

Rights to education, employment, and public speaking.   It was particularly individual protests that won women the right to obtain higher education, to enter professions such as law or medicine, and to speak in public. Small individual victories, then the gradual opening of access to each of these domains, in time laid the foundation for women's admission to the public sphere.[58]

By the 1850s, woman's access to female academies was well established. The Rockford Female Seminary in Illinois, founded in 1852 by Anna Peck Sill and modeled on Mt. Holyoke, would educate leaders of the late nineteenth century like Jane Addams, the founder of the famous settlement Hull House in Chicago, and Elizabeth Griffin, the mother of the famous Abbott sisters—Edith, an economist at the University of Chicago, Grace, a social worker and later director of the Children's Bureau, and Agnes, a pioneer in public health and the first female professor at Harvard Medical School.[59] The great remaining barrier was access to college and university education. Oberlin opened to women in 1837, and Lucy Stone traveled from Massachusetts to Ohio to study there and become one of the first woman college graduates in the country in 1847. The University of Iowa, founded in 1855, was coeducational from the beginning. Of the small colleges, Earlham was founded by Quakers in 1847, Antioch by Horace Mann in 1852, and the College of Wooster by Presbyterians in 1866—all pioneered by educating young women equally along with young men.[60]

Closely intertwined with the battle of women to enter college was the struggle to be admitted to professions such as medicine. In the opening volumes of the *History of Woman Suffrage,* published in 1881 and recounting the first woman's rights conventions of the 1840s and 1850s, it is striking how many women doctors are mentioned as either attending the meetings or corresponding with woman's rights leaders: Harriot K. Hunt, Elizabeth Blackwell, Marie Zakrewska, and others less well known today. Their stories dramatize both the prejudice that they faced and their outstanding contributions once they succeeded. Hunt, for example, born in 1805 and widely known as the first woman doctor, started teaching school in 1827. After a serious illness of her sister in 1830, she learned to practice medicine and was very success-ful in treating her Boston patients. She applied for admission to Harvard Medical School in 1847, was denied acceptance, but was admit-ted in 1850 to hear lectures. The all-male student body so strongly protested that she gave up the attempt. In 1853, however, she was awarded an Honorary Doctor of Medicine Degree from the newly founded Female Medical College of Pennsylvania. Elizabeth Blackwell was also turned away from Harvard Medical School as well as several others before finally being admitted in 1847 to the Geneva College of Medicine in New York. Blackwell founded the New York Infirmary for Women and Children and later instituted training for other women physicians, one of whom—Marie Zakrewska—opened the New England Hospital for Women and Children in 1862 in Boston.[61]

These heroic victories were incorporated into the woman's rights canon to propound a moral: women need to persevere against great odds to be independent because they are everywhere shackled by reli-gious and domestic customs that perpetuate their dependency. "Let the daughters be trained for their responsibilities," said Clarinda I. Nichols, publisher of a newspaper in Vermont, at the Second Woman's Rights Convention in Worcester in 1851. They should be taught self-reliance and some independent means of support.[62] Speakers repeat-edly decried the narrow number of occupations open to women, the insufficiency of their wages, and their exclusion from the law, medi-cine, and ministry. According to Paulina Wright Davis, speaking at the New York Woman's Rights Convention in 1853, women had lost some of the economic independence they had once known: "In the middle ages, we practiced surgery, medicine, and obstetrics. The healing art was ours, by prescription. Restore it to us."[63]

By and large such statements applied to middle-class, educated women, like the leaders themselves. But woman's rights leaders were also concerned with women in humbler occupations, like the new industrial jobs in the textile mills, shoe factories, and printing trades. Davis spoke also of them:

We ask that the avocations which progress and improvement have substi-tuted for all that we have lost be fairly opened to us. . . . You have swal-lowed up a thousand household workshops in every great factory, and we demand our place at the power loom with wages up to the full value of our services. . . . Give us our place at the press, that has displaced the lost art [of copying manuscripts]. For the ruder labor, from which we have been taken and from which the world is now forever relieved, give us the use of those arts of modern birth to which we are so much better adapted than the usurping sex. Dentistry, daguerreotyping, designing, telegraphing, clerking in record offices, and a thousand other engagements which ask neither large bones nor stronger sinews, and which [require] neither the delicacy, nor the retirement, that you hang upon as the propriety of our sex.[64]

Woman's rights advocates were doubtless aware that in mill towns like Lowell young women off the farms were reading and educating themselves even after a long working day. The famous *Lowell Offering* published the poetry and meditations of young women like Lucy Larcom, who moved with brothers and sisters and her widowed mother to Lowell in 1835. Lucy worked in the mills from the age of 12 until her early 20s, then moved west and taught school in Illinois.[65] Although the influx of Irish workers in the 1840s cut short such opportunities for female economic independence and learning, the possibility of new industrial occupations for women, like the professions, held out a hope for escape from domestic confinement.

Working women's associations were slow to develop and form links with the woman's rights movement, however. In the newly industrialized towns where more than half of the mill operatives were female before 1850, women were gladly taking paid employment. They were willing to strike in Pawtucket in the 1820s for better working conditions, in Lowell in the 1830s to protest a rise in room and board without a change in wages, and again in the 1840s for a 10-hour day.[66] But their organizing was separate from the activities of the middle-class women who lectured and wrote on woman's rights and who by 1848 had begun to demand the vote. Only after the Civil War in 1866, with the involvement of Susan B. Anthony in the Equal Rights Association and with the 1868 and 1869 conventions of the National Labor Union, were working women explicitly put on record in support of woman suffrage.[67]

Concurrent with the gains in women's education and professional opportunities came a gradual but momentous change in attitudes toward women's public speaking. Two lecturers from abroad—Fanny Wright from Scotland and Ernestine Rose from Poland—had since the late 1820s tackled such questions as woman's rights, abolition, and the rights of workers. But women born on native soil were at first stymied at every turn when their missionary and reform organizations appeared to usurp male prerogatives in representing the public interest. Both the women's missionary and the moral reform societies had received censure from Protestant clerics. These strictures culminated in a pastoral letter from the General Association of Congregational Ministers of Massachusetts, who in 1837 spoke out against Angelina Grimké's public lectures opposing slavery: "We appreciate the *unostentatious* prayers and efforts of women in advancing the cause of religion at home and abroad, in leading religious inquirers TO THE PASTOR for instruction. . . . [T]he vine whose strength and beauty is to lean upon the trellis work, and half conceal its clusters [should not think to assume] the independence and overshadowing nature of the elm."[68]

Lucy Stone, the valedictorian of her Oberlin class in 1847, refused to write a valedictory speech or attend commencement because she would not be able to deliver her speech. Even the women of Seneca Falls in 1848 asked a man, James Mott, the husband of Lucretia, to chair the meeting because they were so unused to exercising authority in mixed gatherings. But Elizabeth Cady Stanton's maiden speech at Seneca Falls was eloquent, and the Woman's Rights Conventions of the early 1850s recorded many speeches by women. A decade after Lucy Stone had graduated without giving her valedictory, the woman valedictorian at Oberlin was allowed to deliver her speech herself.[69] The change of custom was enormously important, for it symbolized the legitimation of woman's voice in the public sphere along with her responsibility for the home.

Marriage and property rights.   Just as the woman's rights leaders preached self-reliance and a woman's need for independent means of support, they also insisted on the right of a woman to control her own earnings, form contracts, and be an equal guardian of her children. Prevailing practice favored the husband in any contest between a married couple. Ernestine Rose, in her presentation to the Woman's Rights Convention of 1851, sketched the issue in dramatic terms: "and when at his nightly orgies, in the grog shop and the oyster cellar, or at the gaming table, he squanders the means she helped by her cooperation and economy to accumulate, and when she awakens to penury and destitution, will it supply the wants of her children to tell them that owing to the superiority of men she had no redress by law; and that as her being is merged in his, so ought theirs to be?"[70]

By speaking of a woman's being "merged in his," Rose was referring to the common law theory of coverture, by which a woman's property after marriage was controlled by her husband. In theory, the husband's and the wife's interests were the same and that interest was to be ruled by the husband. After marriage a woman's legal existence was suspended; her husband assumed all her debts, and she was not able to maintain legal relationships, to hold property in her own right, or to have rights over children.[71]

Changing economic conditions made these rules increasingly problematic. Husbands sometimes went off to sea, prospected for gold, or settled a new homestead on the frontier and never came back. On occasion they remarried, but left wives behind with no independent recourse for managing joint property or securing it against access by other claimants. Women might also gain independent earnings from household products or seasonal labor, or work in the mills, but with no assurance that their wages were theirs.[72]

These new conditions precipitated widely scattered efforts before the Civil War to revise state property laws to protect the rights of single, married, widowed, divorced, and deserted women.[73] Changes in property law had been proposed from the 1820s on, even before woman's rights leaders became involved. In New York, for example, a judge, concerned that his wife be able to manage and retain her own property, first proposed such legislation in 1836. That year Ernestine Rose worked for a petition to the state legislature. In 1840, together with Paulina Wright Davis and Elizabeth Cady Stanton, Rose circulated a petition and spoke for it before the legislative committee in Albany. But the bill did not pass both houses until 1848.[74]

After the panic and severe depression of 1837, married woman's property laws had appeal because they offered a means to safeguard the financial stability of a family, even when a landlord had lost his property or a husband's business had failed. Between 1839 and 1848, legislation protecting women's property rights was enacted in 7 states[75]; by 1860, 14 states had passed some kind of women's property legislation.

The most liberal laws were enacted in Massachusetts, Ohio, and New York as a result of campaigns by woman's rights advocates. In the winter of 1854, Susan B. Anthony and 60 other women canvassed their counties in New York and gathered 6,000 signatures to petition the legislature for women's rights to control their earnings, to guardianship of their children in case of divorce, and to the vote.[76] The New York law, passed in 1860, provided for the right of women to enter into a contract, to will or to sue, to dispose of their earnings as they chose, to share in the joint earnings of a couple, and to enjoy equal guardianship of children; the Massachusetts law was similar, except for the joint right to the couple's earnings.[77]

A key provision of woman's rights legislation was a woman's legal guardianship of her children and the right of contract. Half a century of women's organizing in benevolent, missionary, and moral reform societies had created a tradition of women's moral authority that was totally at odds with the tradition of coverture. It was a relatively short step to revise the law. Just as higher education, public speaking, and paid employment would later lay a foundation for woman's individual participation in the public sphere, so a married woman's equal right to control her own and her children's interests set the stage for her equal authority to represent the family in the larger community. Both the temperance and suffrage movements expressed outrage at domestic inequality, especially when a woman was paired with an intemperate or improvident man.[78] Woman's rights advocates made property laws a continuing object of their reforms, and between 1869 and 1887, 33 states and the District of Columbia granted women the power to control their wages, and 30 allowed women a separate estate.[79]

While working for legal reform, woman's rights leaders were also criticizing the traditional dependency of women on men and projecting a new egalitarian marriage ideal. Ladies of leisure were the object of feminist scorn. Idle wives lived with their families in boarding houses, ate meals quickly and in virtual silence, then retired to their rooms for some needle work or took a little promenade outside.[80] These women of the urban middle class, absent from the dinners, music, games, and political discussion of men, were prejudiced against work and even avoided education and teaching.[81] Sarah Grimké spoke candidly: "this class of women . . . are taught to regard marriage as the only thing needful, the only avenue of distinction. . . . Fashionable women regard themselves, and are regarded by men, as pretty toys or as mere instruments of pleasure."[82] But the feminists of the 1850s projected an alternative ideal of being active physically, eating properly, and dressing sensibly.[83]

Perhaps the best-known examples of the new marriage ideal were Lucy Stone and Henry Blackwell. Lucy, who kept her own name after marriage, and Henry, a Cincinnati hardware merchant and abolitionist, enjoyed the kind of intellectual and social equality in their marriage that many reformers advocated but few were able to realize. The model had already appeared in the marriage of Quaker reformers James and Lucretia Mott, active in temperance, abolition, and woman's rights. Historian Barbara Solomon has unearthed other, less well-known but impressive partnerships. Hannah E. Myers Longshore, one of the early woman physicians and mother of two children, enrolled at the age of 31 in the Female Medical College of Pennsylvania and received her M.D. in 1851, all with the unfailing support and encouragement of her teacher husband, Thomas Longshore. Mary Frame Myers Thomas, a half-sister of Hannah Longshore, and her husband, Owen Thomas, undertook medical study together, after the birth of their third child, at Western Reserve College in Ohio and then the Pennsylvania Medical College in Philadelphia.[84]

The early woman's rights leaders could also imagine an honorable place for single women, to be treated with respect and encouraged in their ambitions. Likewise, a woman should have the right of divorce if her marriage became intolerable. Elizabeth Cady Stanton, arguing before the New York state legislature in 1861, contended that when marriage became "a mere outward tie, . . . with every possible inequality of condition," it should be dissolved.[85] Just as property rights reform accorded dignity and responsibility to married women, growing attention to the possibility of celibacy and divorce signaled a new ideal of female independence and autonomy.

Abolition.　　Women's commitment to the abolition movement was another key factor in their emancipation. In 1829 William Lloyd Garrison, the leader of American abolitionists, called for three constituencies to join him in the antislavery cause—churches, New England women, and the newspapers. He appealed to women as Republican Mothers to add their voice to the abolitionist cause. In Boston, an African-American woman, Maria Stewart presented her "Meditations" in 1832 to the First African Baptist Church and Society. Garrison published this as a tract and printed three other addresses by Stewart in his antislavery newspaper the *Liberator*. In 1834 Garrison was instrumental in establishing the Female Anti-Slavery Society in Providence and others in Portland, Maine, and Amesbury, Massachusetts. Between 1833 and 1838 more than 100 female antislavery societies were established in northeastern cities and towns, and thousands of American women took part. The groups reached from Boston, Philadelphia, and New York to such western points as Ashtabula, Ohio.[86]

As leader of the abolition movement, Garrison also fathered the woman's rights cause. Through involvement in the antislavery movement, the leaders of the woman's movement could build on its equal rights ideology, the medium of lectures to large audiences, and the strategy of the signature-petition. Garrison's speeches during the 1830s described sexual exploitation of slaves and, along with the essays of Maria Stewart and of Angelina Grimké (in "An Appeal to the Christian Women of the South"), aroused a form of public protest by women that was quite different from that of the church groups or moral reform societies up to that time. In 1834 Garrison mobilized women in a door-to-door petition campaign to abolish slavery in the District of Columbia. This, according to Marilley, was a daring form of engagement that built on the precedent of married women's use of the petition during the American Revolution to request the release of husbands from the army or to protest the exile of helpless loyalist women and children from patriot territory. Petitions, which relied on the rhetoric of humiliation and subordination and had once been women's last political recourse, had become a bona fide instrument of political expression for women joined in the cause against slavery.[87] Their success shocked the legislators, established women's right to petition, and raised the slavery issue in Congress.

Abolition also provided woman's rights leaders with an escape from clerical authority and with a theory of social change. Beginning with the conservative clergy's 1837 attack on the Grimké sisters for public speaking against slavery, continuing to the 1840 meeting of Mott and Stanton at the World's Anti-Slavery Convention in London, and finally maturing after the Civil War and Reconstruction, "the development of American feminism," according to Ellen DuBois, "was inseparable from the unfolding of the anti-slavery drama."[88] Like the moral reform societies and temperance movements, the abolitionists first focused on the moral wrong of holding slaves, then moved on to the political and legal means by which to abolish slavery. In the process they moved "from a framework of individual sin and conversion to an understanding of institutionalized oppression and social reform."[89] Sarah Grimké's reply to the pastoral letter of 1837 denounced belief in the meekness and dependence of women and propounded a new vision:

"Men and women were CREATED EQUAL; they are both moral and accountable beings, and whatever is *right* for man to do, is *right* for woman."[90]

By confronting the oppression and subservience of women and their legal incapacity to affect the system, women with abolitionist experience found an avenue into the secular and political realm. The leaders of missionary societies, moral reform, and temperance had focused primarily on individual reform. The suffragists, with insight born of the abolitionist cause, saw the need to change the institutions of the larger society.[91] In addition, the brutal treatment of slave women gave proof that the delicacy of women was a mere cultural invention that could hardly justify their exclusion from citizens' rights. In her eloquent impromptu speech before the Woman's Rights Convention in Akron, Ohio, on 28–29 May 1851, former slave Sojourner Truth told of her hardships compared with the white ladies who had heavy loads lifted for them, were given rides in carriages, and were helped over mud puddles. "And a'n't I a woman? . . . I have ploughed, and planted, and gathered into barns, . . . and born thirteen chilern. . . . And a'n't I a woman?"[92]

Woman suffrage.   These several streams of activity converged in the woman suffrage movement, which began in the 1840s and persisted until 1920 when its object was won. Lucretia Mott and Elizabeth Cady Stanton first met at the World's Anti-Slavery Convention in London in 1840. Eight years later, in July 1848, when Mott was visiting Seneca Falls, New York, a coterie of friends, many of whom had been active in other causes, called a meeting to be held in the Wesleyan Chapel and met ahead of time in the living room of one of their members to draw up their ideas in writing. They searched for an example and finally settled on the Declaration of Independence, which they then followed as a guide for listing their natural rights and the wrongs done against women. Though unaccustomed to running a meeting or speaking in public, they put forth a "Declaration of Sentiments" that stated the ideals and principles of the woman's rights movement for the next 70 years. This statement claimed that women were free citizens entitled to life, liberty, and the pursuit of happiness. After listing the injustices done by men against women, the meeting resolved that women should have equal rights to teach and speak in public, to exercise "the sacred right of the elective franchise," and to secure for "women an equal participation with men in the various

Angelina Grimké. Library of Congress.

Lucretia Mott. Sophia Smith Collection, Smith College.

Sojourner Truth. Library of Congress.

Elizabeth Cady Stanton and her daughter, 1856. Seneca Falls Historical Society.

trades, professions, and commerce." The declaration was signed by
100 men and women.[93]

Other conventions followed in Salem, Ohio, in 1850, in Akron in
1851, and in Worcester, Massachusetts, in October 1851. There
Elizabeth Cady Stanton spoke of "the violence, rowdyism, and vulgar-
ity which now characterize our Congressional Halls and show us
clearly that 'it is not good for man to be alone.'" Ernestine Rose spoke
against marriage laws and customs that submerge a woman's identity
in her husband's. Woman "should be there to civilize, refine, and
purify him, even at the ballot-box."[94] In Syracuse in September 1852,
Susan B. Anthony read the usual resolutions protesting women's subordination and calling for equal rights to education and to protection
as citizens; Lucy Stone and others called for resistance to taxation
without representation; and Antoinette Brown argued against the conservative interpretation of the Bible that sanctioned the inferior status
and oppression of women. A letter from Stanton called for coeducation.[95] At the New York Woman's Rights Convention of 1853, Clarina
Nichols argued that women should be able to vote in order to have
control over their "moral, intellectual, and social interests" and be
able to protect their children as a mother. "If women were allowed to
vote, the best measures for the good of the community would be carried."[96] The first woman physician, Harriot K. Hunt added, "I desire
to vote that I may sit on school committees . . . I wish to sit on committees where I can see to a better regulation of the healthfulness of
our streets, and the introduction of a higher tone into the topics of
our parlors," and the improvement of public educational opportunities
for girls.[97]

Significantly, women's claims to the ballot and other rights
emerged at a time when admission to citizenship was being significantly expanded to include the "common man." At the time of the
Revolution, it was a man's *property* that allowed him to vote, not his
character, nationality, beliefs, or residence. Within 10 years after the
Revolution, tax paying was beginning to become a substitute for property, and naturalization was instituted to incorporate foreigners as
inhabitants or residents.[98] As the qualifications for voting expanded to
include formerly excluded groups, it seemed logical to include women
as well. In the 1853 Constitutional Convention of the Commonwealth of
Massachusetts, for example, woman's rights leaders argued that taxation and representation should be coextensive and that if women were
subject to punishment they should be able to construct the laws.[99]

During the 1850s, the franchise became the cornerstone of the woman's rights movement. The Seventh National Woman's Rights Convention, held in New York City in 1856, resolved, "that the main power of the woman's rights movement lies in this: that while always demanding for women better education, better employment, and better laws, it has kept steadily in view the one cardinal demand for the right of suffrage; in a democracy, the symbol and guarantee of all other rights."[100]

To ask for the ballot was to challenge women's fundamental economic and social dependence and the doctrine of separate spheres. Political rights implied autonomy and self-determination and the potential for expressing interests different from those of a husband.[101] But these claims for the individual woman had to be reconciled with competing priorities. Which was more important or pressing, for example, woman suffrage or temperance, woman suffrage or the emancipation and enfranchisement of former slaves? On these questions the leaders struggled and eventually diverged.

Before 1860 Stanton and Anthony were active in abolition, temperance, and woman's rights. After the Civil War, their cause became suffrage alone. Woman's rights leaders had hoped that the Fourteenth Amendment would provide suffrage for women as well as African-Americans, but they were bitterly disappointed. The Fourteenth Amendment limited representation of states who denied the vote to male inhabitants and was ratified in 1868. Stanton and Anthony said it would have been so easy to add the condition of sex, and they both actually worked to secure petitions against the Fourteenth Amendment. Lucy Stone had favored rewording the Fourteenth Amendment but still supported it, reasoning that it was better for some rather than none of the disenfranchised to get the vote. Julia Ward Howe supported passage of the amendment as it stood.[102] Northern states, however, in actuality continued to deny African-Americans the vote, and so the Fifteenth Amendment was passed in 1870 to assure that "the right to vote shall not be denied on account of race, color, or previous condition of servitude." The American Equal Rights Association had originally supported universal human suffrage but, under its abolitionist leadership, ended up putting the "Negro's hour" ahead of the vote for women.[103]

The result of the struggle over the Fifteenth Amendment was a split in the suffrage ranks and the founding of two rival organizations in 1869 that gave rise to two major streams of suffrage activity that would persist until the ratification of the federal suffrage amendment in 1920. The state-by-state approach, first exemplified by the admission of Wyoming as an equal suffrage state in 1869, held the potential for gaining woman suffrage through state constitutions; this was the preferred strategy of the American Woman Suffrage Association founded in 1869 and led by moderate suffragists like Lucy Stone and Julia Ward Howe, who in 1866 and 1867 had been ready to concede the "Negro's hour." The second strategy was a woman suffrage amendment to the federal constitution that would grant the franchise across the nation in one fell swoop; this was the preferred approach of the National Woman Suffrage Association led by Stanton and Anthony, also founded in 1869.

Links to abolition thus both helped and hindered the suffrage movement before the Civil War. On the one hand, participation in the antislavery movement provided training in grass-roots organization, persuasion, and politics. But the alliance also hampered progress by diverting attention from women and insulating woman's rights leaders from the reality that theirs was a more difficult and less popular cause.[104]

The closer connection of the American Woman Suffrage Association to the temperance movement would not become evident for at least another decade, after the founding of the Woman's Christian Temperance Union in 1874. By 1870, however, the major elements for the interweaving of domestic and equal rights feminism were firmly in place.

Conclusion: Women's Roles in 1870

The American Revolution set the stage for women's religious, charitable, and temperance associations to accomplish the first major expansion of women's activities outside the home. But it was the woman's rights and suffrage leaders who made explicit the philosophical and legal basis for a role for women in public life. By the second half of the nineteenth century, domestic and equal rights feminism had begun to address the enormous cultural challenge of redefining women's roles.

The cultural problem was to justify and legitimate women's activities outside the home. In three different ways women's groups developed and established a new image of the female ideal. First, by organizing all kinds of religious, benevolent, and reform groups, they dramatized the wide range of women's abilities and concerns. Second, they pinpointed the rules and customs that most needed to be changed by protesting the key forms of sex inequality. Finally, through effective methods of mass persuasion and legal reform, they launched the largest and most successful women's movement known up to that time.

In 1790, even though women had loyally helped during the Revolution by supporting the tea embargo and by raising supplies for the Continental Army, the overwhelming expectation of women was that they would play little part in public affairs. Less than a century later, that expectation had changed. Benevolent and missionary societies and women's religious conversions had established the spiritual and moral equality of women. Moral reform and temperance societies then expanded the expectation of moral equality beyond the boundaries of private spiritual life to the community outside the home. In the words of Barbara Epstein, "Only in the case of something as deeply held and long established as orthodox religious belief, could women bring themselves to challenge the supremacy of husbands and fathers."[105] Destitute children, fallen women, and drunken men were the recipients of their concern. In addition, women entering higher education, working in the mills, or speaking in public staked out claims to equality in intellectual, commercial, and political realms. There was even the suggestion that women's sense of family responsibility and their moral opposition to intemperance and slavery might make them morally superior and more public spirited than men. The "rough, rude, drinking, swearing, fighting men" from whom women were supposed to be protected by not going to the ballot box were the very result of women's absence from politics.[106] Women could bring a refining influence if they were given equal property rights and the vote. By such reasoning it began to seem more desirable to admit women to all the rights and privileges of citizenship than to claim that independent women were unnatural and that they should be represented by men.

All of the many nineteenth-century women's organizations, however, eventually encountered the same roadblock: established male leaders, one after another, tried to hold back or discourage them. First to bear the brunt were the female missionary societies, then the moral reform groups who wanted to censure men for their role in prostitution, third the women in the antislavery groups, and fourth the women in the temperance cause.[107] Rejection of women from higher education and medical and law schools revealed yet another realm of resistance. The value of these challenges to woman's rights was that they put the cause into focus. In being denied the right to speak in public, to hold property, to gain education, to vote or hold public office, woman's rights leaders were forced to confront the common underlying issue of woman's moral, domestic, and civil inequality. Expanding these rights became the task of their movement. Their eventual success in changing the laws meant that they had shifted to some degree the social and cultural boundaries of the feminine role.

The women's movement accomplished this feat through a repertory of methods that grew from its many branches. Membership in women's volunteer groups began in the churches; the respectability of religious activity and Republican Motherhood was used to expand women's power in the home and the community. The right of prayer and religious expression was extended to justify general moral equality, the right of speaking in public, and the adoption of reformist positions on sexuality, temperance, slavery, and woman's rights. Organizational techniques learned in missionary and cent and tract societies were applied to the purposes of moral reform. Women's groups developed a common organizational culture, collected contributions and dispensed funds, held regular meetings and kept records, sponsored lectures and regional conventions, founded auxiliaries in neighboring towns, and fostered overlapping networks of leaders and members.[108] The groups that went beyond moral reform to legal change added still other tactics: gathering of petitions, campaign travel and circuit lecturing, lobbying before the legislature, and direct actions such as trying to vote.

In all of these efforts the advances made by domestic and equal rights feminists were closely intertwined. Had the church women, missionary societies, and moral reform groups not spelled out the moral implications of woman's equality, the woman's rights groups could not have begun. Had the abolitionists and suffragists not pressed their claim to woman's rights in the public sphere, woman's equality as an individual and a family head would have continued partial and unsecured. Together the two types of feminism laid out the full spectrum of woman's potential and power.

Chapter 3

Temperance: The Extension of Woman's Power in the Home

Between the Civil War and the turn of the century, the Woman's Christian Temperance Union emerged as the most powerful force for the enlargement of woman's sphere. By 1873 a temperance crusade had swept upstate New York, Ohio, and Michigan with women's prayer meetings and the closing of saloons. Within a year the WCTU had formed a constitution, elected a national slate of officers drawn from many states, and begun its pattern of regular annual meetings with published minutes. By 1885 there were 44 state WCTU organizations in addition to local groups in Indiana, Washington, and Wyoming Territory, which added up to a total of more than 4,000 local chapters and 70,000 members. A plan of work initially outlined in 1874 had led to 23 specialized departments, ranging from "prison work" to "work among colored people." Two earlier newspapers combined in 1883 to become the 16-page weekly *Union Signal.* By 1895 the WCTU counted roughly 135,000 members and was probably the largest organized body of women in the United States, rivaled only by the various Protestant women's missionary societies combined.[1]

Until recently, the significance of the WCTU achievement was largely measured in terms of its contribution to temperance and prohibition. After the repeal of national prohibition in 1933, WCTU reform goals were often interpreted as defensive and moralistic.[2] Only in the last few years has the contribution of the temperance women to feminism been appreciated as an extension of "domestic feminism."[3] Social or domestic feminism may have been a necessary precursor to "woman's rights feminism," which sought to widen woman's sphere outside as well as inside the home.

The WCTU contribution to feminism can be traced in four major aspects of the temperance movement. First, temperance women developed an *ideology* that linked women's power in the home to their power in the public sphere. Second, the WCTU raised up *women leaders* who were able to articulate the ideals of American womanhood and set goals for the movement. Third, the WCTU constituted a strong *social movement organization* that reached into local communities and linked individual women to the larger feminist movement. Fourth, the woman's temperance movement developed a *reform strategy* linking temperance and woman's rights that mobilized immense support nationally as well as locally.

Historical Roots

One of the most striking characteristics of the woman's temperance conventions of a century ago was their continuity with the religious culture of the times. Meetings opened with prayers; hymns were sung; the speeches of the leaders were studded with references to scripture, the will of God, the love of Christ, and the direction of the Holy Spirit. The founding convention of the Woman's Christian Temperance Union was in fact planned at the annual Sunday School Convention at Chautauqua, New York, in the summer of 1874 and held in November 1874 at a church in Cleveland. The organization of Christian temperance women thus built on the normal round of women's religious activities that were common to every little village and town: weekly church attendance, prayer meetings, and work in the home and foreign missionary societies. Yet the WCTU very soon began to stretch that tradition of female religious activity to include not only social reform but also political power for women. The expansion of woman's role from charitable works to an interest in reform legislation was natural when viewed through the experience of the temperance movement. As early as the 1850s the goal of temperance advocates had shifted from reforming confirmed drunkards to prohibition of the sale of spirituous liquors in any but very large quantities through variants of the "Maine law." This law, first adopted by the state of Maine in 1853, virtually closed the saloons, cut off the sale of liquor by the glass, and constituted the temperance movement's first major step beyond reform of the individual to reform of the society.[4]

During the temperance crusade that swept Ohio and neighboring states in the winter of 1873–74, women took up the cause of closing dramshops by kneeling in snow outside the saloons, singing hymns, and appealing to the conscience of both saloon keepers and patrons. Between 22 December 1873, when Dr. Dio Lewis spoke to an evening prayer meeting in Hillsboro, Ohio, concerning "The Duty of Christian Women," and April 1874 more than 25 Ohio towns had experienced the crusade. For example, in Mount Vernon, Ohio, then a town of 6,000 with 31 saloons, the crusade began on 16 February and in 12 days of prayer 23 saloons had closed. By the first week of April 1874, only six saloons remained where drink was publicly sold.[5] In all of 1873–74 there were more than 300 crusades in Ohio alone. The first president of the WCTU, Annie Wittenmyer, listed and described the dozens of communities in Indiana, Illinois, New York, Pennsylvania, Michigan, Wisconsin, and other states that shared in the fervor of the period. Historian Jack Blocker has examined newspaper accounts and found a total of 911 recorded crusades between December 1873 and November 1874 that involved 57,000 to 143,000 women. The heaviest concentration of crusades was in Ohio, with 307. Indiana, Illinois, Michigan, and New York had more than 50 each. In more than 25 other states and territories there was at least some crusade activity (see figure 3.1).[6]

By November 1874, temperance women, who up to that time were found primarily in local societies and only sporadically in state organizations, were ready to organize on a national level.[7] Unlike the pioneers for woman's rights at the 1848 Seneca Falls convention who found it difficult to speak and designated a man to chair the meeting, the temperance women of 1874 moved confidently toward the establishment of a national association. After four days of prayers, speeches, hymns, and discussion, they had framed a constitution, elected officers, and outlined a plan of work. All of these proceedings were then printed and bound in *Minutes,* which set the pattern for later meetings.[8]

The existing religious culture in which most Protestant women participated thus provided a solid underpinning during the formative stages of the temperance movement. No irreverent rejection of the Bible for its patriarchal bias (which the prominent suffragist Elizabeth Cady Stanton expressed in her later years), no effort to secularize the

Figure 3.1

Woman's Temperance Crusades, 1873–1874

(States Ranked by Women Involved per State)

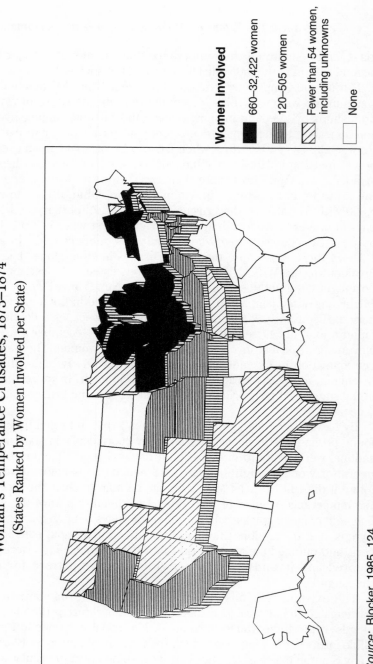

Women Involved

■ 660–32,422 women

▦ 120–505 women

▨ Fewer than 54 women, including unknowns

□ None

Source: Blocker, 1985, 124.

temperance and suffrage appeal (as was typical of the peppery Oregon suffragist Abigail Scott Duniway) were present to sap the WCTU's solidarity or vitality. Instead the temperance union was able to build a large and harmonious organization with strong outreach and a challenging yet compatible appeal to the leading women of most communities.

Soon after the organization was formed, a test of unity came in a debate over whether the WCTU should endorse the franchise for women. Annie Wittenmyer and the older and more conservative leaders said no. Frances Willard, the young corresponding secretary and former dean of the Evanston College for Women, argued that the woman's ballot was necessary for "Home Protection." Willard's view eventually carried; in 1879 she became president of the WCTU, an office that she held until her death in 1898 and that she used to lead members toward an enlarged religious, social, and political role for women.

Through the latter years of Willard's presidency, and especially after her death, the WCTU faced a choice between remaining a broad-ranging reform group and becoming a more narrowly focused political tool for the establishment of prohibition. In the 1880s and 1890s, Willard expressed sympathy with socialist principles in her presidential addresses and touched a vast range of social issues that historian Ruth Bordin has listed as "peace and international arbitration, the spoils system and political corruption, recreational centers for the masses, the double standard, the power of the press, the eight-hour day, the labor movement, poverty, social insurance, the initiative and referendum, the capitalist massacre of miners, starving Armenians, lynching, food reform, woman suffrage, and the fight for woman's rights in the Episcopal church."[9] Reform goals of the WCTU were infused with a concern for social justice and included improvement of conditions for working women and abolition of white slavery. But with the first presidential speech of Willard's successor, Lillian Stevens, in 1899, the focus of the union sharply narrowed. Stevens's concerns were almost entirely with prohibition and temperance; although the broad-ranging departmental structure of the WCTU continued, the single issue of curbing alcohol quickly began to dominate the organization. The pages of the *Union Signal* also reflected the change: while roughly half of its articles before 1900 were devoted to prohibition, the proportion after 1900 rose to nearly 70 percent.[10]

Ideology

In its heyday the Woman's Christian Temperance Union managed to accomplish remarkable growth and exert a wide influence. Central to its success was a distinctive view of the nature of women and men. Temperance women, by and large, saw their own sex as towers of strength and moral courage who were at the same time loving and kind, much like a good mother. Men, on the other hand, were a more unpredictable lot. Some were upright and good; others were well-meaning but wayward and subject to temptation. The drama of women's lives, from the temperance women's point of view, was in finding ways to make their vision of home and society prevail against the mindless disorder and corruption found in the worlds of men.

To document the distinctive features of the woman's temperance ideology, I examined the WCTU newspaper *Union Signal* between the years 1885 and 1915 and developed a set of categories for coding the contents of short stories and reports of major news events (described in appendix A).[11] I compared what I found there with the contents of the major suffrage newspaper, the *Woman's Journal,* to see what was similar and what was different. Many women and a number of historians have claimed that temperance and suffrage were simply a part of the same movement.[12] I discovered that both temperance and suffrage ideologies contained a *gender ideology* that was imbedded in images of women and men, but this ideology differed between the two groups.

Images of women and men.   Temperance women projected an image of their ideal roles and created a complementary image of men. The progressive woman was interested in the ballot, the conservative woman thought it unnecessary. The new man signed a total abstinence pledge and believed in a single moral standard for men and women; the traditional man was unaware of such issues. These traditional and progressive images fell into oversimplified dichotomies, but over time they became further differentiated. New women were not simply "unsexed" immodest creatures, unmindful of their proper place in life, nor were traditional women without weaknesses; there was both a good and bad type of new woman and a good and bad type of traditional woman.

Temperance women focused most on the good traditional woman, a wife and mother, and the bad traditional man who betrayed her with his dishonesty or drunkenness. Between 1885 and 1915, 10–11 percent of the articles in the *Union Signal* contained these two images. Another 8 percent pictured a moral, upright, progressive man. But as shown in table 3.1, only 4 percent pictured the progressive new type of egalitarian woman.

Temperance women were concerned not so much with changing women or with pulling them out of the circumscribed context in which they lived as in seeing that they used all their powers to the full in their domestic and benevolent roles. While more of the suffragists were pioneers in the sense of developing a new public role for women, the temperance women were consolidators, concerned with using women's powers to the full in the female roles that were already accepted.

As to their image of man, temperance women found enough to criticize in man's most basic role as family member that there was no reason to ask for better performance in new areas. Rather than change the boundaries of the male role, they wanted to improve men's performance wherever possible as husbands and fathers. A number of *Union Signal* story plots in the 1880s and 1890s depict an upright and loving wife or mother who suffers because a once promising husband or son is nearly destroyed by drink; the solution is for the man to pledge abstinence.[13] The temperance newspaper had more than four times as many articles on the strengths or inadequacy of men as citizens and family members as the suffragist journal during the same period.

Temperance advocates put their hope in the improvement of men. They saw their feminine duty as one of broadening the sense of social responsibility in men not only in the home but the larger community. The focus of the temperance ideology was to perfect the imperfect man; suffragists, however, were twice as likely to focus their attention on women, as shown in table 3.1.

The image of the mother also pervaded temperance women's reform ideology. Women could alleviate cruelty and misery in the society around them by ministering to others in the public world just as they would in their own homes. As citizen-mothers, they could join their citizen-husbands in caring for society's needy and dependent members.[14] A good man or woman could thus save others from temptation and turn around the life of a community by fellowship, prayer, and education. Such an individual could also persuade others to sign the pledge and whole towns to close their saloons. The *Union Signal*

TABLE 3.1
Images of Women and Men
(*Union Signal* and *Woman's Journal,* 1885–1915)

Type of Image[a]	Union Signal (WCTU)	Woman's Journal (Suffrage)
Women (categories 1–4, appendix A)		
Good new woman	4.3%	15.5%
Good traditional woman	10.0	7.0
Bad traditional woman	3.3	7.5
Bad new woman	0.0	3.0
TOTAL	17.6	33.0
Men (categories 5–8, appendix A)		
Bad traditional man	11.0	4.0
Good traditional man	4.5	0.5
Good new man	7.9	1.0
Bad new man	0.0	0.0
TOTAL	23.4	5.5

[a] No article was counted more than once. Of articles in the *Woman's Journal*, 64 percent did not contain these images. In the *Union Signal*, the comparable figure was 58 percent.

reported one such example in the missionary work of the Reverend Albert Derr, who like the early women crusaders was able to clean up a whole logging town by holding prayer meetings in the largest saloon (at the invitation of the saloon keeper), establishing a choir, getting Bibles, and drawing the lumberjacks to church services where they could enjoy hymn-singing and fellowship rather than frequent the saloons. By the time Derr left town there were only 4 saloons remaining out of the original 11, and 750 people were regularly attending church.[15]

But in a contrasting fictional account, one Joab Robinson, having a large apple crop, ignored the warnings of women and children against the perils of cider and had three barrels made up and put in the cellar.

Confronted with news of the death of his outstanding son, valedictorian and prize winner, he discovered that the boy began drinking the cider when it was sweet, then became addicted to it when it turned hard and was eventually ruined by drunkenness. The father resolved never again to make or taste another drop of cider.[16]

A central theme of these stories is that a virtuous person (often a woman or a good man such as the Reverend Derr) is able to raise up or prevent another (often a man or boy such as Joab Robinson's son) from becoming degraded by drink, gambling, or some other corruption. Compared with the suffrage newspaper, the *Union Signal* imagery was distinctive in picturing most women as "already there"— that is, the WCTU women saw themselves as equal if not superior to men in moral strength and ability to change and improve the world, whereas suffragists were more likely to see men as enjoying the roles and privileges to which they themselves aspired.

The ideal society.   Also imbedded in temperance ideology was a distinctive analysis of the pressing social problems of the day. The worldview of the WCTU, its representation of contemporary social ills, and its remedy for healing them was spelled out in the speeches, editorials, and stories printed in the *Union Signal*. The list of topics is immense: terrible working conditions for women, white slavery, cruelty to animals, education for women, a woman's vulnerability when married to a drunkard, political corruption owing to the buying of votes by liquor interests.

The temperance women pinned these problems on a failure of social responsibility. In a rapidly industrializing society where philanthropic and humanitarian agencies were not yet adequate to their task, women threw themselves into the breach by extending help to those in need. Like the valiant woman of Proverbs who "is open-handed to the wretched and generous to the poor,"[17] a Christian temperance woman found acceptance and praise from religious authorities and her own community for acts of social conscience.

Efforts to enact child labor laws and implement educational and municipal improvements were incorporated into the feminine role by having women represent the interests of the weak to the powerful and in so doing build a broader sense of community.[18] Of all the articles in the *Union Signal* that I sampled between 1885 and 1915, 3 percent outlined the threat of irresponsibility, 16 percent argued the need for a higher sense of responsibility, and 9 percent proposed a humanitarian solution to these problems. Temperance women's primary vehicle for exercising a sense of social responsibility was through expansion of traditional charitable activities that concerned the individual and the home. Between 1885 and 1915, roughly 70 percent of the articles in the *Union Signal* touched problems and issues inside the home compared with 30 percent outside.[19] The particular forms of injustice that temperance women found compelling were the dark side of the loving and emotional aspects of the female role: white slavery (which they delicately referred to under the topic of "social purity"), polygamy (then still practiced among the Mormons), and all other forms of marital or sexual oppression of women. Health and life-style also concerned them; they exposed the dangers of narcotic addiction and patent medicine.[20]

Temperance women's analysis of public problems was framed in largely individual terms. One popular reform was Sabbath observance. Temperance women were steadfast in both individual and collective resolve to cease all labor and forgo entertainments on Sundays. Sabbath observance seemed to promise a restored sense of community in the face of advancing industrialization, growing cities, and a polyglot population of new immigrants with different traditions and values. The foreign and Catholic vote likewise threatened the middle-class, Protestant way of life that was familiar to most temperance women. In their poverty, illiteracy, and general naivete, the new immigrants were thought to be susceptible to drink and vote buying and to contribute to all the social evils of the day.[21]

Agenda for social change. Linked to the temperance women's social analysis was a distinctive formula for social change that began with a personal pledge to refrain from alcohol, extended this commitment to the larger community through charitable and humanitarian help, and eventually culminated in efforts for woman suffrage and prohibition. The ultimate goal on the *Union Signal* agenda was prohibition, although suffrage was usually mentioned as a necessary means to that and other reforms. Also mentioned were more limited goals, such as raising the age of consent (many states permitted marriage at 12 years for a girl and 14 for a boy), instituting scientific temperance instruction in the schools, substituting grape juice for communion wine in churches, and organizing young people in Loyal Temperance Legions.

The pledge as a vehicle for personal reform had been developed during the 1840s and 1850s by the Washingtonians and Sons of

Temperance. The WCTU from the very beginning enjoined its members to ban alcohol from their own homes and communities, and the *Union Signal* honored this commitment by printing related stories. Pledge work expressed not only self-discipline and a sense of social responsibility but also a conviction that personal influence could be the means to improve the whole society.

Compared with the suffragist branch of the feminist movement, the WCTU was more oriented to personal reform and the quality of domestic life than to far-reaching structural change in public life and the social order. Table 3.2 shows that half the articles in the temperance newspaper were focused on personal change, compared with only one-fifth of the articles in the suffrage newspaper. The temperance newspaper emphasized individual change through the pledge and humanitarian and charitable activities for the needy. Consistent with this more individualistic orientation, the temperance paper was also more likely than the suffrage paper to emphasize women's self-improvement and equality in already familiar roles—as housekeepers, wives and mothers, and good citizens of the community. By contrast, the suffrage paper emphasized women's need to attain equality in the spheres from which they had traditionally been barred—higher education, the professions, church leadership, and politics.

Humanitarian work also received attention. News on the departments for prison work, railroad work, soldiers and sailors, young women, social purity, and the National Temperance Hospital conveyed the vitality and potential for improvement that went with direct aid to dependent people.

Prohibition and these other causes supported the case for the woman's ballot. Prohibition promised to solve many social problems in one fell swoop. Temperance women were likely to base their suffrage argument on particular grounds—that women needed the ballot to protect their interests as mothers and wives in community issues or to vote for special reforms such as prohibition. Suffragists, however, were more likely to call for the ballot as a universal human right.[22]

Leadership

The leadership of the WCTU forged its ideology, then created its organization. Early temperance women connected women's domestic interests and their economic and political roles beyond the home. Take this short story from the *Union Signal* as an example. The wife of the

TABLE 3.2
Types of Reform Advocated
(*Union Signal* and *Woman's Journal*, 1885–1915)

Type of Reform	*Union Signal* (WCTU)	*Woman's Journal* (Suffrage)
Individual versus Societal Reform[a]		
Reform or aid for the individual Prison work, anticruelty, antigambling (24.2, 24.3, appendix A)	14	8
Reform of societal agencies Labor laws, educational and civic improvements, peace (24.1, 24.4, 24.5, 24.6, appendix A)	14	32
Reforms in Traditional versus New Roles of Women[b]		
Reform in traditional roles Self-discipline, family equality, temperance for productivity (3, 4, 17, 23.1a, appendix A)	88	23
Reform in new roles for women Political, educational, professional, moral equality (16, 18, 19, 21, appendix A)	35	101

[a] Chi-square = 5.472 with Yates's correction; p < .01 .

[b] Chi-square = 67.964 with Yates's correction; p. < .001 .

mayor belonged to a church group that distributed food and clothing to the poor. After a few months the mayor's wife saw conditions worsen. Unbeknown to her, the mayor had voted for licensing of a saloon to gain needed municipal funds. Not only did their son became a dissolute, but she was seeing more need than ever for handouts from the church.[23] The story clearly implied that these tragic events could have been prevented if women from the outset had been part of the decision making and if the saloon had never been allowed into the town. The early leaders provided models of how this could be done. WCTU leaders did have some access to community decision making, but at first only through their own social position or through prominent husbands and fathers. Women temperance leaders, more than the ordinary population, were able to envision a world in which enlightened wives and mothers might exercise their sense of responsibility in the larger community. Did they possess distinctive characteristics that set them apart from other woman leaders and from the population at large? They came from comfortable to even moderately wealthy families and had access to education, social contacts, and travel well beyond that of ordinary women. Had they experienced and resolved particular conflicts that enabled them to provide leadership to others of like mind?[24] The lives of three WCTU presidents provide some answers.

Annie Wittenmyer (1827–1900), prior to her leadership of the WCTU from 1874 to 1879, was widely known for her work during the Civil War. She mobilized food and hospital suppliers and worked toward getting wholesome food into military hospitals. Born in Ohio, she attended a girls' academy, married a wealthy merchant, and lived comfortably in Iowa where she helped organize a Methodist church and established a free school for poor children. Widowed shortly before the Civil War, she became the secretary of the Soldiers' Aid Society of Keokuk. Having entrusted her surviving child to the care of her mother and sister, she undertook many innovative projects during the Civil War that established her reputation as a leader of women. She was briefly president of the independent Iowa State Sanitary Commission, then set up a model diet kitchen for wounded soldiers in Nashville, and was later active on behalf of orphaned children of dead soldiers. After moving to Philadelphia around 1870, she began writing, visited Lutheran deaconess houses in Germany, and was a leading figure in the Woman's Temperance Crusade of 1873–74.[25]

Frances Willard (1839–98), before becoming president of the

WCTU from 1879–98, was known primarily as an educator. She taught in female academies in Illinois and Pennsylvania and had been president and then dean of the female coordinate college connected with Northwestern University. Although she was born in upstate New York, the family moved to Oberlin so that her father could study theology. (Her mother also took courses there in the 1840s.) In a few years the Willards traveled to Wisconsin by covered wagon, where the family farmed more than a thousand acres. Although Frances had only four years of formal schooling, she entered Milwaukee Female College and later transferred to the North Western Female College in Evanston. She spent two years traveling in Europe with a friend whose father paid for her trip. Never married, she became one of the most famous woman lecturers and writers of her time. Her statue stands in the national Capitol in Washington, placed there by the state of Illinois in 1905.[26]

Lillian Stevens (1844–1914), born in Maine, had a father who was a teacher. She attended Foxcroft Academy and became a teacher herself for a short time in the 1860s. She married a grain and salt wholesaler and moved to his fine family homestead near Portland. With her husband's encouragement she began to substitute reform for household duties and entrusted her daughter to a governess. In Portland in the 1880s she was a familiar sight driving her phaeton from the police station to the friendly inn, carrying out her charitable work for delinquent women and poor children.[27] Stevens was Willard's hand-picked successor and served as president of the WCTU from 1898 to 1914.

Despite their education and relatively comfortable and privileged backgrounds, all three women experienced some personal loss that appears to have influenced their plunge into religious activity and reform work. All but one of Annie Wittenmyer's five children had died in infancy; she herself was widowed at an early age. Frances Willard broke off her engagement with her brother's close friend Charles Fowler in 1861 because she could not love him and shortly after lost both her father and her beloved younger sister Mary to tuberculosis. In 1873–74, the year of the temperance crusade, her career in higher education had also been frustrated by Northwestern University's absorption of the women's college of which she had been head.[28] Loss and disappointment were less obvious in the life of Lillian Stevens. Her biographer mentions only that the death of her only brother in childhood "prompted her first significant thoughts about religion" and in

Frances Willard (center) surrounded by the general officers of the World WCTU. From *The Beautiful Life of Frances Willard* by Anna A. Gordon, 1898.

part made her combine her father's Universalism with its promise of the salvation of all souls with strong support for the Baptists, her mother's denomination.[29]

Whatever their personal reasons for joining the woman's temperance movement, each of the three presidents also shared a third characteristic: they had engaged in some occupation or prior activity as reformer that prepared them for or led them to the type of domestically oriented reform work that was peculiar to the WCTU. Both Wittenmyer and Stevens were concerned with poor children and dependent women. Wittenmyer's administrative abilities during the Civil War were directed to mobilizing a vast network of food and hospital supplies; she later helped to establish an orphanage for veterans' children in Iowa and a retirement home for war widows and nurses in Ohio. Stevens helped organize local institutions to aid and reform delinquent women and children (often taking neglected women into her own home), campaigned for a state women's reformatory, and served as the Maine delegate to the National Conference on Charities and Corrections.

Willard was less involved with charities but was similar to Wittenmyer and Stevens in being oriented primarily to work with women. While still in her 20s she was active in the American Methodist Ladies Centenary Association and at 35, having resigned her position at the Evanston Ladies College, "adrift, with no savings, and deeply unhappy,"[30] she discovered the temperance movement, became secretary of the Illinois state women's temperance association, then its president in 1878, and organized a campaign that gathered 100,000 signatures in support of a state law granting women the vote on local option, a measure that was defeated but that brought out a large vote for local option in the spring of 1880. In the meantime, during 1877 she had worked part of the year as director of the women's meetings for the famous evangelist Dwight L. Moody.

Each of these reformers was to some degree a product of her times, and her role varied according to her age and era. While all of the major leaders had experience dealing with legislatures and the political process, the nature of their political activity changed over time. Before 1880 their primary political instrument was the petition with thousands of signatures. In the 1880s and 1890s they attempted to influence and shape party politics. From the mid-1890s to 1920 they actively lobbied the state assemblies and campaigned through cities and towns to win the votes of both legislators and citizens. Thus Wittenmyer was reinstated in her work for the Sanitary Commission in Iowa after an appeal to the legislature; she carried a massive temperance petition to Congress in the 1870s; and in the 1890s became a lobbyist and proponent of pensions for Civil War nurses. Willard orchestrated the petition campaign for local option suffrage in Illinois in 1878–79, threw WCTU support behind the Prohibition party in 1882, and in 1892 launched an unsuccessful attempt to unify Populist forces by bringing together socialists in the Knights of Labor, the WCTU, and the Prohibition party. Stevens in 1884 helped win a state constitutional amendment for prohibition in Maine, then lobbied for prohibition enforcement, temperance instruction in schools, and better correctional facilities.

But what about the many other leaders, the state organizers, the department superintendents who were not so well known? Were they also well educated and relatively privileged? Did they too have particular personal reasons for choosing temperance as the chief reform activity by which they would devote themselves to public service? Were their leadership roles similarly shaped by prior reform activities and tactically varied according to the times?

Several studies of the WCTU leadership and other women's groups now permit some answer to these questions. Sociologist Joseph Gusfield examined the social position of 593 WCTU leaders in 1885 and 1910. Norton Mezvinsky selected a sample of 153 leaders of the WCTU and gathered as much data as possible on their education, occupation, and marital status. Ruth Bordin tracked two groups of leaders: 110 of the most famous, whom she traced through news clippings and scrapbooks, and a less prominent sample of local and state officers of 1874, 1884, and 1894. Following Gusfield and Mezvinsky but prior to Bordin, I too examined the characteristics of the WCTU leaders, but with a somewhat different purpose. My goal was to see how they compared with equally prominent suffragists. I selected 49 suffrage leaders and 49 leaders of the WCTU and analyzed their biographies (as described in appendix B). The results of all four studies are generally consistent in showing the early WCTU leadership to have been relatively privileged and similar to leaders in other fields with respect to education, occupation, and marital status. Relatively less is known, however, about what made the temperance leaders different from other types of women leaders. My own results suggest that personal loss and religious background may have been distinguishing features.

Privilege, education, and achievements.   Among the major temperance and suffrage leaders, more than half had the equivalent of some college education. A number had academy or seminary training and college or professional instruction beyond that. Their occupations carried responsibilities that in most cases extended well beyond their families. A few were primarily wives and mothers; others were authors. The rest had careers that expressed social concern outside the home. Almost all had been involved in professional or philanthropic service that demonstrated benevolent purpose while it gained public notice.

Through teaching, a woman often combined her good education and professional aspirations to express her sense of social responsibility. If a young woman early demonstrated her academic ability as a student, she was recognized as a potential teacher and encouraged to enter the field. After some success, she could attain a supervisory position. Occasionally, feeling her aspirations limited by school teaching, she would aspire to one of the traditionally male professions, such as law or the ministry. But more often she went into reform work. Annie Wittenmyer, Frances Willard, and Lillian Stevens all traveled this career path. Willard, for example, graduated as valedictorian of her college class, began to teach, entered a supervisory position, then left education for the wider field of social reform.

Perhaps the most popular index of a woman's achievement, however, was her marital status. Some of the earliest women leaders seemed less likely than ordinary women to marry. In fact, the marriage rate of reform leaders was lower than that of the population at large. Whereas about one-fifth of the woman reformers were unmarried, only one-tenth of the general population of women between 35 and 44 years of age were unmarried in 1890.[31] On the other hand, the 80 percent marriage rate of my sample of temperance leaders was higher than that of college women in general in 1895, of whom only about 60 percent would ever marry.[32] Of a sample of prominent women from a variety of fields of endeavor whose autobiographies were collected in 1913 for an edition of *Who's Who in America,* 68 percent were married and 45 percent were mothers, as shown in table 3.3.

Data on the husbands of prominent temperance leaders bear out the impression of a relatively privileged group. Bordin found two-thirds of her sample had husbands in the professions or in business and industry. Gusfield found almost half of his larger and less notable group of WCTU leaders to have husbands in professional or managerial occupations.

Personal loss, religious faith, and home-centered reform.   What brought women into the reform enterprise in the first place? Did their individual interests shape their choice of reform? Was there a particular experience that led to interest in temperance? Popular opinion has it that many of the temperance women were the wives or mothers of drunkards. Actually, of the 98 temperance and suffrage leaders I studied, only one was widely known to have an alcoholic husband—Abby Kelly Foster, wife of the composer Stephen Foster (and she was primarily a suffragist). Matilda Carse of the WCTU lost a son as the result of an accident caused by a drunken driver. Some, like Mary Clement Leavitt, the WCTU world missionary, had been quietly divorced without any public mention having been made of the event or its surrounding circumstances.[33]

Not drunkenness in her family but rather the death of a husband or a child is mentioned in more than one-third of the biographies of temperance women. Only five of the suffragist biographies mention comparable circumstance. The frequent mention of death in the lives of the temperance women suggests that family had a particularly important value for them. When a husband or child was removed by death, the pain of loss could perhaps be softened only by participation in an organization that concerned itself with familylike functions of caring for the weak, healing the sick, giving help to the vulnerable and the childlike. Family was also undoubtedly important to other women but not so salient as to be mentioned with the same frequency in their biographies.

Complementing and perhaps interacting with the distinctive personal history of the temperance women was the likelihood that they belonged to one of the Protestant denominations that especially emphasized salvation through conversion and personal reform. The religion of the WCTU women was overwhelmingly anchored in those churches that had been dominant on the frontier—the Methodist, Baptist, and Presbyterian. Well over half of the prominent leaders of the temperance group were members of one of these American churches that emphasized participation of the laity rather than apostolic succession (as in the Catholic, Lutheran, and Episcopal churches) or Puritan orthodoxy (as in Calvinism and Congregationalism). The

TABLE 3.3

Women Temperance Leaders: Education, Occupation, and Marital Status, 1870–1920

	Samples of WCTU Leaders				Other Leaders
	Giele (N=49)	Bordin (N=110)	Gusfield (N=593)	Mezvinsky (N=153)	Campbell (N=878)
Education					
Elementary school	14 (28%)	8 (7%)		4 (3%)	
Academy, seminary, HS	7 (14%)	45 (40%)		57 (37%)	27%
College, normal school	13 (26%)	35 (33%)		66 (43%)	41%
Post graduate work	9 (18%)				22%
Unknown	6 (12%)	22 (20%)		26 (17%)	
Occupation					
Mother/wife	2 (4%)	28 (25%)			Noncareer 32%
Author, editor, lecturer[b]	9 (18%)	30 (27%)			Arts 21%
Teacher before marriage		17 (15%)			
Educator		33 (30%)			Education 22%
Philanthropist, organizer, all-around reformer	33 (66%)	22 (20%)			
Professions, doctor, minister, lawyer	5 (10%)	14 (12%)			Professions 25%

TABLE 3.3 (cont.)

| | Samples of WCTU Leaders[a] | | | | Other Leaders |
	Giele (N=49)	Bordin (N=110)	Gusfield (N=593)	Mezvinsky (N=153)	Campbell (N=878)
Marriage and Childbearing					
Married	38 (76%)	87 (80%)			68%
Single	11 (22%)	23 (20%)			32%
Mothers	14 (28%)	50 (57%)			45%
Husband's Occupation		(N = 87)			
Professional and semiprofessional—lawyer, clergy, physician, teacher		36 (41%)	100 (17%)		
Business, finance, industry		23 (26%)	158 (27%)		
Farmer		2 (2%)	14 (2%)		
Other		4 (5%)	321 (54%)		
Unknown		22 (25%)			

[a] Sources: Giele (1961, 148–49, 152–53); Bordin (1981, 163–75); Mezvinsky (1959, chap. 3); Gusfield (1963, 130) totals for 1885 and 1910 only; Campbell (1976, 77, 210, 317) describes a sample of prominent women whose autobiographies were used for a 1914 edition of *Who's Who in America*.

[b] Lecturer is grouped by Giele with philanthropist and organizer and by Bordin with author and editor.

traditions of the frontier churches had early been shaped in accordance with the need for individual ethics and purity in the isolated habitations of newly settled land. These churches had supported temperance as one of the major means of assuring individual self-discipline and morality. Congregationalists were also active in the early temperance efforts at the opening of the nineteenth century, but they were never so consistently successful on the frontier as the Baptist, Presbyterian, and Methodist groups.[34]

The theme of individual morality developed by the frontier churches paralleled woman's concern with temperance. In part because of their religious heritage, temperance women found it natural to turn their attention to the uplift of the individual. The blending of religion, personal loss, maternal concerns, and educational and career achievement combined to bring them out of the home and into public life. The quality of individual life mattered deeply to them. They saw its relevance to family life and the community. By pursuing moral reform and uplift of the individual, they believed they could also better the larger society.[35]

Temperance women were furthermore distinctive in the types of reform in which they engaged. The latter half of the nineteenth century offered all sorts of possibilities: suffrage, temperance, corrections and charities, settlement houses, trade union work, child welfare, women's education, and community improvement. Temperance women seemed not so much interested in general civic improvement and structural reform as in the immediate alleviation of misery. Through charitable activities and personal involvement they offered direct help and services to people in need. The WCTU therefore gave more attention to charitable work, nursing, prison and jail work, social purity, and anticruelty than to general work for the advancement of women in education or employment. Table 3.4 shows how the personal histories, religious roots, and reform interests of the temperance women all fit together in a coherent emphasis on help for dependent persons rather than on a more radical challenge to women's subordinate status.

Later leaders.   Though centered primarily on change in individuals and the family, temperance leaders increasingly accepted the larger women's movement, even though their place in it became more specialized. From the beginning of woman's rights agitation, the histories of suffrage and temperance were closely intertwined. A number of woman reformers, such as Susan B. Anthony, Elizabeth Cady Stanton,

TABLE 3.4

Background of Temperance and Suffrage Leaders, 1870–1920

	WCTU	Suffrage
Religious Background[a]		
Denominations of the frontier		
Methodist, Baptist, Presbyterian	31	7
Denominations of established communities		
Congregational, Unitarian, Universalist,		
Quaker, Episcopalian	10	24
Denomination not ascertained	8	18
	49	49
Missionary Experience[b]		
Active in foreign missionary societies	17	1
Not active in foreign missionary work	32	48
	49	49
Reform Experience[c]		
Advancement of women		
Clubs, education, working women's issues	4	16
Helping others		
Nursing, charities, prison and jail work,	15	4
purity, anticruelty	19	20
Personal Loss[d]		
Mention of death of husband or child	18	5
No mention of death of husband or child	28	35
	46	40

[a] Chi-square = 24.76; p < .001. Classifications of denomination based on Niebuhr (1957, 141–54, 167).
[b] Chi-square = 15.312; p < .001 with Yates's correction.
[c] Chi-square = 7.130; p < .01 with Yates's correction.
[d] Chi-square = 6.445, p < .02 with Yates's correction. Only those leaders were counted whose biographies appeared in publications that mentioned personal facts such as death of husband or child.

Amelia Bloomer, and Mary Livermore, had worked for temperance and suffrage. Some of the earliest and more evangelically oriented WCTU leaders, such as Annie Wittenmyer, however, were outspoken in their opposition to becoming involved in an issue such as suffrage, which would drag their skirts "through the mire of politics."[36]

These two opposing attitudes toward suffrage were reconciled under the leadership of Frances Willard in 1879–98. Throughout this period it was official WCTU policy to promote what Willard called the "Home Protection Ballot," a limited form of suffrage that would permit women to vote in local option elections. In a number of states during the 1880s and 1890s, the top leadership of temperance and suffrage societies was often identical. Zerelda Wallace, wife of a former governor of Indiana, in 1875 spoke before the legislature of the state on the subject of temperance. Finding that a temperance memorial bearing signatures of 10,000 women had been ignored because they had no vote, she organized and became president of the Indianapolis Equal Suffrage Society. She was also president of the Indiana WCTU in 1874–77 and 1879–83 and served as the head of the franchise department of the WCTU in 1883–88.[37]

After the Civil War, Mary Livermore, then living in Illinois with her husband, a Universalist minister, edited her own suffrage newspaper, the *Agitator,* and was elected the first president of the Illinois Woman Suffrage Association. When her family moved to Massachusetts, she became one of the editors of the *Woman's Journal* and was eventually elected president of the American Woman Suffrage Association. An extremely popular lecturer, she toured the country, giving in all more than 3,000 lectures on topics ranging from temperance to "What Shall We Do with Our Daughters?" From 1875 to 1884 she was president of the Massachusetts WCTU.[38]

In Louisiana, Caroline Merrick, wife of the chief justice of the state supreme court, was one of the founders and leading officers of both the Equal Rights Association and the state WCTU. In Tennessee, Lide Meriwether was president of both state temperance and suffrage organizations in their early years. J. Ellen Foster of Iowa, an ardent suffragist and prominent Republican party worker, also served as president of the Iowa WCTU. Hannah J. Bailey of Maine headed the Maine suffrage association from 1891 to 1897 and served as the national superintendent of the peace department in the WCTU, from which position she tirelessly worked for international arbitration and world peace.[39]

By 1900, however, it was more difficult to maintain a nearly equal involvement in both movements. While suffrage gained popularity, the prominence of the temperance leaders declined. Contributing to the long-term decline of the WCTU was a change in leadership. The number of prominent leaders dropped as old leaders left to become active in other groups or as new leaders failed to enter. Of the 49 prominent leaders of the WCTU whose biographies I examined, only 9 were important in the period after 1895. In later years, the era of Frances Willard was glorified and used for fund-raising efforts. Gusfield, in his extended study of the leadership, found a steady decline in the social status of the leaders after 1900.[40] At the World's Congress of Representative Women in 1893, a number of women prominent in the WCTU gave addresses on social purity, philanthropy, and temperance education. But the majority of the speakers were even then more identified with suffrage and other causes than with temperance.[41]

Other women who continued to be active in both suffrage and the WCTU seemed to shift their main identification to suffrage. Ella Stewart and Catherine Waugh McCulloch of Chicago were secure enough in their own identity to describe objectively the disdain of suffragists for the WCTU.[42] These two socially prominent reformers from Chicago had early been active in the WCTU and remained on its board of national lecturers, but became increasingly active in suffrage.

Organization

Although the WCTU bore the marks of a quasi-religious movement, it was neither the captive of any one religious group nor a solely religious entity. Instead the WCTU advanced women's position as moral and upstanding members of local churches and communities and thereby helped to construct a broader identity for temperance women as citizens of the state and mothers of the nation. Thus the temperance cause, although it bore religious overtones, was not narrowly sectarian but ecumenical.

The challenge of encompassing many states and regions pushed the WCTU to create an organizational structure that reproduced the federal-state differentiation of national government. The president of each state branch was a vice president of the national organization. At the same time, specialized departments spanned territorial boundaries and handled specific mandates, such as scientific temperance instruction or work among Indians. Binding all these activities together were the lecture tours of organizers, the state and national conventions, and the weekly newspaper that kept the many parts of the organization in communication with one another.

State unions and the growth in membership. State representation broadened over time. In the founding convention of 1874, five-minute reports came from only six states: Ohio, Massachusetts, Michigan, New York, Indiana, and Vermont, although the District of Columbia, Illinois, Iowa, Maryland, New Jersey, Pennsylvania, and Wisconsin were also organized that year. By 1880, however, there were 22 state organizations and by 1885 there were 51 state and territorial units. Virtually the whole country had been organized in the span of a decade.

The corresponding secretaries of the state and national organizations reported precise statistics on chapters and membership in each state. States kept track of the number of meetings and types of activities held, dues collected, expenses paid, and pieces of literature handed out—all of which were recorded each year in the minutes of the national convention. A phenomenal amount of activity was under way wherever there was a state temperance union: state fairs, lobbying on behalf of pending legislation, sponsorship of speech contests, special publications, and annual state conventions for which the most established states had their own printed minutes. Departments also pursued their specialized goals at the state level, and in the case of the department of work among colored people such activity had by 1910 resulted in a total of 11 state organizations of black women's temperance unions (Arkansas, District of Columbia, Florida, Georgia, Louisiana, Maryland, North Carolina, South Carolina, Tennessee, Texas, and Virginia).

Especially impressive, in addition to the sheer volume of activity, was the steady growth of the WCTU membership at the local level. Numbers rose rapidly—from 14,000 in 1879 to 52,000 in 1883 to 70,000 in 1885.[43] Ohio, where the crusade began, in 1895 reported 600 local chapters, 94 district and county chapters, 12,300 active and honorary members, 1,350 Loyal Temperance Legions for youth, and 700 young women added that year to the young women's temperance auxiliaries. Other states with large memberships were New York with 840 chapters and 22,000 members, Pennsylvania with 667 chapters and 19,000 members, and Illinois with 650 chapters and 15,000 participants. By 1910 membership in New York, Ohio, Pennsylvania, and a number of midwestern states had nearly doubled, while it rose more gradually or held steady in New England, along the eastern seaboard, and in the South. These developments are summarized in the maps of WCTU membership for 1883, 1890, and 1900 shown in figures 3.2, 3.3, and 3.4, respectively.

Just how broad was the rank and file? For reasonably well-educated women in small communities the WCTU appears to have been a major vehicle for their personal emancipation. Chapters must have averaged 15 to 20 members, smaller in the villages, with more than 100 in the cities. Particularly in the smaller towns, the WCTU was the thinking woman's organization, allied with a number of progressive causes. They helped poor transient men and women in the big cities; they put pressure on the medical profession to rely less on alcohol as a means of treatment; they introduced physical education and scientific temperance instruction in the schools. In the recollection of the eminent Chicago sociologist Everett Hughes, who recalled the interest of his own parents in feminism, temperance women were almost synonymous with the enlightened leadership of the local community:

I was brought up in southern Ohio a few miles from Washington Courthouse and have among my possessions a book called *The Crusade at Washington Courthouse,* which belonged to my mother. In the parsonages in which we lived there were many meetings of the WCTU. They were in those cases, almost without exception, made up of the leading women of the community, the wives of the leading businessmen and professional men, my mother as wife of the minister, and perhaps some people less prominent. They were not the wives of drunkards or ne'er-do-wells. Very few of them, so far as I know, had ever had any problem of drink in their families. This same lot of women talked about boiling the baby's milk, about general sanitation, about improving education, about child labor laws, and about all the rest of it. They seemed to be interested in general social improvement and were, I suppose, the progressive women of their time in many respects.[44]

The relative density of WCTU membership suggests that temperance work was likely to be popular in smaller cities and towns of the middle Atlantic and midwestern states, a distribution that correlated with the strength of the frontier churches, Methodist, Baptist, and Presbyterian. In these locations it is likely that the WCTU was the most progressive and activist women's organization available, certainly much more politically involved than either the missionary societies or the women's clubs. And into these less urban areas the

Figure 3.2
Woman's Temperance Union Membership, 1883
(States Ranked by Members per 100,000 Residents)

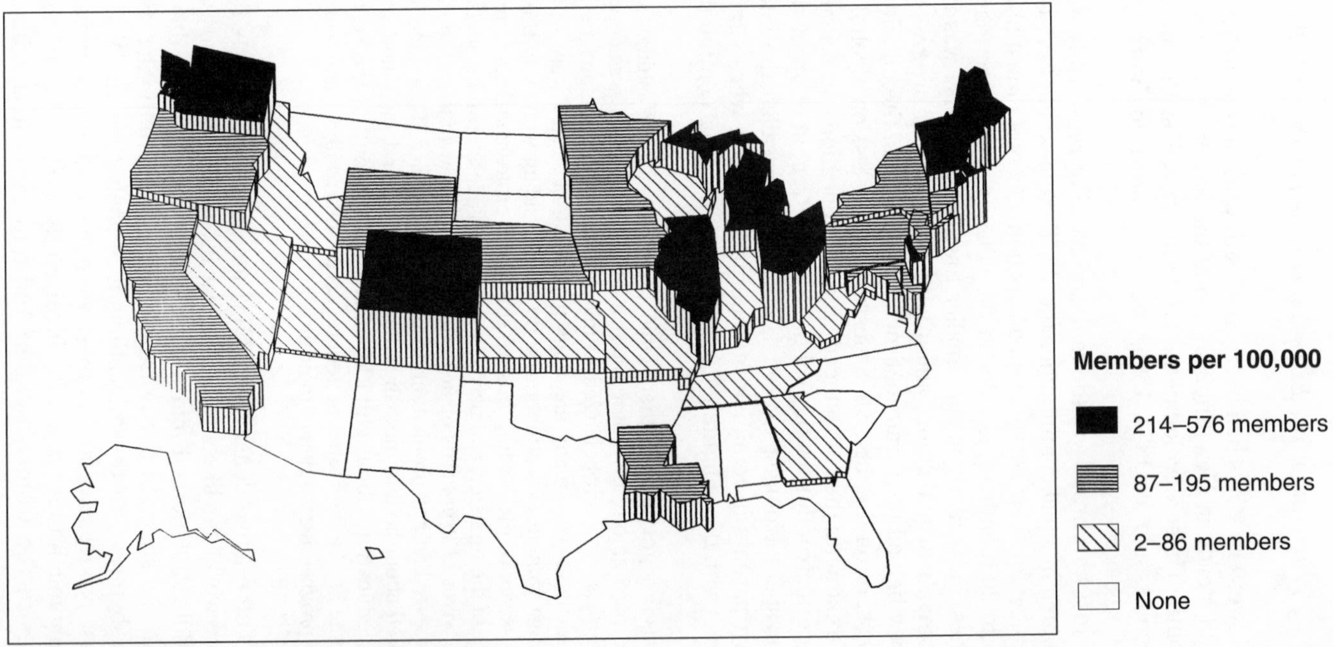

Members per 100,000

■ 214–576 members

▥ 87–195 members

▨ 2–86 members

□ None

Source: NWCTU Minutes, 1883, 68–107.

Figure 3.3
Woman's Temperance Union Membership, 1890
(States Ranked by Members per 100,000 Residents)

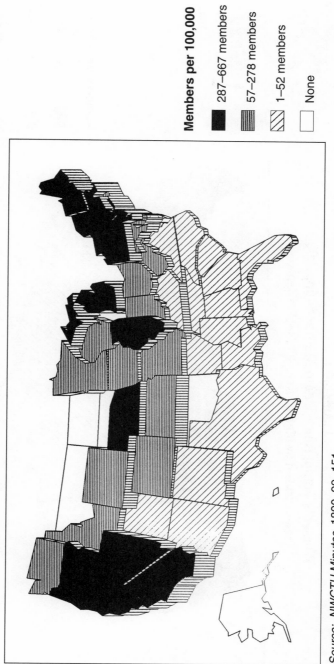

Members per 100,000

- 287–667 members
- 57–278 members
- 1–52 members
- None

Source: NWCTU Minutes, 1890, 99–151.

Figure 3.4
Woman's Temperance Union Membership, 1900
(States Ranked by Members per 100,000 Residents)

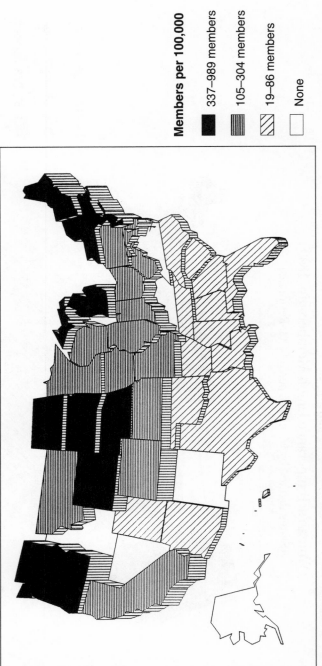

Members per 100,000

- ▉ 337–989 members
- ▥ 105–304 members
- ▨ 19–86 members
- ☐ None

Source: NWCTU Minutes, 1900, 113–39.

suffrage organizations, the women's trade union groups, and the college women's suffrage league were less likely to penetrate. Thus simply as a membership group that expanded women's horizons to concern with the public good, the WCTU appears to have made a contribution to female emancipation.

The WCTU had always had a broader organization than suffrage. In the 1880s when suffrage groups existed mainly in very large cities, the woman's temperance unions extended to smaller cities but were still predominantly urban. With time, however, the unions pushed into even smaller towns.[45] But this outreach probably exacted a cost that diminished the cosmopolitan and progressive stance of the organization. In a report on the work of local temperance unions in Tennessee, Lide Meriwether described the outlying unions as mainly concerned with speaking contests and lectures that used illustrations of the stomach to demonstrate the effects of alcohol on the body, whereas in Memphis the unions were interested in prison and jail work, social purity, and suffrage.[46]

In the 1890s, before the new burst of energy that came to suffrage in the following decade, it was sometimes the WCTU that kept feminism alive. Mary Livermore, in an 1894 letter to Alice Stone Blackwell, daughter of Lucy Stone and Henry Blackwell, wrote of the aging and thinning of suffrage ranks in her town north of Boston while the WCTU continued to grow:

We have no Suffrage League in Melrose. In three years, we lost by death and removal every member of sense and influence belonging to the League, nearly forty in all . . . All who remained were members of the W.C.T.U., and in my absence they voted to disband, and unite with the W.C.T.U., which they did. I haven't the heart to start another.

We have a W.C.T.U. of nearly 400 members, and *I don't know of one who is not a suffragist.* We have a Superintendent of Franchise, and as I am a member, I keep the organization up to the mark.[47]

Departments and the plan of work.   Specialized departments cut across state and territorial boundaries and reflected temperance women's expanding agenda for social reform. The plan of work outlined at the first convention in 1874 listed such activities as organization, making public sentiment, juvenile temperance societies, the pledge, and such goals as the institution of coffee rooms and fountains. These ventures fell into five principal domains that within the next few years would become the province of one or more departments headed by a national superintendent and would be reproduced in most states. The number of departments grew rapidly from around 20 in 1880 to roughly 40 in 1895 and thereafter.[48] *Organizing* fell to such departments as juvenile work, the young woman's branch, and the support of lecturers and organizers. *Outreach* was the purpose of work among colored people, foreigners, Indians, lumbermen, miners, railroad employees, and soldiers and sailors. *Publicity and education* were advanced through scientific instruction, state and county fairs, temperance literature, and the Woman's Temperance Publishing Association. Departments for *alcohol substitution* changed their names over the years, but at one time or another included friendly inns and reading rooms, unfermented wine, and antinarcotics. Finally, a number of departments were dedicated to *personal and social reform:* prison and jail work, evangelistic work, social purity, temperance legislation, franchise, and relation of temperance to labor and capital.

We have already seen the accomplishments of the organizers in the phenomenal growth of state unions and local membership. Much of the early development was due to the tireless efforts of Frances Willard, who toured the country giving an average of one lecture a day between 1874 and 1883, staying with local townspeople, paying her train fare, and sending occasional checks to her mother from the modest donations collected.[49] The WCTU missionary Mary Clement Leavitt traveled around the world between 1883 and 1891, visiting and organizing temperance work in Australia, New Zealand, India, Africa, and Europe; she everywhere circulated the "Polyglot Petition" against the international traffic in opiates and stimulants and was responsible for most of the 7.5 million signatures that had been collected by 1895.[50]

Certainly one of the most impressive activities on the books of the WCTU was its organization of a number of special constituencies that formed participating units in the whole. Branches for youth and young women formed part of the larger state and national organization. African-American women had their own local and state units, at first designated by such names as Sojourner or Harper, later by number, as in Texas No. 2.

Then there was outreach to extend the temperance message into groups known for their vulnerability to alcohol or the attractions of the saloon: inebriate women, miners, lumbermen, railroad workers, soldiers and sailors. Of particular interest for the history of the temperance movement were the attitudes and stance of the WCTU toward "foreigners." Sometimes bitter WCTU statements contrasting denial of

"Home of the Intemperate." From *Fifty Years History of the Temperance Cause* by J. E. Stebbins, 1876. Courtesy of the Frances E. Willard Memorial Library, Evanston, Illinois.

"Singing Outside the Saloon." From *Fifty Years History of the Temperance Cause* by J. E. Stebbins, 1876. Courtesy of the Frances E. Willard Memorial Library, Evanston, Illinois.

suffrage for themselves with its availability to poor, uneducated, immigrant men are an indication of WCTU nativism. These pronouncements gave their own Anglo-Saxon Protestant heritage a place of
central importance while resisting the cultural and political changes
threatened by hordes of wine- and beer-drinking Catholic immigrants
from Central and Southern Europe. Nevertheless, the WCTU took up
work with the new immigrants. In 1888 the WCTU established a
department for work among foreigners that faced the problems of the
new immigrants in philanthropic rather than recriminating terms. By
the turn of the century, WCTU women were active at various ports of
immigration both in the East and among the Chinese in California.[51]

Efforts to substitute nonalcoholic beverages for wine and spirits in
many respects encountered remarkable success over the 50-year
period between 1870 and the establishment of prohibition in 1919.
Aside from the Episcopalians and Lutherans, most Protestant
churches replaced communion wine with unfermented grape juice.
Alcohol was banned from state dinners at the White House during the
administration of Grover Cleveland. Thousands of Sunday schools and
youth groups routinely circulated the pledge and secured signatures
almost as a matter of course. Conscientious matrons excluded brandy
and any other form of spirits from sideboard and pantry. Moreover,
the WCTU campaigned against the opium traffic and all other addictive narcotic substances. By 1910 a new climate of opinion had been
established that made the social use of alcohol in good society the
exception rather than the rule.

From the beginning WCTU leaders showed their understanding of
the importance of publications and education to spread their message.
Beginning with the founding convention in 1874, the organization
addressed the need for a newspaper and how to support it. By convention time in 1875 six issues of the monthly *Woman's Temperance
Union* had appeared, with Annie Wittenmyer as publisher and Jane
Fowler Willing as editor. In 1883 the *Union Signal* became the official
weekly newspaper of the WCTU. Within a year it was the most popular temperance journal in the country, with nearly 14,000 subscribers,
and by 1890 it was the largest women's paper in the world, with a circulation of nearly 100,000. Even more impressive was the fact that this
16-page weekly was almost entirely produced by women. The
Woman's Temperance Publishing Association, which published it
along with other periodicals for children and 2 million leaflets a year,
employed 111 people, of whom 89 were women.[52]

The grandest purpose of the union, however, was personal and social reform, and contribution to progressive social change became the legacy for which the WCTU will most be remembered. Among the most active departments were social purity, scientific temperance instruction, and franchise, each of which helped to win numerous changes in state laws over the 40-year period between the WCTU's initial decision in 1879 to endorse political action by working for the franchise and the adoption of the constitutional amendments for prohibition in 1919 and suffrage in 1920. Temperance women visited prisons and looked to the proper conditions for women prisoners. They encouraged the introduction of police matrons in some of the large cities. Some, like Lillian Stevens of Maine, were appointed by the governors of their states as representatives to the National Conference of Charities and Corrections under the presidency of Jane Addams.[53] Taken together the departments succeeded in framing a broad reform agenda that dovetailed with the goals of other progressive groups but also raised consciousness and stretched the political awareness of the rank and file of ordinary middle-class women.

Reform Strategy and Accomplishments

It took almost half a century from the founding of the WCTU in 1874 to win national prohibition with the passage of the Eighteenth Amendment in 1919 and to obtain woman suffrage with the Nineteenth Amendment in 1920. While working for temperance and prohibition the WCTU broadened women's civic horizons by quietly fostering the expression of feminist principles among the moderate middle class. Temperance women helped to construct the modern welfare state by extending their caregiving and good housekeeping to municipal and national government. Finally, the WCTU directly advanced the cause of suffrage by at first supporting limited forms of franchise, such as school, municipal, and local option suffrage, and later full suffrage.

Temperance as a vehicle for feminism.   By building on the woman's temperance crusade and wrapping themselves in the symbols and language of the churches, women's temperance advocates subtly expanded the feminine role from hearth to public arena.[54] In their very first convention the WCTU established circulation of the pledge, organization of local temperance societies, and promotion of mass meetings as the first order of business. The pledge read as follows: "I hereby solemnly promise, God helping me, to abstain from all distilled, fermented and malt liquors, including wine and cider, and to employ all proper means to discourage use and traffic in the same."[55]

By pledging themselves, their children and their households, "banishing alcohol in all its forms from the sideboard and the kitchen," keeping an autograph pledge book on their parlor tables, and carrying one in their own pockets, Christian temperance women propounded an implied feminism.[56] They pressed for the moral and social equality of the sexes and organized on behalf of women's rights and interests.

The plan of work outlined at the first annual convention of 1874 was largely a plan for missionary work by means of individual charity and conversion, what at that time was termed gospel temperance. Specific articles addressed the issues of unfermented sacramental wine, temperance coffee rooms and water fountains in every town, homes for inebriate women, and clubs for reformed men. From one perspective these reforms might be understood as regressive attempts to preserve a rural, Protestant, nativist way of life in the face of rapid urbanization and immigration.[57]

But the WCTU emphasis on individual responsibility and self-discipline that was embodied in the pledge and such charitable institutions as homes for inebriates can also be given a more progressive interpretation. These admittedly parochial pursuits represented the simplest means to extend women's traditional maternal concerns beyond the home. How else was a woman without vote or profession to reform the world? Her primary instruments of power were those of the mother, cook, homemaker, and churchgoer. She could refuse to marry a man who drank.[58] She could bring up her children to abstain.[59] As a hostess she could emulate the practice of such public figures as wives of U.S. presidents who from 1877 to 1897 banned wine and liquors from their public entertainments, or William Jennings Bryan, whose "dry" dinners were said to be popular with foreign envoys.[60] In her own modest way she could provide coffee, tea, water, unfermented wine, safe lodging, and a sympathetic ear to replace the drinks sold in saloons or the uncertain shelter usually meted out to the drunk and disorderly. As early as the 1850s women's temperance groups had provided shelter, food, and clothing to wives of drunkards and women who themselves were alcoholics.[61] In the early years of the WCTU Frances Willard herself actively participated in daily meetings at Lower Farwell Hall in Chicago, working with individuals, bringing them to the point of taking the pledge, helping them keep it once taken, and assisting and counseling the families of drunkards.[62] Such efforts won wide approval; as Willard's biographer Mary Earhart noted, temperance was more popular than suffrage because it was "so much easier to see a drunkard than to see a principle."[63] Eventually these simple beginnings would generate more ambitious and far-reaching proposals to build the conditions for temperance and health into the very foundations of the larger society.

Municipal housekeeping and the origins of the welfare state. After gospel temperance the next step to expanding women's roles as citizens was to understand that their maternal and wifely skills were needed not just in the home, the church, and the neighborhood but in the halls of government. In the words of one writer for the *Union Signal,*

the management of a city is but a larger form of housekeeping, and men working at it alone have introduced the same untidy, unsystematic, spend-thrift ways that they do into their own habitation when they keep bachelor's hall. It is not good for man to be alone anywhere, and least of all when he sets up housekeeping individually or by municipal organization. When the women of New York City band together it is first of all to clean the filthy sweating dens. Their gospel is first of all a gospel of soapsuds.[64]

Temperance women shared an interest with women's clubs and suffragists in a number of progressive causes that were eventually institutionalized in broader government programs: prison reform, children's health, betterment of women's working conditions, and pure food and drug laws.[65] But in two areas especially, the WCTU had a unique and enduring impact on the social conscience and laws of the nation: in matters relating to social purity, or the sexual exploitation of women, and to the establishment of scientific temperance instruction in the schools.

Social purity. The quest for social purity was associated with missionary work to heathen women and Mormons, establishment of women's prisons, the crusade against the white slave traffic, efforts to raise the age of consent, and efforts to improve conditions for working women. As early as 1875, the WCTU had a committee for suppression of the social evil that in 1883 was renamed social purity and that between

1885 and 1895 waged a remarkably successful campaign to raise the legal age of consent, a necessary foundation for bringing charges against abusers and procurers.[66] A department for suppression of impure literature was established in 1884, a department of Mormon work in 1886, and a department for sex education in 1910. In their understanding of the connections between violence, sexual abuse, and drunkenness, the WCTU presaged modern feminist discoveries that alcohol abuse, prostitution, cruelty, pornography, and delinquency of women are often linked.[67]

Temperance women developed their first concern for social purity through the churches. One of the continuing purposes of women's foreign missionary work had been to liberate the "heathen" women of India from moral enslavement in the zenanas, or harems, in which they lived.[68] In America temperance women felt similar compassion for the white slave or the Mormon wife who was part of a polygamous household.[69] Temperance women at first used preaching, prayer, and rescue houses to help fallen women. Temperance women helped gather 100,000 signatures on a petition to the Michigan legislature to establish a reformatory for girls in 1879.[70] They then turned to purity campaigns and legislative action to accomplish enlightenment and protection.

In 1885, when Frances Willard became head of the social purity department, the work gained particular significance. A young physician, Kate Bushnell, made a trip to the lumber camps in northern Michigan and Wisconsin and returned with reports of women being kept there that outraged WCTU members, who had pledged "to treat all women with respect and to protect them from wrong and degradation."[71] For a time the temperance group placed hope in legal reform and focused on raising the age of consent. In 1887, the age at which a girl could consent to "her own ruin" was as low as 10 in 15 states. Sample legislation developed by the WCTU called for means of dealing with the "increasing and alarming frequency of assaults upon women and frightful indignities to which even little girls are subject": "We, men and women of _____, State of _____, do most earnestly appeal to you to enact such statutes as shall provide for the adequate punishment of crimes against women and girls. We also urge that the age at which a girl can legally consent to her own ruin be raised to at least eighteen years."[72]

By 1895, the number of states with the age set at 16 or above had been doubled to 20. But the age of consent was still 7 in Delaware and

10 in Alabama, South Carolina, Georgia, and Florida. From the beginning the WCTU contended that vice was related to the liquor traffic, and some suffragists, like Anna Howard Shaw, very strongly supported this position. Most suffragists, however, pointed to the need for better employment opportunity: "[T]he great protection is the ability of young girls to earn their living by congenial labor. All the social purity societies do not equal the trade schools as a preventative," claimed the Reverend Anna Garlin Spencer at the 1908 suffrage convention.[73]

In the 1880s, even though Frances Willard took active interest in the labor movement, most conservative women were oblivious to the problems of working women. Official investigations and reports described unbelievable poverty, crowding, and lack of concern for women's health and well-being in the sweatshops and tenement rooms where they did piecework.[74] Helen Campbell's *Prisoners of Poverty* (1900) and the labor report of 1888, *Working Women in Large Cities,* gave ample description of the cramped working conditions and crowded tenements that were conducive to immorality among women factory workers.[75] But in general temperance women tended to put more emphasis on the establishment of a single moral standard, a "White Life for Two," than on the improvement of women's working conditions. A 1905 article in the *Union Signal* voiced the central tenet of the purity rule: "Let us away with the double standard of morality. Let us teach our boys and all the world that vice is vice as black and abhorrent in men as in women. Let us teach that a fallen woman is no more fallen than a fallen man."[76]

Scientific temperance instruction. A second major thrust of temperance women was instruction of children about health, physiology, and effects of alcohol on the body. One historian has said that the institution of scientific temperance instruction in the textbooks and schools of the nation was "the most distinctive contribution of the WCTU to the temperance movement in the United States."[77]

A variety of themes came together in the WCTU drive for scientific temperance instruction: temperance women's maternal concerns for children; distrust of the medical uses of alcohol and alcohol-based patent medicines; and progressive ideas about health, physical education, and physiology.[78] In their founding convention in 1874, WCTU women noted that Catholicism was to be admired and emulated for its concern with training children and youth; they called for similar effort

A MERRY CHRISTMAS

UNION SIGNAL

AND WORLD'S WHITE RIBBON

"THOU HAST GIVEN A BANNER TO THEM THAT FEAR THEE: THAT IT MAY BE DISPLAYED BECAUSE OF THE TRUTH."

Volume XXIII.—No. 48. Issued Weekly.   CHICAGO, December 16, 1897.   [Price $1.00 Per Year in Advance.

Union Signal and World's White Ribbon

Organ of the National W. C. T. U.   ...FOR 1898...   Organ of the World's W. C. T. U.

STATUTORY PROHIBITION

Is the objective point for the year. The UNION SIGNAL will report the campaigns. All W. C. T. U. lines of work will be discussed by eminent leaders, and reform movements by other societies will be noted. All of the notable writers can not be named, nor the good things they will present, but below are a few of them:

CORRESPONDENTS

Rev. Carl F. Eltzholtz.	Mrs. Mary T. Burt.
Mrs. Mary A. Ward Poole.	Josiah W. Leeds.
Henry J. Osborn.	Rev. O. W. Stewart
Mrs. Margaret B. Platt.	Mrs. Clinton B. Smith.
Mrs. S. M. I. Henry.	Mrs. Helen M. Stoddard.
Miss Elizabeth P. Gordon.	Miss Frances B. Callaway

STORY WRITERS

Marietta Holley.	Estelle M. Amory.
Ella Beecher Gittings.	Louisa A. Nash.
Max Johann, M. D.	Rev. J. F. Cowen.
Eliza E. Cartwright.	Emma P. Seabury.
Mrs. E. Craft Cobern.	Ada Melville Shaw.
Sarah K. Bolton.	Harriet Francene Crocker.

CONTRIBUTORS

Mary A. Lathbury.	Mrs. Clara Hoffman.
Mary G. Stuckenberg.	Rev. George M. Hammell.
Mrs. Marion Baxter.	Mrs. Mary H. Hull.
Miss Harriet Orcutt.	Rev. Frances E. Townsley.
Rev. Amos R. Wells.	Mrs. Helen L. Bullock.
Mrs. Helen M. Barker.	Grace H. Dodge.
Dr. Sarah Hackett Stevenson.	Mrs. Anna M. Vail.
Lillian F. Lewis.	Dr. Booker T. Washington.
Jennie Fowler Willing.	Mrs. Booker T. Washington.
Mrs. Mary F. Lovell.	Mrs. Henry Blair.
Mrs. Mary Jewett Telford.	Prof. A. A. Hopkins.
Louise Manning Hodgkins.	Rev. C. H. Mead.
Rev. J. A. Adams.	Rev. James Dunn.
Mrs. Joseph Cook.	Henry D. Lloyd.
Prof. Graham Taylor.	John G. Woolley.
Katharine Lente Stevenson.	Rev. Charles E. Bently.
Mrs. Frances E. Beauchamp.	Dr. Herrick Johnson.
Rev. Charles G. Ames, D. D.	Mrs. Leonora Lake.
Dr. T. D. Crothers.	Kate Lunden.
	Mrs. E. R. Chase.
	Prof. Richard T. Ely.
	Jane Addams.
	Josephine Shaw Lowell.
	Prof. Martha Foote Crow.
	Mary B. Willard.
	Ellwood Pomeroy.
	Rev. Louis Albert Banks.
	Prof. Sarah F. Whiting.
	Mrs. Louise S. Rounds.
	Prof. Samuel Dickie.
	Prof. E. J. Wheeler.

OUR ROUND-THE-WORLD MISSIONARIES

will describe their progress, the drink customs of the countries they visit, and the helps and hindrances to the advancement of Temperance.

Miss Jessie Ackermann.	Mrs. J. K. Barney.
Miss Clara Parrish.	Mrs. Helen L. Bullock.
Miss Vincent.	Miss Cummins.
Miss Shaffner.	Miss Erickson.

Correspondents will report Practical Temperance and Reform work from forty odd countries. Some of these are:

Miss Agnes Slack, England.	Mary S. Powell, New Zealand.
Gwyneth Vaughn, Wales.	Elisabet Selmer, Scandinavia.
Miss Amelia Pemell, Australia	Miss Olif Johannsdottir, Iceland
Mrs. E. Mac Kerrow Moody, South Africa.	
Mrs. F. P. Bowen, Constantinople.	

FRANCES E. WILLARD will continue to write editorials, paragraphs on current topics, bits of travel, and upon many subjects of interest to our world-wide constituency.

LADY HENRY SOMERSET will contribute Studies in Black and White, or Stories of the London Slums, and write of the progress of Temperance in England.

MRS. MARY H. HUNT will discuss Scientific Temperance laws, anti-alcohol sentiment among educators and scientists.

MARION A. MAC BRIDE—Domestic Science.

FLORENCE KELLEY—Indirect Helps to Temperance.

CHARLOTTE PERKINS STETSON — Home Cooking and Intemperance.

MRS. MARY L. WYATT and MRS. M. LOUISE FORD will contribute occasional stories for the Children's page.

Mrs. Frances J. Barnes,	Carrie Lee Carter,	Ida Clothier,
Belle Kearney,	Mrs. Ella A. Boole,	Belle H. Mix,

and others, will furnish the Y news and much that will be interesting and instructive to young women.

MRS. KATHARINE LENTE STEVENSON

besides other contributions, will offer a course of study to the unions through the Local Union column every other week, beginning with the first issue in January. Alternate weeks she will answer questions and give helpful hints to the workers.

REV. WILBUR F. CRAFTS and MRS. MARGARET DYE ELLIS (Members of the Third House) will put our readers in touch with the work in the interest of Christian Citizenship and reform legislation at Washington, D. C.

DR. MARY WOOD-ALLEN, MRS. JESSIE BROWN HILTON, and others, will write articles to mothers and fathers on Home Training.

State and Territorial Press Superintendents will furnish regular reports from their respective fields, and the W. C. T. U. News column will continue to give short items gleaned from many sources.

THE CURRENT EVENTS PAGE WILL BE CONTINUED.

The Union Signal for the full year contains 800 Pages as it stands, or a quarto volume of 3,200 pages, or sixteen volumes of 200 pages each for $1.00

FIFTY CENTS TO MINISTERS.

Union Signal masthead. Courtesy of the Frances E. Willard Memorial Library, Evanston, Illinois.

by temperance women to instruct the young. Less than two years later, in a speech to the International Medical Convention held in Philadelphia, Annie Wittenmyer emphasized that alcohol had no food value, was of questionable medical use, and might lead to addiction.[79] Progress in temperance education was rapid from that point forward.

The National Temperance Association in 1877 endorsed school lessons in temperance and approved the first physiology text with temperance content that was used in Indiana. In 1878 the WCTU established a department of scientific temperance instruction, with Mary H. Hunt at its head.[80] The following year state unions in Maine, Massachusetts, Vermont, Connecticut, Iowa, Minnesota, and Indiana brought the issue before local school boards. School suffrage was passed in 1881 in Massachusetts, a direct outgrowth of the efforts of temperance women and prohibition forces to influence the schools.[81]

For the next 20 years, with the backing of an 1881 WCTU resolution "to enact laws requiring the study of alcohol in its effects upon the human system in all schools supported by public money," Hunt traveled widely and pursued a strategy of getting state legislatures to institute temperance instruction in the public schools. In 1897 such laws were on the books in 41 states and the District of Columbia. By 1903 only Georgia was without such a law. It was estimated that in 1901–1902 some 22 million children received scientific temperance instruction.[82]

Important consequences ensued for publishers, textbook content, curriculum, and teachers. Publishers turned their books over to Hunt and her assistants for suggestions and revisions. By 1891 the WCTU department had endorsed 25 books. But such success also brought charges of inaccuracy and venality. A blue-ribbon "committee of fifty" polled school teachers in regard to the texts and reported 47 books rated "good" and 86 "bad."[83] Nevertheless, the WCTU met with amazing success in its efforts to institutionalize its goal of temperance instruction. Laws were passed and implemented through steady pressure on publishers, teachers, and legislators.[84] As with their efforts to raise the age of consent, WCTU activists gained valuable knowledge of how to mobilize a constituency, petition legislatures, and lobby for the reforms that they so ardently desired. But this experience brought home ever more painfully the realization that to be fully effective they needed the vote.

Justifying equal rights for women.   As a bridge from charitable works to political action there was no more important group than the

Woman's Christian Temperance Union. As they worked for such reforms as local option, higher age of consent, and temperance instruction, conservative temperance women who had once questioned the need for the vote began to see its importance. The leaders were even more advanced in their understanding that the franchise was needed. As Bordin notes, they "had acquired lobbying skills and knew their way around legislative chambers; they could testify before committees and were well aware of the harassment value of the right of petition. They represented the largest and most geographically widespread body of women to acquire political action skills in the history of the republic to that date."[85]

It should be recognized, however, that there is another widespread view of the WCTU, held by some of their contemporaries as well as modern historians, that the group were primarily singing and praying evangelists rather than hard-headed political activists bent on equal rights for women. Suffragists in the 1870s thought the woman's temperance crusade a pathetic display of misguided faith in God to get rid of liquor and drunkenness instead of a rational appeal to legislators to change the laws and grant women the vote.[86] More recently, historian Jack Blocker has characterized the temperance and suffrage advocates as following "separate paths." Suffragists, he says, had more faith in state action, whereas the crusaders had been disappointed by the failure of antiliquor laws to protect them and had thus taken to the streets; the WCTU's main subsequent interest in the woman's ballot was not as an end itself but to put teeth into law enforcement.[87]

Certainly the WCTU arguments for woman suffrage did have a more "particularistic" quality than those of the suffragists. Temperance women were more inclined to justify the need for the ballot as a means to the particular end of establishing a liquor-free society rather than as a universal civil right due women as citizens (Aileen Kraditor has termed this an *expediency* rather than a *justice* argument). In my content analysis of the *Union Signal* and the *Woman's Journal,* I found the proportion of "particularistic" suffrage arguments very much higher in the temperance newspaper (61 percent versus 9 percent).[88] But the nearly 40 percent representation of universalistic reasoning for suffrage among temperance advocates should not be ignored.

In reality the WCTU positions for both suffrage and temperance were intertwined in complex ways. You would think from reading the *Union Signal* that the millennium might come either way. With either the woman's ballot or prohibition, the community would be a safer place for wives and children; brewers' greed and political corruption would lose their influence on government; newly empowered women and righteous leaders would find a way to world peace.[89] As the WCTU position on woman's rights and prohibition evolved over a period of almost 20 years, both reforms became part of a standard platform in which their benefits were intertwined. This symbiotic relationship was primarily responsible for both the strengths and liabilities that the WCTU contributed to feminism.

WCTU support for suffrage. In 1875, at the second annual convention of the WCTU, a telegram came from the American Woman Suffrage Association then meeting in New York City: "The American Woman Suffrage Association bids your convention God-speed. Soon may women, armed with the ballot, help make laws which concern human welfare."[90] But it was not until 1879, when Frances Willard was elected president, and 1881, when a committee on the franchise was organized, that the WCTU took an unequivocal stance on woman suffrage. Up to that time there was considerable division over whether the organization should support even a limited franchise for local option or prohibition (an idea first introduced at a convention in 1875). Conservative forces opposed suffrage of any kind: Wittenmyer argued that the churches would object if suffrage were introduced; even the "home protection ballot," made famous in 1877 by Frances Willard's petition campaign in Illinois, was defeated in the 1878 convention: "*Resolved, That as the responsibility of the training of the children and youth rests largely upon woman, she ought to be allowed to open or close the rum shop door over against her home.*"[91]

With Willard's ascendancy to the presidency in 1879, however, suffrage support rapidly gained among temperance women. In 1882 state and national franchise departments began to work for the vote on temperance issues; by 1883 a resolution favoring equal and unlimited suffrage for women was adopted by the annual convention. From that point forward the WCTU was the most effective grass-roots organization to promote the woman's ballot. Numerous state suffrage campaigns relied on the WCTU for local strategy and tactics to help pass state suffrage referenda: Iowa in 1883–84 and 1916, Kansas for its municipal suffrage bill in 1887, Colorado in 1893, California in 1911, South Dakota and West Virginia in 1916.[92]

WCTU support for suffrage was not, however, universally regarded as an unmixed blessing, especially by the more militant suffragists.

Temperance women settled more easily for a limited school, municipal, or local option franchise. Their suffrage activities also aroused powerful and unwelcome opposition from the liquor interests. How then did the WCTU contribute to the suffrage cause? Was its attachment to prohibition a progressive or reactionary force?

Progressive or retrograde feminism? Historical judgment about the contribution of the WCTU to suffrage has yielded a mixed verdict. The national disillusion with prohibition during the 1920s and repeal in 1933 cast a shadow over organizations such as the WCTU that had campaigned for the federal prohibition amendment. Historians of both suffrage and temperance were inclined to criticize the WCTU for its seeming narrowness in the way it championed suffrage and other reforms.[93] Rather than directly claim equal rights for women, the WCTU argued that they would use the ballot for "home protection." Instead of devising new political and social mechanisms for a more complex urban society, they preached the gospel of soapsuds and clean government: prohibition and woman suffrage would be sufficient to turn back the tide of corruption, control the ignorant "foreign vote," and frustrate vote buying by politicians and saloon keepers.[94] In addition, the organizational dynamics of the WCTU itself seemed to argue more for a reactionary than a progressive role in history. By 1900 Ella Boole, president of the New York WCTU, noted that drinking among women was on the increase in fashionable society.[95] Even though by 1915 the General Federation of Women's Clubs had endorsed prohibition, temperance women began to feel left behind and resentful.[96] Anna Howard Shaw and Mary Garrett Hay left positions in the WCTU to become prominent in suffrage. Other, less well-known state and local leaders in a number of instances were first active in the WCTU when it was the only women's reform organization available in a small town, and then became active in suffrage when they moved to a larger town or when suffrage clubs became more widespread.[97]

WCTU hostility toward suffragists appeared in Illinois, Pennsylvania, Iowa, and South Dakota with reports that the WCTU women felt bitter toward the more socially influential women who were entering the suffrage field. Nor evidently did suffragists consider the WCTU members to be their equals. Ella Stewart wrote in 1915 of the Pennsylvania suffragists, "They haven't liked the WCTU suffrage campaign, I hear. Have snubbed the temperance women unmercifully."[98]

Understandably then, a half-century after the passage of suffrage and prohibition, the conventional wisdom had it that the suffragists were more forward looking and more important to the first feminist movement than temperance women. But contemporary scholarship makes clear that this evaluation must be revised. It is true that the WCTU couched its feminism in moderate and conciliatory language, in part because of its long involvement with churches and the Prohibition party. But it is also true that the political agenda of the WCTU led forward rather than backward. Its organization and membership in many places kept suffrage sentiment alive when the official suffrage associations were tiny or nonexistent. And although it provoked opposition by the wets, the WCTU did actually form the backbone of many suffrage campaigns that in the end helped win the federal amendment.

It was particularly the WCTU's unflinching support for the Prohibition party from 1884 on that gave pause to many feminists and even some temperance advocates. Jane Ellen Foster of Iowa, a prominent Republican, opposed the WCTU's stated policy of supporting only the Prohibition party; in 1884 she fought the issue openly, but lost and took the majority of Iowa and a few Pennsylvania and other unions with her to form the Non-Partisan WCTU.[99] Ohio women in 1885 had similar objections to partisanship. Nevertheless, Willard argued for the sole support of the Prohibition party on the grounds that even conservative women would become politically involved if they could forward the cause of prohibition.[100] She addressed the Ohio WCTU as follows:

Dear Sisters, . . . You are also to bring the amenities of the parlor into the turbulence of public life. Abundantly you have proved, by your wisdom, courage and patience in the eleven years since the Crusade, that you are capable of this. Politics is the witch's broth of our times. Into its seething depths you are to cast the one ingredient which alone can purify and sweeten. I mean your influence. You have not ballots, and you have not money; but what riches of clear and thoughtful brain, true heart and helpful hand you are bringing to the only party that has dared declare itself for an outlawed liquor traffic and a protected home![101]

Willard had reason for her claim. The Prohibition party of Kansas, for instance, at its 1884 convention had resolved in favor of civil service reform, antimonopoly legislation, cheap postage, governmental currency, *woman suffrage,* suppression of polygamy, election of U.S.

officials by direct vote of the people, better regulation of the railways, and impeachment of officials for election fraud.[102] Corruption was real; the Citizen's League of Chicago in 1885 found the liquor power "so entrenched in county politics as to render practically void their attempts to enforce laws against sale of liquor to minors and husbands."[103]

But by 1900 even sympathizers had turned critical of the narrow Prohibition party platform. The *Union Signal* complained, "It does not embody that other principle [the ballot] which once made the prohibition platform appeal so forcefully to the homemakers and home keepers of this nation."[104] Moreover, WCTU help with petitions for prohibition aroused opposition from the liquor lobby to suffrage campaigns. Carrie Chapman Catt and Nettie Shuler found in Iowa and Ohio that "the two factors, wet and dry, had exactly the same effect in nullifying the woman suffrage struggle. The wets were opposed to suffrage, but trying to keep their opposition sub rosa. The drys were in sympathy with suffrage but restraining their sympathy" for fear of doing harm.[105]

Yet on balance, despite these drawbacks from close association with the prohibition cause, the WCTU did far more good than harm where suffrage was concerned. Willard forged a moderate ideology for suffrage that brought homemakers and churchgoers into the feminist fold. In her only speech before the Senate Suffrage Committee in Washington, Willard combined a firm argument for equal rights with a sentimental appeal on behalf of mothers:

I suppose these honorable gentlemen think that we women want the earth, when we only want half of it . . . we ask you that they be allowed to stand at the ballot-box, because we believe that there every person expresses his individuality. . . . I ask you to remember that it is women who have given the costliest hostages to fortune, and out into the battle of life they have sent their best beloved into snares that have been legalized on every hand . . . I charge you, gentlemen, give woman power to go forth, so that when her son undertakes life's treacherous battle, his mother will still walk beside him clad in the garments of power.[106]

As a result of her centrist stance, Willard was able to build an organization with far broader appeal than the suffrage associations. During the long barren years between attaining school and municipal suffrage in the 1880s and the final drive for a federal suffrage amendment that began in 1914, the WCTU was often the core women's group that held suffrage activities together. In Colorado, for example, between a failed suffrage campaign in 1877 and victory in 1893, the WCTU became the state suffrage leaders' primary recruitment organization. Not only did the suffrage campaign prepare the way for the WCTU reforms in the following decade, but "the WCTU goals and infrastructure," according to Marilley, "in turn served as hospitable platforms to the demand for woman suffrage."[107] In Massachusetts in 1891, the venerable Mary Livermore wrote suffragist Lucy Stone of the sharp decline in suffrage ranks and the key role of the WCTU in supporting suffrage in the town of Melrose, where she lived: "It is impossible to keep up the two separate organizations—especially as the W.C.T.U. has between 300 and 400 members, maintains a franchise department, and elects an out-and-out woman suffragist as its superintendent."[108]

A similar interdependence also occurred in the South. Belle Kearney, who was later to become a state legislator in Mississippi, Caroline Merrick, a Louisiana temperance and suffrage leader, and Lide Meriwether of Tennessee all came to public prominence as advocates for women in their activities for the WCTU.[109] In West Virginia, the state president of the WCTU, Mrs. Yost, also served as vice president of the state suffrage organization, and a 1915 report to the *Union Signal* mentioned the spread of suffrage sentiment. "About half our speeches, given by request, are out and out suffrage speeches."[110]

The 1875 greeting of the American Woman Suffrage Association to the second annual convention of the WCTU now rings prophetic in its reverse, "Soon may women, armed with the ballot, help make laws which concern human welfare." It was women's work for human welfare that helped arm them with the ballot.

The Larger Significance of the WCTU

More than a century after the Woman's Christian Temperance Union began, there is a new and proper appreciation of its role in the emancipation of women. Rather than a merely parochial evangelical group of praying women, the WCTU became the single most important catalyst for the metamorphosis of women's roles. From wives and mothers who were once confined to home and church, the women of the WCTU became the gadflies to the moral and social conscience of the community; in the process they discovered their future place as citizens in the public sphere. This remarkable transformation was realized through the interplay of four factors necessary to any successful social movement: an *ideology* that voiced the ideals of the membership, *leaders* who inspired the loyalty of followers, an *organization* that effectively recruited others while pursuing its goals, and *an agenda, or strategy,* for reform that was consistent with group ideals yet also capable of being accomplished.

WCTU ideology, as revealed through the pages of the *Union Signal,* pictured traditional wives and mothers as the primary anchors of goodness in the community and men and boys as especially vulnerable to temptation and their own human frailty. Women became instruments of power primarily through extension of their traditional maternal concern for their own children and family members to all children, all families, all women. The result was a reform ideology that at first was primarily oriented to personal and individual change and cloaked in religious language and manner. With time, however, women's emancipation and suffrage came to be seen not so much as the outward signs of equality but as the necessary tools for accomplishment of women's good works.

The leaders had in their own lives experienced both the privileges and the personal loss that led to an ideology of caring and social reform. Like suffrage leaders, many had gone beyond the local school to receive education in an academy. A number had served as teachers, then broadened their activities to wider areas of social reform. Yet when compared with the suffrage leaders, slightly more of the temperance women had been married, and significantly more were described in their biographies as having lost a husband or child. More of them also came from the nonconformist Methodist, Baptist, or Presbyterian churches that emphasized individual moral reform. In their lives the constricted home orientation of most traditional women was transformed into a passionate concern for the welfare of the whole community.

State and national organization of the Christian temperance women became the vehicle for expansion of their movement and accomplishment of personal and social change. Between 1885 and 1900, with several hundred thousand members in the United States and other countries, the WCTU became what was probably the largest secular organization of women in the world. State units comprised many local chapters and pressed for state legislation on issues ranging from women's prisons to temperance instruction in the schools. The local WCTU was often the grass-roots organization for promotion of woman suffrage as well as prohibition. A system of specialized departments at the national level was mirrored in state and local activity: departments such as juvenile work and young women to address organizational needs; departments such as work among colored people, foreigners, and miners for outreach; temperance literature and state and county fairs for publicity; reading rooms and unfermented wine for alcohol substitution; and prison and jail work, social purity, and the franchise for personal and social reform. WCTU goals dovetailed with those of other progressive groups, and efforts to realize them stretched the social consciousness of ordinary women and helped accomplish the subtle transformation of the traditional private and home-oriented feminine role into a broader ideal of the caring woman citizen.

The WCTU reform agenda produced a number of accomplishments: raising the age of consent in almost every state, instituting scientific temperance instruction in the schools, educating thinking women to their need for the ballot. Methods at first drew on the successful techniques of prayer meetings and religious revivals, with their focus on individual conversion of the drunkard or saloon keeper. But gospel temperance soon gave way to municipal housekeeping and then to political campaigning. Results were remarkable: grape juice replaced communion wine, "dry" dinners became the new standard of entertaining, millions of school children learned the dangers of alcohol, white slavery and physical and sexual exploitation of women were openly recognized, and by 1885 this conventional middle-class reform organization was fully behind the franchise for women! State temperance leaders were often state suffrage leaders. An organization of women that began with members afraid of dragging their skirts through the mire of politics emerged a standard bearer on behalf of women as citizens for social welfare.

Chapter 4

Suffrage: Women as Citizens

By the end of the Civil War a number of people believed that voting rights for women would not be long in coming. Women who had opposed slavery, bravely helped with volunteer work, sat at the bedside of wounded soldiers, or supplied the army hospitals from behind the lines with food and bandages seemed quite deserving of being counted full citizens.[1] But the Fourteenth Amendment, passed by Congress in 1865, granted civil rights to former male slaves only. The Fifteenth Amendment, passed by Congress in 1869, dealt only with the enfranchisement of black men. By 1870 several suffrage organizations had been formed to work for the woman's vote. Each mounted a series of valiant efforts to win equal representation. At first there were short-term demonstrations—women trying to vote in several states or resisting taxation. Next came petition campaigns to allow women to vote for school boards, municipal offices, or local option. Finally, sporadic attempts to revise state constitutions were expanded into a drive for the federal suffrage amendment, which was finally ratified in 1920.

The entire movement took almost a century. In the words of Carrie Chapman Catt, the tireless organizer and head of the National American Woman Suffrage Association,

To get the word male . . . out of the constitution cost the women of the country fifty-two years of pauseless campaign . . . 480 campaigns to get Legislatures to submit suffrage amendments to voters . . . and 19 campaigns with 19 successive Congresses. Millions of dollars were raised, many in small sums, and expended with economic care. It was a continuous, seemingly endless, chain of activity. Young suffragists who helped forge the last links of that chain were not born when it began. The suffragists who forged the first links were dead when it ended.[2]

Why did the suffrage movement take so long? Why did suffragists achieve acceptance later than temperance advocates? Woman suffrage, more than temperance, required a radical change in the definition of women's roles. Suffragists had to construct a longer ladder of women's roles that reached from that of wife and mother to that of citizen. Once achieved, the suffragists' vision helped socialize women to higher and broader levels of responsibility and made possible the perception that public roles of male and female were fundamentally similar. Women as well as men became obligated to take responsibility for political corruption in city government, assimilation of immigrants, and labor unrest.

These views were not accepted, however, until suffragists mounted a social movement that proved their political capability. Suffragists first had to develop an *ideology* of change in women's roles that drew on American ideals of freedom and equality. Second, *leaders* emerged from earlier woman's rights groups to live out a new version of the female role and recruit others to their cause. Third, individual reformers constructed an *organization* to make decisions, set priorities, and persist from one contest to another. Finally, suffragists won the support of the larger society through an *agenda, or strategy,* for structural change that appealed to many and varied groups—Catholics as well as Protestants, workers as well as owners, and new immigrants as well as the native born. All these developments occurred during the 50-year period between the emergence of the two major woman suffrage associations in 1870 and the adoption of a constitutional amendment that granted women the franchise in 1920.

Historical Background

After the establishment of woman's property rights during the 1850s, the major issue became woman's right to vote. According to historian Ellen DuBois, the great significance of the woman suffrage movement was that it radically bypassed woman's oppression within the family to demand instead her "admission to citizenship."[3] Until 1867 it appeared that suffrage might be extended to women along with former slaves through a constitutional amendment. The National Woman's Loyal

League in 1862–63 collected more than 400,000 signatures to present to Congress in support of the Thirteenth Amendment for the ending of slavery. Earlier canvassing activities of Elizabeth Cady Stanton and Susan B. Anthony had laid the groundwork for such a petition campaign. After the war, suffragists helped to form the American Equal Rights Association in 1866 to work for the franchise for both women and blacks. The Kansas Campaign of 1867, however, which pitted black suffrage against woman suffrage, made leaders like Stanton and Anthony decide that woman suffrage should be an autonomous feminist movement. Never again would they risk having the women's vote played off against another major reform.

In September 1868 Anthony formed the Working Women's Association in New York, which organized wage-earning women to demand their own enfranchisement. Two months later a group of proabolition suffragists led by Lucy Stone and Antoinette Blackwell formed the New England Woman Suffrage Association to counter the political initiatives being made by Stanton and Anthony.[4] In 1869 these fledgling organizations gave way to two major new suffrage associations that carried forward the cause for woman's rights along lines similar to their predecessors.

The more radical National Woman's Suffrage Association (NWSA), founded in 1869, broke sharply with the abolition tradition and advocated woman's rights first and foremost. Through their woman's rights newspaper the *Revolution*, Stanton and Anthony took a series of positions on labor questions, divorce reform, birth control, and the inconsistencies of the Bible that radically challenged the accepted conventions of the day. Their association with George Francis Train (a "Copperhead" Democrat and southerner who opposed the Fourteenth Amendment) and their opposition in 1869 to ratification of the Fifteenth Amendment (on grounds that it put black enfranchisement ahead of women) was a source of disappointment to their former allies in the abolition movement.[5] The NWSA managed to live from convention to convention through the associations and correspondence of a handful of leaders. Lacking a strong local organization to work for state suffrage referenda, NWSA sent its national leaders to state and regional conventions and was less in touch with local conditions than if it had been able to rely on an indigenous local leadership.

The more moderate, Boston-based American Woman Suffrage Association (AWSA), also founded in 1869, built on the legacy of the New England Woman Suffrage Association and maintained an alliance with the old abolition cause. Leaders included such respected male reformers as Wendell Phillips and prominent women like Julia Ward Howe, author of the "Battle Hymn of the Republic," and Mary Livermore, head of the Sanitary Commission during the Civil War. Long-time feminists were also among them: Lucy Stone and her husband, Henry Blackwell; her sister-in-law Antoinette Brown Blackwell; and pioneering female professionals such as Universalist minister Olympia Brown and physician Harriot K. Hunt.

Instead of repudiating the cause of the former slaves, the American Woman Suffrage Association accepted the priorities of the abolitionists. Believing that the years immediately following the Civil War were indeed the "Negro's hour," this group was willing to stand aside temporarily to allow passage of the Fifteenth Amendment granting former male slaves the franchise. Local and state chapters sprang up that were linked by representation on a national board. A successful newspaper, the *Woman's Journal*, was issued from Boston. Membership numbered in the thousands, and links were formed to the churches and to the women's temperance organizations.

The early suffrage movement had no parallel to the temperance crusade of 1873–74, unless one counts the few sporadic attempts by women to vote such as occurred on presidential Election Day in 1868, when 172 women in Vineland, New Jersey, cast their ballots to vote. In 1870 the elderly Grimké sisters, veterans of abolition and the early woman's rights movement, set out in a winter storm leading a delegation of 40 women to vote in Hyde Park, Massachusetts. Caroline Burnham Kilgore (who later became the first woman lawyer in Pennsylvania) tried to cast her ballot in 1871. The venerable Susan B. Anthony led a group of 16 women to vote in the 1872 presidential election in Rochester, New York, was then arrested and indicted for voting illegally, and was finally pronounced guilty and fined $100. Voting protests also occurred in Ohio in Geauga County each year from 1871 to 1876.[6] But such demonstrations never amounted to a widespread movement of the kind that preceded the rapid growth of the WCTU.

Suffragists were more inclined to change the law itself. In a number of states they made a direct appeal to constitutional conventions. One of the most dramatic instances was the New York State Constitutional Convention held in 1867, at which the petitions for woman suffrage represented roughly 20,000 signatures. Despite the eloquent arguments of Elizabeth Cady Stanton and others that the word "male" should be removed from that phrasing indicating who should vote, the measure was defeated. In Pennsylvania the culmination of the pre–Civil War woman's rights movement came with the suffrage debates at the Constitutional Convention of 1872–73. Advocates of the franchise for women argued that suffrage was a natural right, that many women had no men to represent their interests, and that women would contribute as well as men to the conduct of public office. But the majority of the Committee on Suffrage recommended against it. Similarly, in Ohio during the Constitutional Convention of 1873–74, many local suffrage groups, such as that from Toledo, unsuccessfully petitioned the convention for woman suffrage.[7]

It soon became clear, however, that there would be no quick resolution of the woman suffrage impasse. It was not a question of simply accepting women's ballots at the polling places or of having the state conventions circumvent opposition by adopting a provision for woman suffrage in the state constitution. There had to be a long slow process of winning more supporters to the cause, educating the general public, and then finding the legal mechanisms that would admit women to full citizenship.

Up until 1893 there was a rough division of labor in which NWSA pressed the Congress for a federal suffrage amendment and AWSA worked for state referenda and more limited forms of suffrage, such as the municipal, school board, and local option vote for women. But by 1890 the aims of the two groups were beginning to merge. Memories of the bitter division between the radicals Stanton and Anthony and the moderates Stone and Blackwell over the Kansas Campaign of 1867 had begun to fade. Support for partial suffrage was leading to acceptance of full suffrage. In 1893 the two arms of the suffrage movement united to form the National American Woman Suffrage Association (NAWSA).

NAWSA had the basis for a two-pronged federal and state approach to suffrage. Greatest energy went into securing suffrage amendments to state constitutions (as Wyoming did when it became a state in 1869) and mounting state referendum campaigns for presidential suffrage (such as succeeded in Colorado in 1893). But the state route was a slow and discouraging process, which after 1913 was overtaken by a return to the strategy of seeking a federal amendment. Nevertheless, the state campaigns eventually paid off by raising consciousness and helping to elect sympathetic officials. In the last analysis, greatest support for adoption of the federal suffrage amendment came precisely from those states that had already affirmed woman's right of franchise at the state and local levels.[8]

Ideology

Like temperance, suffrage had a gender ideology, but one that emphasized equality of the sexes rather than differentiation. In their social analysis, suffragists located the major social problems of their day in conditions outside rather than inside the home. And in their reform agenda, suffragists focused primarily on access to equality through higher education, legal rights, equal pay, and the ballot rather than through personal reform and the limited forms of suffrage advocated by temperance women.

Between 1885 and 1915 slightly more than half (57 percent) of the suffrage articles in the *Woman's Journal* concerned reforms outside the domestic realm, such as education, employment, religion, and government. By comparison just under half (48 percent) of the articles in the *Union Signal* dealt with similar issues. Suffragists also gave attention to woman's status within the home and to the effects of temperance on the family, but in smaller proportion than the Woman's Christian Temperance Union (17 percent versus 26 percent).[9]

Gender ideology.   Suffragists believed that women *as women* could do something significant outside their homes. Like temperance women, some suffragists wished to extend motherhood into public life. Julia Ward Howe expressed women's capacity to turn motherly concern into work for the public good: "The neglected child, wandering about the streets to learn the lessons of meanness and of crime. . . . At the sight of him, oh! women, let your woman's hearts be touched. Let your blessed motherhood put itself at interest, multiply itself so as to embrace him, the homeless, the friendless."[10] But the majority of suffrage statements were less focused on women's maternal role. Where the WCTU newspaper cited the weaknesses of men and the needs of children, the suffrage newspaper treated women as central figures. Almost twice as many stories in the *Woman's Journal* as in the temperance newspaper had women as their principal character (33 percent versus 18 percent).[11]

Suffragists admired what might be called good "new" women. Such women were not afraid to depart from a submissive and homebound role. For example, the *Woman's Journal* carried a story of two girls in a remote area who, seeing the malfunction of a railroad signal, courageously ran to where they could stop an oncoming train and prevent a collision that would have taken 600 lives. The story concluded, "Surely such young women as these deserve to be voters!"[12] Other articles described the life and work of women who were famous scholars, illustrious graduates of colleges and universities, and pioneer members of the clergy.[13]

Twice as many suffrage stories pictured women as the competent, intelligent, and pioneering new type as the good "traditional" type. Suffragists affirmed women's inherent equality with men. They ridiculed the fragile dependent women so much admired by traditionalists.[14] Temperance women, however, focused more on the motherly qualities in traditional women. Good traditional women in the *Union Signal* were twice as frequent as good new women.[15]

The suffragist vision of the new female role departed from tradition in two ways. First, suffragists challenged the time-honored assignment of instrumental (task-oriented) activity to men and expressive (caregiving) responsibility to women. Temperance women, in contrast, focused more on the emotional and expressive value of the wife and mother's role, as shown in table 4.1.[16] In a *Woman's Journal* article in 1900, MIT professor Ellen Richards urged women to adopt scientific and efficient methods usually thought characteristic of men: "The secret of success in housekeeping as well as in manufacturing, lies in the right use of methods and machinery."[17] One *Woman's Journal* contributor even suggested some role reversal in traditional male and female duties. Having observed an efficient male chef in a Pullman dining car, she playfully suggested the possibility that "man is divinely ordained to cook and wash dishes. A careful review from Genesis to Revelation [reveals that] . . . the only rebuke administered to woman by the Divine Master was for too much serving of meat and pie by the frugal Martha; his praise being given to the wise Mary who eschewed the kitchen range and chose the better part, that of wisdom and learning."[18]

In a second way suffragists challenged the traditional feminine role by claiming that women could handle greater moral, economic, and legal responsibility than they were then allowed in the household and community,[19] the church,[20] and the state. In their newspaper, the suffragists touched on themes of women's equality and responsibility five times as often (72 versus 14) as the temperance newspaper (see table

TABLE 4.1
Ideology of Suffrage and Temperance Papers, 1885–1915
(Number of Articles)

Themes in Articles	*Union Signal* (WCTU)	*Woman's Journal* (Suffrage)
Instrumental versus Expressive Focus[a]		
Instrumental emphasis on woman's managerial and productive role in the home	1	33
Expressive emphasis on woman's maternal, moral, and emotional role in the family	17	7
Universal versus Particular Reasons for Vote[b]		
Universal arguments based on equal protection of interests or equal political responsibility	14	72
Particular arguments based on maternal interests, cleaning up politics, or need for reform such as prohibition	22	7

[a] "Instrumental" based on categories 17.1, 17.2, 17.3 and "expressive" based on categories 17.4, 17.5 in appendix A. Chi-square with Yates's correction = 27.210; $p < .001$.
[a] "Universal" based on categories 16.1, 16.2 and "particular" based on categories 16.3, 16.5 in appendix A. Chi-square with Yates's correction = 33.085; $p < .001$.

4.1).[21] In the household, for example, a woman was often an equal partner when she helped the family over a spell of adversity by raising income from her flock of hens and her churn.[22] In the church, women ordained to the ministry demonstrated equal capacity with men for moral and religious leadership.[23] In public affairs, women through their interest in parks, schools, and community life showed their capacity for understanding and running local governments.[24] Women's interest in peace in some ways made them seem even more competent than men to shape national policy.

Social analysis.   Suffragists' image of the new woman nicely fitted their social critique. Society had failed to develop women's talents to the full and, by so doing, suffered the ravages of poverty and social exploitation that could be eradicated if women were full citizens. Not only could the woman's vote allow her to protect her own and her children's interests, but it would itself be a tool for economic and public progress.[25] Through their common efforts for the vote, suffrage as well as temperance women expressed a sense of responsibility for others.[26] The *Woman's Journal*, however, was more interested in the reform of social structures than of individuals. Suffrage articles more often had an instrumental emphasis and mentioned the need for peace, better schools, improved working conditions, and civic improvement, while temperance articles focused on expressive methods such as helping children, prisoners, or poor women (see table 4.1).

Education and economic independence. Suffragists knew that the prerequisites for political equality were education and economic independence. Women's intellectual achievements helped to further the suffrage cause by enabling women to enter the world of public affairs.[27] Repeatedly they argued that every girl should be taught some means of self support. "In this way much of the misery of life would be avoided and our girls would not sit down and dream out romance after romance, and waste the best days of their life in foolishness."[28] A certain Mr. Shearman who had trained many women to operate typewriting machines in a business office was reported by the *Woman's Journal* as saying, "Never think of marriage until you are able to support a husband."[29]

The need for economic independence grew with the increasing population of single women. In 1900 Charlotte Perkins (Stetson) Gilman stated unequivocally, "We have not yet fully realized the social value of the unattached women of our century." While she conceded that a large surplus of women could lead to an increase in prostitution, she emphasized the potential productivity of single women: "Instead of being absorbed, contented, wholly occupied and limited by their own families, we have now the heart and mind and ever serviceable hand of woman turned loose to serve the world in general. The power of love undrained by its natural recipients, is freed for wider use. . . . The educational, religious, charitable, philanthropic, reformatory, and generally humanitarian work of this age, is largely done by single women."[30]

Nonetheless, uneducated and untrained women thrown upon their own resources were vulnerable to prostitution. Temperance women addressed this concern with their department of social purity, homes for working girls, and campaigns against the traffic in women. Suffragists, however, were more likely to emphasize the need for training and good wages as preventives. As early as the 1860s, Caroline Dall had delivered her famous lectures, later published in *College, Market, and Court*, which portrayed the link between the low wages of working women and the prevalence of prostitution in the poorer districts of New York and other cities around the world.[31] After the Civil War Susan B. Anthony reported the activity of working women's associations in the *Revolution* and called for the ballot as a means to ensure equal pay for equal work.[32]

Educational and economic inequality, however, continued right up to the eve of the suffrage amendment. Women in the garment factories and shops of the large cities were low paid, living on the edge of misery. Mercenary and unethical employment agencies perpetrated frauds on innocent girls seeking work.[33] Many girls chose to work in offices or retail stores where conditions were pleasanter, even though in some cases hours were long and factory wages were higher.[34] In 1915 suffragists were still calling for equal educational and economic opportunity in language that echoed the 1848 Declaration of Sentiments at Seneca Falls: "We do not receive equal pay for equal work. . . . We work in factories, stores, and offices, yet we have nothing to say about the conditions under which we work. We are obliged to attend school, yet we have no voice in shaping the policy of the school board."[35] Suffragists thus argued that occupational and professional equality were the means to citizenship as well as the symbol of it.[36]

Political power and social justice. As women entered professions and developed interests outside the home in child welfare, school improvement, conservation, and pure foods (as in the Pure Food and Drug Act of 1906),[37] their primary instrument of power became the *ballot*.[38] Alice Stone Blackwell wrote in a *Woman's Journal* editorial, "Until women have the ballot . . . their interests never will be fully represented, and what is worse, the moral and humanitarian interests of society will not be fully represented either."[39]

To advance their cause suffragists, like the temperance women, especially before 1890, used religious and moral imagery to make their point. One delightful fantasy written by a member of the local suffrage society in Henry County, Indiana, pictures the effect of a "work-to-rule" strike where local ladies actually *live* the life enjoined by St. Paul. Veiled and secluded in their homes, unavailable for church and temperance work, they convince the local conservative minister of the need for suffrage and a broader role for women.[40] Other articles argue that women's entry on the political scene will give them more to think about than "puddings and pies".[41] Women's votes will curb prostitution, remove the grog shop from the street corner, protect children from economic exploitation, and clean up polling places and politics, as it was said to have done in Colorado and Arizona.[42]

But in general suffragists' arguments for the franchise were always more secular and more universal than those of the WCTU. The goal of getting women out of the kitchen was transformed into an effort to expand the number of states with equal guardianship, property rights, and equal pay.[43] Maternal concern for poor and exploited children was translated into a legislative platform that included proper and effective child labor laws, good public schools, and decent food and housing laws.[44] *Woman's Journal* articles implied that women's rational and knowledgeable approach to municipal government would benefit the park system, street cleaning, disposal of garbage, light and water systems, the fire department, and general housing concerns.[45] A drop in infant mortality in Kansas from 1914 to 1915 was reported to be the direct result of women's work with the board of health.[46]

Suffragists' primary focus was the ballot. Roughly a third of all *Woman's Journal* articles between 1875 and 1915 contained arguments for the woman's ballot, compared with about a fifth of *Union Signal* articles. In addition, suffragists' reasoning was almost always "universalistic," that is, based on claims of equality and justice as ends in themselves. Temperance women, however, were more likely to give "particular" or expedient reasons for the ballot by depicting it as a means of achieving specific ends, such as raising the moral tone, cleaning up politics, or voting for prohibition (see table 4.1).[47]

Consistent with the broader, more universalistic focus of the suffragists was their insistence on neutrality with respect to the use of the vote. Suffragists held the vote to be the inalienable right of all, regardless of sex, color, or creed, even though they sometimes expressed bitterness that less well-educated immigrants and former slaves could vote while they could not.[48] In an 1880 *Woman's Journal* editorial Thomas Wentworth Higginson stated the suffrage philosophy: "I do not think we shall succeed, or deserve to succeed, until we rest our claim on the right of women to vote on every measure, whether they vote for or against it."[49] Anthony echoed that sentiment in 1890 on the occasion of the merger between the American and National Woman Suffrage Associations, "I want our platform to be kept broad enough for the infidel, the atheist, the Mohammedan, or the Christian."[50]

Suffragists thus voiced their belief that the ballot was an instrument of power to which all were entitled. Whether a means for equal protection or a tool for social reform, it was part of woman's natural right.

Leaders

The distinctive character of the suffrage movement emerged from the lives of its leaders. Rather than try to improve women's intimate or domestic lives, suffrage women emphasized justifying their place in the public sphere. Suffragists defined their reform as a universal and inalienable right; they claimed the rights of men for women. *Woman's Journal* articles on "Women in the Press," "Women in Science," and "Colleges and Alumnae" periodically celebrated notable women for their professional accomplishments and public contributions. An article on a woman scholar working at Harvard's Peabody Museum concluded that "in science, at least, men are glad to recognize valuable work, whether men's or women's."[51]

Such ideas were truly radical for their times. As early as the 1830s and 1840s, woman's rights activists envisioned a world in which women spoke in public, went to college along with men, and entered professions like law, medicine, and the ministry. Stanton suggested in 1852 that a woman have the right to ostracize her husband for drunkenness and in 1850 that she have the right of divorce. These ideas were viewed as an open threat to the home, and cartoons depicting the new woman wearing trousers and smoking cigars treated them with skepticism and derision.[52] It was as if the application of the rights of men to freedom, representation, and material success were indecent when applied to women.

Susan B. Anthony and Elizabeth Cady Stanton, c. 1880. Seneca Falls Historical Society.

Lucy Stone. Sophia Smith Collection, Smith College.

Carrie Chapman Catt. Library of Congress.

What kind of woman could even think such radical thoughts, let alone stand up to the ridicule of being thought mannish, rebellious, and a potential destroyer of the home? Stanton and other feminist pioneers must have been so rooted in an alternative view of women that they could withstand the censure that came their way. Feminism must have provided for them another frame of reference through which they could justify their pioneering behavior.

The lives of several exemplary suffragists suggest what may have been distinctive about their background and motivation. Each was immensely talented, even brilliant, as a thinker, organizer, and public speaker. All grew up in relatively prosperous middle-class families in rural areas or small towns. All gained an education quite beyond the typical women of their generation. But despite their unusual gifts, each was keenly aware of her disadvantaged status as a female and even in childhood questioned the conventions that deemed women inferior.

Elizabeth Cady Stanton (1815–1902) grew up in Johnstown, New York, the daughter of a lawyer and a mother whose family were leading landowners. Although there were servants at home and Elizabeth had the advantages of learning Greek and Latin from the local parson and a year at the Troy Female Seminary, she resented the clear preference her parents had for sons and the fact that because she was a woman she could not, like her brother, enter nearby Union College.

Through Gerrit Smith, a cousin well connected with the leading abolitionists and other reformers of the day, she met her husband, lawyer Henry Stanton. They spent their honeymoon at the World's Anti-Slavery Convention in 1840, where the women delegates were not accorded official recognition and where Elizabeth met Lucretia Mott (with whom she would later issue the call for the Seneca Falls woman's rights convention in 1848). After several years in Johnstown and then Boston, the Stantons settled in Seneca Falls, for which Henry was briefly a delegate to the New York State Senate. They had seven children. After Elizabeth's signing of the Declaration of Sentiments at Seneca Falls in 1848, the Cady family pressed her to recant, but unsuccessfully.

Stanton began working with Susan B. Anthony (1820–1906) of nearby Rochester in 1851 for the New York state Daughters of Temperance; it was the beginning of a close and long-lasting collaboration between the two for the cause of woman's rights. Younger than Stanton and without the responsibilities of husband and children,

Anthony was freer to travel and organized county-by-county canvasses for woman's rights. Stanton was known for her writing and speaking skills and for her winning personality; Anthony, a teacher and a Quaker, for her exceptional organizational abilities and political acumen. By the end of her life Anthony had become the symbol of the woman's movement.

In 1863 Stanton and Anthony organized the National Woman's Loyal League, which gathered thousands of signatures on behalf of the emancipation of slaves. The two toured Kansas in 1867 to campaign for a state suffrage amendment and a year later started the newspaper the *Revolution* in New York. In 1869 they founded the first national woman suffrage organization (NWSA) to work directly for a federal suffrage amendment. During the next decade Stanton lectured widely on topics of coeducation, marriage and divorce, and enlightened childrearing. She was the first woman to address the New York State Senate, speaking on behalf of married women's property rights, and served as the NWSA's president until 1890.[53]

Lucy Stone (1818–93) experienced even harsher discrimination than Stanton in comparison with her brothers. Although her father paid for the college education of his sons, he refused to help his daughter except by a loan she was required to repay. By teaching summers she eventually saved enough money to spend one year at Mt. Holyoke Seminary and finally, when she was 25, entered Oberlin College. The first Massachusetts woman to graduate from the full four-year program in 1847, she fought many battles throughout her early adulthood on behalf of women. At Oberlin female students were not allowed to debate in public; she protested by forming a clandestine female debating society. Awarded honors at graduation, she refused to write a commencement address that only a male would be allowed read. When abolitionists asked that as an organizer she refrain from mixing woman's rights with the antislavery cause, she won their permission to speak on woman's rights during the week and abolition on weekends. In church matters she voted her convictions, even though women's votes weren't counted. Her speech at the 1851 Woman's Rights Convention in Worcester, Massachusetts, was credited with converting Susan B. Anthony to the suffrage cause. At the time of her marriage to Henry Blackwell in 1855, she was one of the first feminists to keep her maiden name, thereby giving rise to a new expression—a *Lucy Stoner*—to refer to a married woman who kept her own name.[54]

Following the Civil War Stone helped to organize the American Equal Rights Association, which worked for both African-American women and woman suffrage. After serving as president of the New Jersey woman suffrage association in 1868 she moved with her family to Boston, where she became one of the leading New England suffragists. In 1869 she helped to found what was considered the more moderate wing of the suffrage movement, the American Woman Suffrage Association, with headquarters in Boston. She was also the principal founder and editor of the suffrage newspaper, the *Woman's Journal*, which for an unbroken span of 47 years served as the "voice of the woman's movement," not only by publishing the official proceedings of the major suffrage organizations but by articulating the central tenets of feminism.

Carrie Lane Chapman Catt (1859–1947) represents the younger generation of woman's rights leaders. She was born on a farm near Ripon, Wisconsin, then moved with her parents (both of whom completed high school) to Charles City, Iowa, when she was seven. Even while a youngster she noticed the inequality of women and asked why her mother didn't go to town with her father to vote for Horace Greeley against Ulysses S. Grant in 1872, a query that she long after remembered was met with ridicule because she had assumed that women could vote!

Like the earlier generation of woman's rights leaders, Carrie Lane was bright and intellectually independent. With only a fraction of the needed tuition provided by her father to attend Iowa State Agricultural College, she earned the rest by teaching school. Since female students were excluded from military training, she started the Ladies Military Company, which drilled with broomsticks. She also defied the traditions of the college literary society by speaking in public. She organized a debate on woman suffrage, held offices in the literary society, and practiced parliamentary procedure, presumably to be able to run a meeting if she ever had the opportunity.[55]

While still in her 20s Carrie Lane rose from teacher to school superintendent in Mason City, Iowa, then married the local newspaper publisher Leo Chapman in 1885. After his untimely death only a year later, the young widow worked on a San Francisco newspaper for a year, then returned to Iowa, where she rapidly rose in the Iowa Woman Suffrage Association. Her second husband, George Catt, in 1890 explicitly agreed that she would be free to travel and pursue her suffrage activities for two months every spring and every fall. Known for her organizational genius and campaign work, she had by 1895 become the chief organizer of the relatively new National American Woman Suffrage Association and in 1900 was elected its president. She resigned in 1904 because of illness but returned to that office from 1915 to 1920 to implement her famous "winning plan" of state-by-state referenda that laid the groundwork for adoption of the federal suffrage amendment.[56]

All in all, these pioneer suffrage leaders came from middle-class backgrounds with parents who were in farming, business, or the professions. In general, they gained an education far beyond what was typical for their day. But, perhaps most notably, they were nonconformists with respect to the traditional feminine role. They spoke in public, dressed unconventionally or engaged in physical exercise unusual for women, tried to vote, and in other ways rebelled against the sex-role norms of their day. Their lives raise the question of whether other suffrage leaders shared some of these same distinguishing characteristics. In what respects were they different from their counterparts in the woman's temperance movement?

Family background and education.   With respect to their socioeconomic origins, most suffragists were rather similar to temperance leaders in social class as well as education. Neither group was very poor, nor did they generally come from families with large land holdings or big-city wealth. They grew up in small towns, on prosperous farms, or in business and professional families.

A slightly larger number of suffrage women, compared with temperance women, had college and professional training, even before 1900, as shown in table 4.2, but leaders from both groups were likely to have attended a female academy, college, or university. They often had records of outstanding academic achievement and then taught school at some point in their careers. For example, Frances Willard of the WCTU and Carrie Chapman Catt of NAWSA had each graduated as valedictorian in her college class. Each began teaching and then entered a supervisory position: Willard as president of the Evanston Ladies' College and Catt as a superintendent of schools in Iowa. Both then left education for the wider field of reform. Another suffrage leader, Belva Lockwood, candidate for president on the Equal Rights party ticket in 1884 and 1888, began as a teacher in a district school, then headed several seminaries, became a lawyer, and was the first woman to be admitted to the bar of the Supreme Court. Table 4.2 shows that the educational background and teaching experience of the temperance and suffrage leaders were comparable, especially among the first generation.

Marital status and occupation.   Perhaps the key popular indicator of femininity was marital status. Because suffragists were thought mannish relative to other women, they were often imagined to be less attached to family than ordinary women or temperance women. Actually, however, there was no difference in the frequency with which suffrage and temperance leaders married, had children, and to all appearances lived the accepted domestic role of wife and mother, as shown in table 4.3. The popular allegations must have been due to the stereotypes of the suffragists.

A comparison of the occupations of WCTU leaders with those of suffrage leaders also shows very little difference in their overall occupational distribution. Almost half of each group played the more traditional roles of homemaker, writer, or philanthropist, while the other half were in what were for women pioneering professions—medicine, the clergy, law, or lecturing and organizing, as is also shown in table 4.3.

Early woman lawyers read law with a husband or a local lawyer, then passed the state bar examinations without other training. Married lawyers, like Ada Bittenbender of the Nebraska WCTU and the Chicago suffragist Catherine Waugh McCulloch, practiced law with their husbands[57]. Editors and journalists like Alice Stone Blackwell of the *Woman's Journal* and Elizabeth Boynton Harbert of the WCTU were associated with women's papers or wrote the women's column for a large city newspaper.

For those women interested in the ministry, a great deal depended on the willingness of their denomination to ordain them and give them a parish. The suffragist Olympia Brown was ordained in 1863 in the Universalist church, where attitudes toward women preachers were more liberal than in some other denominations. Fifteen years later, the Methodist Episcopal church refused to ordain prominent WCTU member Anna Howard Shaw despite her graduation from theological school; she then joined the Methodist Protestant church, where she was finally ordained.

TABLE 4.2
Education of Temperance and Suffrage Leaders

Highest Level Attained	Leaders Prominent 1870–1920		Leaders Prominent 1870–1895	
	WCTU	Suffrage	WCTU	Suffrage
Public and private schools	14	10	13	5
Academy or seminary or more	29	31	21	15
Academy or seminary	(7)	(4)	(5)	(3)
College, institute, normal school	(13)	(16)	(11)	(7)
Professional	(9)	(11)	(5)	(5)
Not ascertained	6	8	6	5
TOTAL	49	49	40	25

Teaching Experience of Suffrage and Temperance Leaders, 1870–1920

Level of Position[a]	Suffrage Leaders	WCTU Leaders
Grade or high school	8	8
Supervisory position	7	7
Seminary teaching or administration	0	2
College training or administration	3	6
	18	23

[a] Highest level attained.

TABLE 4.3
Marital Status and Occupations of Prominent Suffrage and Temperance Leaders, 1870–1920

Occupation[a]	Suffrage Leaders	WCTU Leaders
Traditional roles		
Mother or wife	2	2
Author	1	2
Journalist, editor	7	7
Philanthropist	11	13
	21	24
Lecturer, organizer	13	17
New roles for women		
Physician	0	1
Minister	4	2
Lawyer	4	2
All-around reformer	4	3
	12	8
Not ascertained	3	0
TOTAL	49	49

Marital and Family Status	Suffrage Leaders	WCTU Leaders
Marriage		
Married	37	38
Single	11	11
Not ascertained	1	0
	49	49
Motherhood		
Mention of children	16	14
Mention of no children	1	1

[a] Other than teaching. Many of the leaders were teachers at one time or another.

Region, religion, and involvement in reform. Temperance women were more likely to come from the Midwest, West, or South, whereas more suffrage leaders came from New England and the Mid-Atlantic states (see table 4.4). The religious backgrounds of the suffragists were also associated with the mercantile and settled eastern seaboard—Congregational, Unitarian, Universalist, and Quaker; several were Episcopalians. Moreover, a number of the suffragists' biographies did not include information on religious affiliation; religion evidently played only a small part in their lives. In contrast, well over half of the temperance leaders (31 out of 49) were from the denominations that had flourished on the frontier—Methodist, Baptist, and Presbyterian—compared with only a fraction (7 out of 49) of the suffrage leaders. The WCTU leaders were more likely to be oriented to individual reform and moral uplift, such as could be found in foreign missionary work. The dominant theme of the early work of ladies' foreign missionary societies was the personal salvation of women despite their confinement to harems or seraglios.

The denominations characteristic of the suffragists all had a strong tradition of identifying religious concern with community concern. Congregational and Unitarian churches represented the established church in New England; Universalism grew out of that tradition. Through their testimonies Quakers sought to relate religious insight to everyday life, not only with respect to individual self-discipline but also with respect to social justice, the responsibilities of citizenship, and such issues as slavery. Thus among the suffrage and temperance women who were prominent before 1900, the temperance women were significantly more active in missionary society work; the suffrage leaders, in antislavery, as shown in table 4.4.

There was also within the Quaker and Unitarian groups a strong tradition of equality for women. Quakers had women preachers from very early times who traveled to evangelize and organize new meetings throughout the East.[58] Sex equality was upheld in Quaker education and in the right of women to speak in meetings. Among Unitarians the prominence of Margaret Fuller and her conversation groups in the intellectual society of Boston in the 1830s were also symbol and precedent for intelligent women's critical commentary on their own roles and the structure of society.

Sex discrimination and innovation. Why were the suffragists so innovative with respect to the conventions surrounding women's

TABLE 4.4

Regional and AntiSlavery Activity of Prominent Suffrage and Temperance Leaders

Region of Origin[a]	Suffrage Leaders	WCTU Leaders
East, Mid-Atlantic	28	19
Midwest, West, or South	21	29
	49	48

	Leaders Prominent 1870–1895	
Reform Activity[b]	Suffrage Leaders	WCTU Leaders
Active in antislavery	7	2
Not active in antislavery	18	38
	25	40

[a] Chi-square with Yates correction = 2.396; p < .10 for one-tailed test.
[b] Fisher exact probability test, p = .01173.

roles? Perhaps they were particularly subject to discrimination or especially sensitive to it, and participation in a movement for women's emancipation was their way of overcoming these barriers. A number were denied entry to a college, a university, or a profession because of their sex. Comparison of the biographies of 17 temperance and 18 suffrage women listed in *Notable American Women* who were born before 1840 shows that suffrage women were more likely to encounter barriers or opposition to their activities than temperance women. At least a third of the suffragists encountered some form of family opposition, compared with only one of the temperance women. And several suffragists had overcome some civil or legal barrier or had faced opposition to public speaking or to their educational or career activity, compared with *none* of the temperance women (see table 4.5).

The suffrage women also appear to have been somewhat more willing to risk innovative behavior on behalf of women's equality. More suffragists were responsible for such new practices as keeping their own

TABLE 4.5

Barriers and Innovations in Leaders' Lives
(NAW sample born before 1840)

	Temperance (N=17)	Suffrage (N=18)
Type of Barrier Experienced		
Family opposition	1	7
Public speaking	0	5
Education	0	3
Civil or legal	0	3
Career	0	2
Type of Innovation		
Organizational leadership	15	12
Public speaking	13	15
Writing	10	13
Economic self support	3	6
Higher education	1	5
Other (cremation, name change, etc.)	2	8

Note: For a description of the methods used to describe the NAW sample, see appendix B.

names after marriage, trying to vote, refusing to pay taxes, or entering a profession such as law that had traditionally excluded women. The suffragist Lucy Stone was the first woman in New England to request that she be cremated on her death in 1893. A comparison of the early temperance and suffrage leaders listed in *Notable American Women* shows that in a number of ways, such as organizing, public speaking, and writing, temperance and suffrage women were similar with respect to innovation. But in such areas as being self-supporting and entering new fields of higher education, proportionally more suffragists than temperance women were pioneers (see table 4.5).

The direction of feminist involvement. The career trajectory of several suffragists began with temperance work. Stanton was president of the New York Woman's State Temperance Society she and Anthony formed in 1852 to protest exclusion from the regular state temperance organization. In the early 1850s Anthony was as active in the Daughters of Temperance in New York as in woman's rights. But it was rare for the woman reformer who began with suffrage to gravitate toward temperance.[59]

Until the 1890s suffrage activity was held much more suspect than temperance. The WCTU could count thousands more in membership than state and local suffrage leagues. In the 20 years prior to 1900 the suffrage cause gradually became more respectable. Where Anthony had once held meetings in bare lecture halls to eke out enough money to cover expenses and keep the movement going, there were now teas and receptions with prominent social leaders. Lillie Devereux reported on a New York suffrage reception in 1890: "About four hundred guests were present, including many persons of social prominence, who do not usually attend such gatherings."[60]

Hannah Solomon attributed the change in status of suffrage women to the great influence of the 1893 women's meetings at the Columbian World's Exposition in Chicago: "Its congress of representative women converted a surprising number of people, men included, to the point where suffrage actually became fashionable!"[61] Other evidence for the growing prestige of the movement came from the New Orleans *Picayune* in 1903, when the National American Woman Suffrage convention was held in that city. The *Picayune* described the audience at the convention as "not only deeply interested and sympathetic but . . . representative of the finest culture in the city and state."[62]

At the national level, the degree of leaders' prominence did not change so much as the nature of their prominence. The qualifications that early suffragists brought to their roles were most often educational achievement or professional expertise. Leaders after 1895, however, were more likely to come from regionally prominent families or from an elite known for their charity and philanthropy, such as Mrs. O. H. P. Belmont, Harriet Lee Laidlaw, and Mrs. Edward Dreier of New York, Laura Clay of Kentucky, and Ruth Hanna McCormick of Cleveland and Chicago.

For budding leaders, the suffrage movement after 1900 provided a challenging opportunity for growth and development. Women were needed who could travel, speak, and help to organize local campaign activity, and in the later years they were much more likely to meet with political success. Catt and others had created a viable organization. Investment of time and energy held promise not just for a handful of visionaries but for a broad class of privileged women who were newly awakened to interest in public affairs.

Organization among the Suffragists

Despite its many similarities to the temperance movement, the suffrage movement had different goals, structure, membership, and allies.[63] The WCTU took off easily after 1873, growing rapidly and spreading into the Midwest and the South and building a strong base in the mainstream Methodist, Baptist, and Presbyterian churches. The suffrage organization, however, was small and fragmented and concentrated among a few pioneer feminists primarily in the Northeast. Not until after 1900 did suffrage activity become important in other parts of the country as well as among both working-class and college women.

Suffragists were generally more advanced or radical than the WCTU in their beliefs about women's roles. They therefore encountered greater difficulty in establishing their cause, a condition reflected in their internal divisions, their smaller and narrower membership base, and their later discovery of social and political allies.

Internal division.   It is striking that the organizational unity of the WCTU was never equalled by the suffragists. The division, even at the founding of the two suffrage associations in 1869, signaled major disagreements over the scope and timing of suffrage objectives. The NWSA and the AWSA had both grown out of the American Equal Rights Association, which immediately after the Civil War worked for the enfranchisement of both women and former slaves. But the two suffrage associations differed in the speed with which they felt woman suffrage could be accomplished. The National, under Stanton and Anthony, opposed postponement of woman suffrage until after African-American suffrage. The American, led by Lucy Stone and other New Englanders, accepted the concept of the "Negro's hour"; their more gradualist approach also better accommodated the moderate and conservative temperance women. Although the National and the

American merged in 1890, another split was in the making between 1912 and 1917. Differing with what she considered to be the conservative policies of the NAWSA's Congressional Committee, committee chair Alice Paul, a social reformer educated in New York and London, withdrew with other more radical suffragists in 1913 to form the Congressional Union for Woman Suffrage; this group later merged with the Woman's Party to form the National Woman's Party in 1917.[64]

Why was there such an organizational contrast in the history of the WCTU and the suffragists? The WCTU had a single national body, strong state and local organizations, published minutes, a substantial budget, and cohesive plan of action. National WCTU records and headquarters even now are located in the WCTU library in Evanston, Illinois, next to Frances Willard's home. No such centralization existed in the suffrage movement. The suffragists were spread between two national organizations; neither achieved the bureaucratic stability and integration of the WCTU. From 1903 to 1909 the headquarters of NAWSA were located in the hometown of its treasurer, Harriet Upton Taylor, in Warren, Ohio, and only after 1910 were moved to New York City.[65] To this day the suffrage records are scattered in handwritten accounts, the *Woman's Journal*, various state histories, and the six volumes of the *History of Woman Suffrage*.[66]

The suffrage organization was probably more fragmented because its members had the more radical goal of achieving political equality for women in a society that was still patriarchal, and different factions formed because they disagreed on how quickly to pursue that goal. In contrast, temperance women presented a united front by making feminism the tool of their reform rather than the object of it. Since the WCTU's stated goal was the control of alcohol, they adopted the methods current in the larger temperance and prohibition movement and avoided the appearance of radicalism. The WCTU and the more moderate AWSA were allies because they shared a gradualist stance in working for limited forms of suffrage such as the municipal and school board vote (although a few AWSA suffragists were always wary of the "home protection" ballot as nothing more than a temperance tool).[67] The more radical NWSA deliberately avoided too close a tie to temperance. As late as the 1890 merger of the NAWSA, Anthony voiced concern that the suffrage cause not become a mere "annex to the W.C.T.U." and thereby shift its focus from the federal amendment to partisan support of a single cause.[68]

A narrower membership base.   From the distance of a century, it is clear that the temperance and suffrage organizations had different histories and goals. Both groups worked for the woman's franchise, and the leaders were similar in being middle class and educated. But the less conventional religious, vocational, and family backgrounds of the suffragists made it more difficult for them to recruit membership among women of the rank and file than for the WCTU.

Nevertheless, the suffrage organization grew dramatically between 1890 and 1920. Before 1890 there was widespread prosuffrage sentiment in the new western states, even though the membership of the suffrage associations was tiny. As a number of these states gained full or even partial woman suffrage (such as Colorado in 1893), suffrage society membership understandably receded. But on the rapidly urbanizing eastern seaboard, despite the defeat of state referenda in New York, Pennsylvania, and Massachusetts, suffrage participation intensified. Weak and delayed support were found primarily in the border and deep South. But even there—in states such as Louisiana, Kentucky, or Maryland—dramatic gains were evident by 1910.[69]

By using records of state dues (10 cents per member) paid to the NAWSA in 1892, 1910, and 1914, I have calculated membership rates per 100,000 population, as shown in table 4.6. States above the median are primarily from New England or the Mid-Atlantic, with a sprinkling from the Midwest. States below the median are generally located in the Midwest and border South. The states with no organization at all are either western or southern.

From 1892 to 1914 the state suffrage organizations varied considerably in size and vigor. Kansas, for example, had a rank of 10 in 1892, reported no dues at all in 1910, and then dropped to 38 by 1914. On the other hand, there were two definite trends indicating steady overall growth. More states were organized in 1910 than in 1892 (36 versus 29). Six more appeared in 1914: Alabama, Florida, Montana, Nevada, North Carolina, and North Dakota. In addition, the median suffrage membership per 100,000 population rose dramatically from 8 in 1892 and 17 in 1910 to 54 by 1914. Several eastern states were able to extend suffrage clubs into almost every county or major town. In Massachusetts, as in New York, all counties were organized. By 1914, 83 out of 88 counties were organized in Ohio, and 66 out of 83 counties in Michigan.[70]

The dynamics of these changes can be understood only by comparing the histories of those states that experienced a dramatic rise in membership with those that declined and those that remained steady. No study has yet supplemented the more than 20 existing state suffrage histories with a quantitative analysis of which sectors of the population gave most suffrage support. As a preliminary effort of that kind, I have analyzed changes in suffrage support by county in the state of New York from 1894 to 1917. The 1894 signature campaign for a state constitutional amendment gathered almost 300,000 signatures, of which roughly 120,000 came from women. A 1915 campaign for a state suffrage referendum that was run by the New York Woman's Suffrage Association enrolled almost 500,000 persons by county of residence; that number rose to more than a million by the referendum campaign of 1917.[71]

Comparison by county across these three events shows that consistently strong suffrage support came from upstate, the old "burned over district" that had ignited numerous social and religious movements, ranging from anti-Masonic demonstrations and nativism to temperance, Mormonism, and the 1848 suffrage meeting at Seneca Falls.[72] In 1894 all but one of the top fifteen counties in suffrage enrollment per capita were from this region, and in a number of them, both upstate and in New York City, the WCTU was credited with having done a great deal of the local work.[73] By the campaigns of 1915 and 1917, however, the strongest support had shifted steadily eastward and downstate; in the later campaigns only half of the top fifteen counties were west of Utica, as shown in figures 4.1, 4.2, and 4.3.

These trends reflected Catt's efforts begun in the 1890s to extend suffrage clubs into more cities and towns and into the South.[74] New campaign methods and more aggressive outreach also came from Alice Paul and the Woman's Party. Suffrage organizers experienced newfound success in urban areas and among populations where their issue had earlier been unpopular or taken for granted. In New York, as well as other states, they formed alliances that reached beyond their traditional constituencies—the WCTU, the small-town middle class, and native-born Protestants—to the concerns of immigrant, working-class, and college women.

Late success in popular appeal. Suffrage alliances with other supportive groups were slow in coming. The WCTU had found a natural base in the churches, but the more radical and secular style of the suffragists worked against such easy association. As historian Karen Blair notes, "The very boldness of the suffrage movement limited its appeal."[75]

TABLE 4.6
State Membership Rates, NAWSA, 1892, 1910, 1914
(Membership per 100,000 Population[a])

Region	1892	1910	1914
Northeast and Mid-Atlantic			
Maine	42.4	33.2	26.9
New Hampshire	—	69.6	150.8
Vermont	—	16.0	16.9
Massachusetts	16.9	47.0	193.1
Rhode Island	32.4	28.0	34.1
Connecticut	13.7	22.4	672.6
New York	16.7	45.1	87.8
New Jersey	8.3	13.0	172.3
Pennsylvania	4.9	13.6	65.2
Low	4.9	13.0	16.9
High	42.4	69.6	672.6
Median	**16.7**	**28.0**	**87.8**
Midwest and North Central			
Ohio	11.0	18.4	29.4
Indiana	2.3	5.2	79.9
Illinois	15.7	16.8	88.7
Michigan	4.8	4.6	35.6
Wisconsin	—	2.9	42.8
Minnesota	4.6	14.5	73.4
Iowa	19.6	28.9	62.9
Missouri	1.2	3.2	39.5
North Dakota	—	—	174.7
South Dakota	17.2	36.6	85.6
Nebraska	6.1	16.5	83.9
Kansas	14.7	—	11.8
Low	1.2	2.9	11.8
High	19.6	36.6	174.7
Median	**8.6**	**15.5**	**68.2**
South Atlantic, East and West South Central			
Maryland	2.8	84.0	127.6
District of Columbia	47.0	31.7	196.4
Virginia	—	3.4	48.5
West Virginia	—	9.0	14.1

TABLE 4.6 (cont.)

Region	1892	1910	1914
South Atlantic, East and West South Central (cont.)			
North Carolina	—	—	9.1
South Carolina	4.4	—	19.8
Georgia	1.5	1.1	53.7
Florida	—	—	38.8
Kentucky	4.1	39.3	43.7
Tennessee	2.8	1.6	127.3
Alabama	—	—	54.1
Mississippi	—	3.6	8.9
Arkansas	4.4	—	—
Louisiana	8.0	39.3	103.3
Oklahoma	—	6.0	6.0
Texas	—	1.2	45.4
Low	1.5	1.1	6.0
High	47.0	84.0	196.4
Median	**4.1**	**4.8**	**43.7**
Mountain and Western			
Montana	—	—	359.0
Idaho	—	—	—
Wyoming	—	—	—
Colorado	7.3	6.3	10.8
New Mexico	—	—	—
Arizona	—	—	—
Utah	331.8	53.6	—
Nevada	—	—	1,219.5
Washington	14.0	39.4	—
Oregon	—	12.6	14.9
California	1.6	41.0	25.2
Low	1.6	6.3	10.8
High	331.8	53.6	1,219.5
Median	**10.7**	**39.4**	**25.2**

[a] Membership figures are estimated from dues payments (at 10 cents per member) recorded in NAWSA *Proceedings*, January 1893, 151–54; NAWSA *Forty-Sixth Annual Convention*, 1914, 55–57. Membership rate per 100,000 population was calculated using census figures on total population of each state in 1890 and 1910. See U.S. Department of Commerce, Bureau of the Census, 1913. Thirteenth Census of the United States, *Population 1910*, 1:57.

Figure 4.1

New York Campaign for Woman Suffrage, 1894

(Counties Ranked by Women's Signatures per 1,000 Residents)

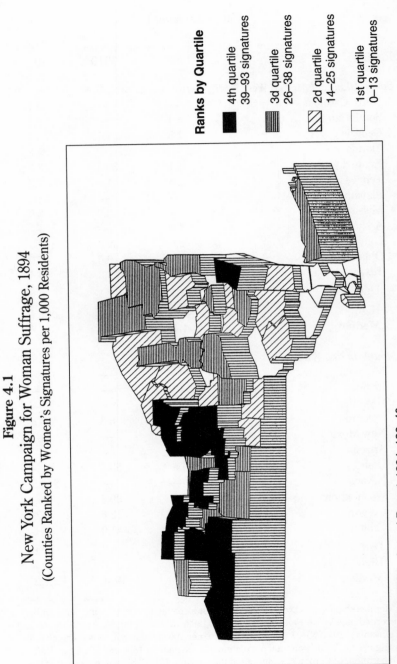

Ranks by Quartile

■ 4th quartile
39–93 signatures

▥ 3d quartile
26–38 signatures

▨ 2d quartile
14–25 signatures

□ 1st quartile
0–13 signatures

Source: NYSWSA, *Annual Report,* 1894, 139–40.

Figure 4.2
New York Campaign for Woman Suffrage, 1915
(Counties Ranked by Women's Signatures per 1,000 Residents)

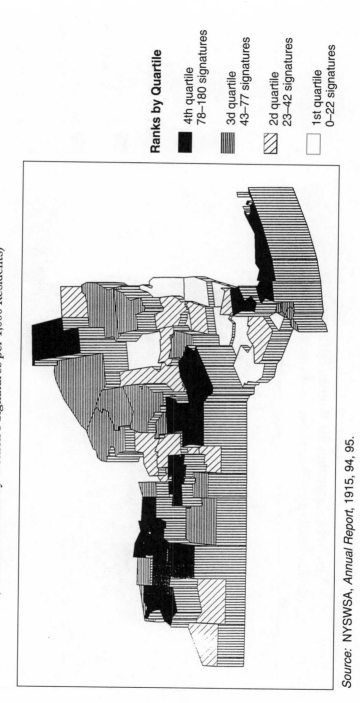

Ranks by Quartile

4th quartile
78–180 signatures

3d quartile
43–77 signatures

2d quartile
23–42 signatures

1st quartile
0–22 signatures

Source: NYSWSA, *Annual Report,* 1915, 94, 95.

Figure 4.3
New York Campaign for Woman Suffrage, 1917
(Counties Ranked by Women's Signatures per 1,000 Residents)

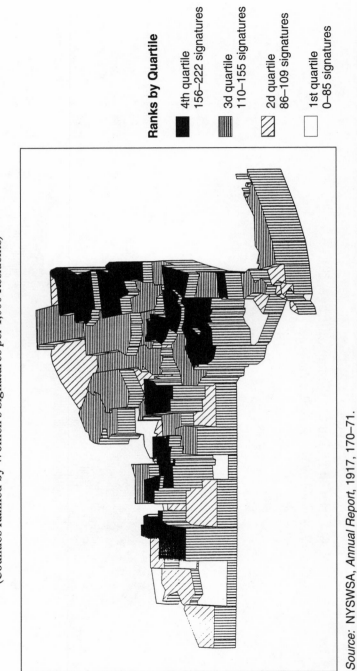

Ranks by Quartile

■ 4th quartile
156–222 signatures

▥ 3d quartile
110–155 signatures

▨ 2d quartile
86–109 signatures

☐ 1st quartile
0–85 signatures

Source: NYSWSA, *Annual Report,* 1917, 170–71.

Rather than stemming simply from membership recruitment, growing suffrage sentiment resulted from a socialization process by which women began to chafe against the old limits of their circumscribed roles. There were three main pathways by which women came to demand their full rights as citizens. One originated in rural Protestant areas; a second among the urban middle class; and the third in big cities with Catholic and Jewish working women, many of them immigrants.

The largest group of supporters were rural Protestants based in the small towns of New England, New York, and the Midwest. Settlers in the five mountain states that established woman suffrage before 1900 expressed some of the same values, and Mormonism in Utah and Idaho also proved favorable to the enfranchisement of women.[76] In Michigan, the Grange and the WCTU cooperated with the state Equal Suffrage Association, were joined by the state Association of Farmer's Clubs in 1910, and by the Daughters of the American Revolution in 1913.[77] An 1884–85 list of state and national WCTU leaders reveals that 60 percent were from small towns with populations under 10,000.[78] Suffrage sentiment in New York was also initially strongest in small towns and upstate counties, as shown in figures 4.1-4.3.

Similar support for suffrage developed among southern women, albeit somewhat later than in the North. Historian Anne Firor Scott describes the process of women's intellectual and social emancipation that laid the foundation for political involvement. "The biographies of hundreds of women show the same progression: missionary society, temperance society, woman's club."[79] Women's initial church work became more secular and nondenominational under the auspices of the WCTU. The literary societies extended their mission beyond literature and the arts to current social problems, such as women's education and children's health. It was but a short step into local politics and cognizance of the need for woman suffrage. Although only four southern states ratified the federal suffrage amendment (Arkansas, Kentucky, Tennessee, and Texas), all the southern states had some degree of suffrage organization as early as 1896.[80]

A second stream of suffrage support came from the progressive and reform-minded urban middle class who dominated the suffrage movement after 1900.[81] Suffragists demonstrated that women's votes ensured social provision and "clean government." States with woman suffrage were more likely to have workman's compensation laws, an eight-hour day for working women, and pensions for widowed

mothers.[82] The ratio of articles in the *Woman's Journal* that advocated such reforms from 1900 to 1915 was exactly double the proportion from 1880 to 1895 (26 percent versus 13 percent). By 1909
NAWSA included committees for work in industry, churches, education, civil rights, and peace.[83] This agenda reflected the combined
influence of the Progressives, a new generation of college women,
and club women.

The Progressive element in suffrage support was a meld of
Populist, temperance, and Republican sentiments, working for what
one historian has termed "municipal gas and water socialism."[84]
Where the Populists had roots in the Grange hall and alliances with
the working class, the Progressives focused on reforming the cities
through settlement houses and sanitary regulations. They represented
the solid middle class, most of whom voted Republican (although the
WCTU had briefly tried to pull them toward the Prohibition party).[85]
They were largely Congregationalist or Unitarian, with a number of
Quakers among the women and some Jews among the very wealthy.
Protestant, Catholic, and Jewish leaders also endorsed woman suffrage.[86] The heroines of this Progressive middle class were the new
college-educated women like Jane Addams of Hull House, Lillian Wald
of Henry Street Settlement, and Florence Kelley of the National
Consumers' League who worked to end child labor and establish pro-
tective legislation for working women. College women organized in
the College Equal Suffrage League in 1906. Women college presidents
Mary Woolley of Mt. Holyoke and M. Carey Thomas of Bryn Mawr,
along with Maud Wood Park, founder of the College Equal Suffrage
League, spoke at a college evening at the national suffrage convention
in 1906. College women helped in state suffrage campaigns in
Massachusetts, New York, and Pennsylvania. The California College
Equal Suffrage League claimed in 1903 that they had organized 30
chapters and 3,000 women in the northern part of the state.[87]

But most numerous, and ultimately most influential among the middle class, were thousands of club women. The General Federation of
Women's Clubs (formed in 1889) lent its full support to the national
suffrage campaign in 1914. In Illinois, along with the WCTU, among
the chief supporters of Progressive reform were the Illinois Social
Science Association and the Chicago Woman's Club, with its four
departments devoted to home, education, philanthropy, and reform.[88]
The *Woman's Journal* as early as 1900 had reported the many good
things being done by women's clubs: "funding of public libraries, . . .

THIS DEALER GIVES HER NO CHOICE

Woman's Journal cartoon ridiculing suffrage opposition, 1912. Library of Congress.

the creation and support of kindergartens, vacation schools, and playgrounds for poor children, the establishment of a State Board of Education [in Delaware], the successful candidacy of women for school trustees."[89] In 1915, after 65,000 women's club members had lent their support to the suffrage referendum in Massachusetts, the *Woman's Journal* commented again: "When the women's clubs advanced from the study of ancient art and Browning's poetry to the study of the community around them; when they widened their field from amusement and self-culture and began to work for legislation to promote human welfare, they were bound to become suffragists."[90]

Against this backdrop of support from rural Protestants and the urban middle class, suffragists faced the challenge of winning converts from the *non*-rural, the *non*-Protestant, and the *non*-middle class. It was the seamstresses, milliners, and laundry workers who brought the backing of these groups to the suffrage movement. They lived in big cities like New York and Chicago; they were Catholic and Jewish; and rather than sharing the Republican or Prohibitionist leanings of the suffragists, they were more likely to sympathize with Democrats and Socialists. These urban, working-class women were brought into the suffrage movement through their own unionizing efforts, membership in Irish or Italian Catholic or Russian Jewish communities, and help from such organizations as the Women's Trade Union League (WTUL), founded in 1903 as a new and powerful coalition of middle-class and working women.[91]

Unionizing activities of working women were particularly alien to middle-class Progressives who favored cross-class alliances rather than the class struggle as a means of social change.[92] But crowded and unsafe working conditions and deceitful employment practices in the garment district of New York City fomented a strike in 1909–10 that involved 20,000–30,000 women workers. Working girls of 16 and 17 were thrown into jail for daring to join the picket line. A tragic fire in the Triangle Shirtwaist factory caused many to jump to their death from as high as 10 stories up. The result was not only mobilization among strikers for woman's rights but growing sympathy among middle-class suffragists for the plight of working women.[93]

Ties to Catholic and Jewish immigrant culture also aided the rise of working women. Before 2,000 people in Cooper Union young Clara Lemlich, a Russian Jewish immigrant, rose to the platform (after speeches by Samuel Gompers and other dignitaries) and electrified the audience with a call to strike. She spoke briefly in Yiddish; then the crowd joined together in raising their right hands and taking the old Jewish oath: "If I turn traitor to the cause I now pledge, may this hand wither from the arm I now raise." Another powerful speaker was Irish laundry worker Maggie Hinchey, who toured New York's ethnic neighborhoods with an Italian flag in the Italian neighborhoods, a Greek flag farther downtown. Such women built support for woman suffrage on very different ethnic and religious traditions from those of the suffrage movement's founders.[94]

Despite such heroic efforts on behalf of suffrage, however, middle-class women found it difficult to welcome the workers as equals.[95] The talented Clara Lemlich, for example, was let go as an organizer for the Women's Trade Union League. The famous historian Mary Beard wrote to Leonora O'Reilly, "It has been my dream to develop working women to be a help in the awakening of their class, but Clara can't make good along the line she has attempted this winter. . . . She has *no* initiative."[96]

Nevertheless, working women helped to win important additional constituencies for the suffrage cause. Middle-class women became less distrustful of wage labor and gained insight into the needs of working women and children. Suffrage conventions first included reports on industrial work in 1886 and regularly after 1893.[97] By 1910, state federations of labor in a number of the eastern states had passed resolutions for woman suffrage, as did the National Federation of Labor.[98] Working-class Catholics who had opposed woman suffrage because of its threat to parochial schools gained sympathy for suffrage as they saw its usefulness to working people. These were important changes that helped such states as Massachusetts to be among the first industrial states to ratify the Nineteenth Amendment in 1919.[99]

Strategy and Tactics of Suffrage Reform

The ideology, leadership, and organization of the suffragists focused on equal rights for women. But by 1900 equal rights was so identified with the woman's ballot that suffrage was understood to be the primary goal of the feminist movement. Why had the objective become so specific? And how did the movement enlist support, fend off opposition, and finally win its goal?

The theory of social movements suggests several key factors in success. *Resource mobilization theory* points to the importance of membership drives, mailing lists, and fund-raising to build a constituency and base of support for the movement.[100] *Frame alignment* and "new social movement theory" focus on movement activities that create a fit between the values and goals of the activists and those of the wider population.[101] *Structural-functional theory* explains a movement's success by its ability to fill a social need. Sociologist Miriam Johnson has recently interpreted the contemporary feminist movement in structural-functional terms as a process of "adaptive upgrading" in which women's roles became more diverse, gave rise to new and higher expectations, extended privileges to women that had previously been denied, and then assimilated these new norms to the culture of the larger society.[102]

Similarly, I too interpret the woman suffrage movement as a means for upgrading women's roles, but at an earlier stage, when the primary problem was to extend women's responsibilities beyond the family into the public sphere. I find that resource mobilization, frame alignment, and structural-functional theories, when integrated, point to four tactical issues the movement had to confront to win the federal suffrage amendment:

1. *Defining the public problem* and challenging certain key rules that barred women from political access. Suffragists learned to argue that women's wider and more diverse responsibilities called for the basic rights of citizenship that were symbolized by the vote. Feminists thus specified suffrage as *the* goal and succeeded by focusing all efforts on attaining it.

2. *Mobilization of support* from large numbers who would advocate for woman suffrage. This was accomplished through "adaptive upgrading" of the image of women's capacities and showing that the ballot was a means for all kinds of men and women to solve their own problems and reach their own individual and social goals.

3. *Alliance rather than conflict* to transcend class, racial, ethnic, regional, and ideological divisions. The movement accomplished "inclusion" of women in the electorate through an integrative process of consensus building rather than polarization.[103]

4. *Cultural incorporation* of female suffrage as an integral part of American democracy and family life. Through "value generalization"

the purposes of the feminist movement were joined with those of the larger society and came to seem a natural part of belief in equality.

Defining the public problem.   For a social movement even to exist, it has to define what sociologist Joseph Gusfield has termed the "public problem" that is the target of its reform.[104] Suffragists met this challenge by specifying (1) *lack of the vote* as the key problem of women; (2) suffrage through the *federal suffrage amendment* as the key goal; and (3) the *increase in "suffrage" lawmakers and "suffrage" voters* as the key political strategy for achieving these ends.

Among some historians it has been fashionable to fault the early feminists for their benighted trust in suffrage as the solution to all women's problems. Kraditor and O'Neill, for example, treat the focus on suffrage as short-sighted because it failed to address women's confining roles in the home and the workplace.[105] Woman suffrage, however, almost certainly would not have been granted as soon as it was without the feminists' narrower and more manageable definition of the public problem as women's lack of political access rather than a more radical and global denouncement of women's domestic and economic oppression.

How to define the public problem was not at all obvious, even to the feminists. In one state after another the suffragists tried several strategies before pinning their hopes on a federal amendment. Before and after the Civil War, the principal appeal was to state constitutional conventions. Some new western states like Wyoming, Utah, and Idaho actually complied and entered the union with woman suffrage already established. In other states like Pennsylvania, Massachusetts, Michigan, or Ohio, where constitutional conventions failed to respond, local and state suffrage groups between 1870 and 1890 asked limited forms of suffrage from their legislatures. After 1890 a third tactic became widespread: the state referendum. But the results were discouraging. Between 1890 and 1918, 29 state referenda were lost; only 14 won. After 1910, however, the push for a federal amendment finally took center stage. Suffragists' political strategy for attaining their goal had two parts: one was aimed at lawmakers; the other at convincing the voters. The Woman's Party was especially responsible for getting the amendment out of Congress. NAWSA used state-by-state campaigns to gain voters in each state who would eventually support the federal amendment.

Pressure on the lawmakers came primarily from the Woman's Party (which originated in 1912 as the Congressional Committee of NAWSA and then became the Congressional Union). Alice Paul and her band of young militants repudiated the ladylike methods of the mainstream suffragists, who had been content to work within the established political structure. Imitating the bold methods of the British suffragists, they used novel forms of disruption, proving that, in the words of William A. Gamson, "feistiness works."[106] They targeted the members of Congress to get the suffrage bill out of committee, then through both chambers. To keep up the pressure they turned all their firepower on key political contests, promising to defeat any senator or representative of the "party in power" (the Democrats) even if he personally favored the suffrage amendment.[107]

Catt of NAWSA, on the other hand, favored a more moderate approach. She emphasized the need for a two-pronged effort to build up victories on state referenda as well as to lay the groundwork for the three-fourths majority of states that would be needed to ratify a federal amendment. As in the successful Idaho referendum campaign of 1896, which focused at the district or precinct level, Catt proposed a similar strategy for winning the federal amendment.[108] According to her "secret plan" suffragists would concentrate their energies on increasing the number of states in which women could vote, using any one of three different tactics: amendment of state constitutions by referenda; action of state legislatures to confer presidential suffrage; or gaining the right to vote in party primaries (especially important in the southern states).[109]

But in the meantime, Congress dragged its feet in voting on the federal amendment. Again Alice Paul's group put on the pressure. In the winter of 1917–18, they picketed in front of the White House, were arrested, then suffered imprisonment and forced feeding. Such treatment pointed up a contradiction between President Wilson's support of democracy in the rest of the world during World War I while ignoring what was happening to women in the Capitol. Finally, the amendment was reported out of Congress and sent to the states for ratification in June 1919. A Democratic representative from Arkansas told two Woman's Party organizers, "All this agitation, the lobbying, the persistence never ceasing, often to us men very irritating like grains of sand in the eyes, has nevertheless hastened your amendment by ten years."[110]

When the amendment went to the states, Catt's plan was again tested in action. States like Wyoming, Colorado, and Illinois had instituted presidential suffrage for women. Voting women in other states had helped to elect representatives who fostered more positive attitudes toward suffrage in subsequent elections. In only a little more than a year after Congress had sent the federal suffrage amendment to the states, the Nineteenth Amendment was enacted in August 1920, by vote of the Tennessee legislature, the thirty-sixth state to ratify.[111]

Mobilization of new sources of support. To achieve this success the suffrage movement had to mobilize a consensus that would become a majority.[112] Suffrage had to evolve a rhetoric and a mobilization strategy that moved with the demographic changes already afoot in the wider population. This meant outreach beyond traditional rural and small-town supporters to a more varied urban population. Time after time the suffrage campaigns noted their success in the rural areas. After a defeat of the 1900 Oregon referendum that was attributed to the city vote, the *Woman's Journal* commented, "Our appeal must be made, first of all, to the farmers, next to the miners, mechanics, and intelligent working men, last and least of all to our city populations."[113]

Yet rural support represented the past rather than the wave of the future. Painfully, between 1896 and 1910, a period suffragists termed the "doldrums," the faithful saw the traditional methods of the old guard fall by the wayside and in their place emerge new and energetic, but unfamiliar methods that reached beyond the converted to involve college women and working people as well as the skeptics and the unconvinced.

The old guard used the convention method that had brought the leaders together annually since the first woman's rights conventions of the 1850s. By 1900 these occasions had become depressingly irrelevant and boring. Maud Wood Park was appalled by a NAWSA meeting she attended in a church basement in Washington, with only about 100 women present. She saw the need to attract a new group of better educated and more energetic women, and with Inez Haynes formed the College Equal Suffrage League (CESL) in Massachusetts in 1903. By 1904 Harriot Stanton Blatch (Elizabeth Cady Stanton's daughter) was forming a CESL in New York. In 1906 NAWSA asked Park to form other branches around the country; and by 1908 M. Carey Thomas, the president of Bryn Mawr, had organized a national association of the CESLs.[114]

In Massachusetts, Park pioneered many of the new methods that would be adopted throughout the country. With Mary Hutchinson

Page of the Boston Equal Suffrage Association for Good Government (BESAGG), she contacted women in all religious denominations and teachers' societies, sent speakers to chapters of the Massachusetts Federation of Women's Clubs, and set up booths at agricultural and county fairs. She took advantage of the 1903 annual meeting in Boston of the Women's Trade Union League and by 1909 reported that 235 unions supported woman suffrage. From the English militants the young Massachusetts suffragists also adopted open-air speaking tours, and in the summer of 1909 held dozens of open-air meetings in the small mill towns of Massachusetts. They even opened a storefront on Boston's Tremont Street, with the stated purpose of making suffrage "picturesque." In the Massachusetts suffrage campaign of 1915, Park made a deliberate attempt to get the support of politicians in Boston's Catholic wards. She had lived among Catholic voters when she worked in a settlement house in the city's South End.[115]

The College Equal Suffrage League was the first to use the automobile for campaigning. Quickly the idea spread to New York, Ohio, and California. In 1909 the New York CESL organized the first suffrage parade. Within a few years the parade became perhaps the best-known hallmark of the suffrage movement. By 1913 some 8,000 to 10,000 women marched in Washington on the occasion of President Wilson's inaugural. And other parades, larger and even more colorful, followed. The 1915 parade in New York counted 30,000 marchers and 25 bands.[116]

Another new technique was political organization by occupation. In New York prior to the 1915 referendum the suffragists directed leaflets and street meetings for a whole week to 240,000 street-car men. There was a day for barbers, two days for brokers, and also time for street cleaners. The Empire State Campaign Committee distributed its message in 26 languages to newspapers across the state and held street dances on the Lower East Side for the Irish, Syrian, Italian, and Polish communities and concerts for the French and the Germans.[117]

Alliance rather than conflict.   Because woman suffrage had long been associated with the temperance movement and with the white, middle-class, native-born, Protestant population, there was an ever-present danger that suffrage would alienate all others: those who drank alcohol, the Catholics, the foreign born, the working class, and nonwhites. One of the suffragists' achievements was to transcend these polarities of class, race, and gender role by defining suffrage in unqualified terms as a universal right.

Difficulty arose first around prohibition. Temperance support for suffrage was long-standing. As early as 1875 the *Woman's Journal* reported that 59 percent of Massachusetts legislators favorable to prohibition had also voted for woman suffrage, compared with only 16 percent of those against prohibition.[118] Support from the WCTU was also a key factor in the first state suffrage referendum victory in Colorado in 1893 and in many other state campaigns.[119] But by the same token, the most notorious opponents of suffrage were the brewers and distillers. Suffragists calculated that dealers were making huge contributions ($4–6 million per year) to defeat suffrage because they thought it spelled prohibition. Neil Bonner, president of the National Retail Dealers' Association, addressed the liquor dealers in 1912: "We need not fear the churches, the men are voting the old tickets; we need not fear the ministers, for the most part they follow the men of the churches; we need not fear the Y.M.C.A. for it does not do aggressive work, but, gentlemen, we need to fear the Woman's Christian Temperance Union and the ballot in the hands of women; therefore, gentlemen, fight woman suffrage."[120]

In Ohio in 1914, the woman's ballot was crushed between the saloon and antisaloon forces. In Oregon, Abigail Scott Duniway fumed at the bumbling of suffrage and temperance leaders that needlessly stirred up resistance from the foes of prohibition.[121] Suffrage leaders eventually saw the need to dissociate temperance and suffrage by broadening the issue of suffrage and making it an end in itself—one of equal rights and "personal liberty in governmental matters." Catt wrote to a suffrage organizer in Missouri, "We stand a great deal stronger when they do not know our party and when, indeed, we do not represent any party in particular."[122] In later years, suffrage leaders who favored prohibition were careful to label their opinion as personal rather than the official view of the group.[123]

A second threat of polarization stemmed from concern over increasing the illiterate black, Catholic, and foreign vote. In 1889, the Reverend Olympia Brown had contrasted well-educated women lacking the vote with their political inferiors, "all the riff-raff of Europe that is poured upon our shores."[124] Some suffrage advocates even suggested that the vote be extended only to those who were educated and who could give proof of citizenship, arguments particularly welcomed in parts of the South.[125] But Carrie Chapman Catt, like Susan B.

Anthony (who wanted suffrage broad enough for "the infidel"), cautioned against too narrow a definition of suffrage or identification with single-interest groups.[126]

A third major source of opposition was what Anne Firor Scott and Andrew Scott term "a vast reservoir of male disquiet which surfaced whenever women appeared to be making progress toward their goals."[127] But this general disagreement came from females as well who believed in the existing sexual division of labor and found it threatening to extend woman's rights (and responsibilities) beyond the home. Antisuffrage associations formed in more than 25 states. Between 1912 and 1918, through their newspaper the *Woman's Protest*, women against suffrage argued that it would have negative consequences for society and for women. Their work helped to coalesce the opposition that came from many quarters: the old upper class who feared a socialist insurgency, southerners worried about race suicide, and assorted conservatives concerned about loss of femininity and decline of the family.[128]

To their objections the best answer was a continued gain in suffrage support from women's clubs, church groups, and labor unions. In California, in the successful campaign of 1911, pamphlets were issued showing that 36,000 women in organized labor, 35,000 women in the California Federation of Woman's Clubs, 6,000 in the state WCTU, and more wanted to vote.[129] Then the tide turned.

Cultural incorporation of women's equality.   Historians repeatedly ask why woman suffrage was not achieved in any more than four states prior to 1910.[130] Part of the answer lay with the changing strategy, tactics, and alliances of the woman suffrage movement. But there were also changes in the audience. In later years, ordinary women were more likely to be involved outside the home in volunteer associations or paid employment. With fewer children and more education in 1920 than in 1870, they had more time available and took more interest in the public sphere. The rapid increase of women in the professions, social work, and benevolent associations was a sign of women's capacity and concern for issues beyond their personal lives.

Among white women the birth rate dropped by almost half between 1800 and 1900, from more than seven to between three and four children per woman of childbearing age. The ratio of preschool children to women of childbearing age also dropped by 10 percent between

Woman's Journal masthead. Library of Congress.

1890 and 1920. In addition, more women were thrown upon their own resources as the divorce rate in urban areas grew from 10 to 21 per 1,000 married women between 1890 and 1920.[131]

Educational opportunities were also expanding. In 1870, there were 500 high schools in the entire country. By 1900 that number had risen to nearly 6,000. Girls benefitted from the expansion of the public high school even more than boys. In 1898, only 41 percent of the public and private secondary-school population were boys, while 59 percent were girls.[132] Although there were many more men in college, the number of women in college rose rapidly between 1870 and 1920. The University of Michigan enrolled its first woman in 1870; Cornell in 1872. New women's colleges opened during the same period: Smith and Wellesley in 1875; Bryn Mawr in 1885; Barnard in 1889; and Radcliffe in 1894. By 1920, 34 percent of all college graduates were women, compared with only 15 percent in 1870.[133]

Industrialization and urbanization created new jobs for women outside the home and showed that the image of woman as dependent and incapable of public responsibility was altogether antiquated. In 1870 only 16 percent of all females more than 10 years old were in the paid labor force, compared with 28 percent in 1920. The figures were much higher for ethnic and black women: as early as 1900, 25 percent of white women with foreign-born parents and 43 percent of black women were in the labor force.[134] In 1870 half of all employed women were in domestic service and one-quarter in agriculture. In just 40 years the 1910 census reported a sharp drop in both these occupations (from 51 to 34 percent in domestic service and from 24 to 16 percent in agriculture), while the proportion of women employed in professional, manufacturing, trade, and clerical occupations doubled (from 24 percent to 49 percent).[135] There were only five woman lawyers or notaries in the whole country according to the 1870 census, but almost 15,000 by 1910. An equally remarkable increase occurred among woman physicians and healers (from 551 to 14,941) and among clergy and religious and charitable workers (from 67 to 9,574). The representation of women on college faculties doubled from 12 to 26 percent during the same period.[136]

It was not just the exceptional woman who experienced this change. The broad rank and file were likely to have tasted some wider political or charitable responsibility outside their families through church groups, the WCTU, the Grange, a woman's club, or a union.[137] Women's missionary societies in 1915 claimed 3.5 million members.

The WCTU in 1911 with 245,000 members was the largest women's organization in the United States. Roughly 100,000 women were affiliated with women's clubs in 1896 and 1 million by 1914.[138] If one counted all these women plus those in the 17 states where women had been granted school suffrage by 1910, the number undoubtedly would have added up to millions who had some degree of experience with public issues and sympathy with the suffragists.[139]

Just as there were changes in the audience, the suffrage leaders had also slightly changed their message to one more easily assimilated by ordinary women. Women's competence for public service was by 1920 understood in a new way—as compatible with her role as wife and mother—that a democratic society should recognize. A pamphlet for the 1911 California suffrage campaign argued that women should be allowed to vote because "women are human beings . . . women are not identical with men—they have special interests. . . . Women are mothers, they deserve honor and power."[140] In the suffrage literature, pictures of little tots began to appear over the caption "I wish Mother could vote."[141] Pamphlets entitled "Jane Addams Wants to Vote" presented her arguments that women needed the ballot in order to be good wives and mothers and to ensure the health, cleanliness, and education of their children. Women could not rely on "influence" to affect political affairs; it was not the proper mode of approach in a democracy where husbands and brothers and sons had the right to express their own opinions. According to Jane Addams, the heroine of the settlement house movement, "Many women today are failing to discharge their duties to their own households properly simply because they do not perceive that as society grows more complicated it is necessary that woman shall extend her sense of responsibility to many things outside of her own home if she would continue to preserve the home in its entirety."[142]

At the same time there was declining emphasis on the purely egalitarian arguments for suffrage. In the early period before 1895, 29 percent of the articles in the *Woman's Journal* called for the ballot as a means to give women equal political status. After 1895, the egalitarian argument appeared in only 16 percent of the articles calling for suffrage. The broadening of specific reform objectives accompanied a more complex and differentiated image of women. Just as women were being portrayed as more feminine, the reforms that suffrage advocated were increasingly aimed at helping others rather than women themselves.

By assimilating women's need for political power to their authority as mothers, the woman suffrage movement established women's right to citizenship. What had yet to be worked out was how women would use the vote. The decades after 1920 would demonstrate the further interweaving of maternal and equal rights feminism in American public life.

The Accomplishment of the Suffragists

In contrast with the temperance women, whose main achievement was to bring women out of the home, the suffragists staked out a place for women in public life. They made a radical critique of women's existing subordination to men. They forged their way into colleges, the law, medicine, and the clergy, and proved that women were just as capable as men. By envisioning a world in which women would have equal rights as citizens, they won the vote that enabled women at last to inhabit the public world.

At the center of the suffragist ideology was an image of the "good new woman" who was responsible for reforming church, state, and society. Suffragists analyzed social problems as primarily stemming from flaws in social structure rather than personal morality. Their solutions therefore emphasized the importance of education and economic independence to help women be truly independent. They also sought political power and social justice in society to enable women's voices to be heard. They wanted to clean up politics and institute equal guardianship, property rights, and equal pay for women. They sought child labor laws, public schools, food and housing laws, and ways to lower infant mortality. To them, equal justice and the vote were ends in themselves more than a means to some particular goal, such as temperance or child welfare.

The personal lives of the suffrage leaders revealed their passion for change and their toughness in the face of rejection. They were innovators, and they dared to question the common belief that women were inferior to men. Some were nonconformists. They tried to go to professional schools from which women had been barred. A few spoke in public, dressed unconventionally, advocated physical exercise, tried to vote. In family background and education they were not so different from the temperance leaders. They had been to a female academy, to college or university. They came from middle-class families that were linked to the farms, commerce, or the professions. They were just as likely to marry and have children, and, like the WCTU leaders, roughly half had been teachers. But the suffrage leaders came more often from the Northeast or Atlantic seaboard and the established religious denominations of the settled East (Congregational, Unitarian, and Quaker) rather than the denominations that turned on personal reform (Methodist, Baptist, or Presbyterian). Whereas many lives of the temperance leaders mentioned a family loss, the suffrage leaders had been denied opportunities because they were women. More of their biographies mention barriers to achievement as well as innovations. Altogether, the suffrage women had personal histories that fitted them for undertaking a radical reform.

Organizationally, suffrage was marked by internal divisions from the very start, probably because of its quite radical goal. After an early start in 1848, and yearly conventions up to the Civil War, two woman suffrage associations formed in 1869 with somewhat different goals and methods. The moderate American Woman Suffrage Association led by Lucy Stone stood by and let former slaves win suffrage before women. The radical National led by Stanton and Anthony focused on the single goal of equality for women. These two organizations joined forces as the National American in 1893, but further splitting occurred between 1912 and 1917 with the departure of Alice Paul, who favored such militant tactics as picketing the White House and launching hunger strikes, to form the Congressional Union and its successor, the National Woman's Party. Together the moderates and radicals gradually extended their organization downward into local communities and diversified their message to reach urban, ethnic, and working groups. They had been slow to form alliances and never had a natural base in the churches (as did the WCTU). But by organizing state-by-state votes on suffrage referenda they ultimately created a broad base of support.

Their long struggle taught suffragists the tactics and skills that extended their base beyond rural Protestants to the diverse ethnic and working groups of the big cities. The vote became the great symbol of equality as well as a tactical goal. The old-guard methods of meeting in annual conventions and listening to speeches declined markedly after 1900. Automobiles and suffrage parades brought new excitement and drama to the cause. Involvement of college women, club women, and trade union women, as well as outreach to city workers from street-car men to stockbrokers, sent a message that the women's vote was in the interest of all the people rather than a narrow group. Woman suffrage was finally incorporated into American law and domestic culture after it found a following among traditional as well as modern women.

Ultimately, it was both a change in audience and a change in the message that brought the suffrage amendment into the U.S. Constitution in 1920. Between 1890 and 1920, rapid demographic changes had created a new type of woman—more educated, more likely to have been employed, and with fewer children and slightly greater vulnerability to divorce. These women were also more likely to have had real experience in public roles through church work, women's clubs, or partial suffrage in the states that permitted it. At the same time, the conversion of vast and diverse groups to the suffrage cause had subtly changed the message of the reformers. They were quietly joining the interests of mothers and families with the interests of women who wanted justice and equal treatment in public life.

Chapter 5

Women's Rights and Feminist Caregiving since 1920

What is the significance of the early woman's movement for American feminism today? Modern American women continue to care for families and children, but their family roles interfere with their presence and power in the public sphere. It is no longer said that "Woman's place is in the home." But modern women more than men continue to make compromises in their careers to care for sick children and aged parents. Until justice for women means that husbands, fathers, and brothers will take a larger role in family life, it is likely that women's equality will remain illusory.

In the face of this harsh reality, the temperance and suffrage movements illustrate three important points for modern-day feminists. First, the early leaders were inspired by the challenges and difficulties in their own lives to envision the new social order in which they wanted to live. Second, they organized and pressed their agenda for social change until they won a wider following. Finally, they welded their claims on behalf of others together with claims on behalf of themselves. United for social responsibility as well as for individual rights, their cause could not be turned aside.

This chapter brings the story of these two streams of the American woman's movement up to the present. Although there have been many gains, modern feminism appears at something of an impasse. In 1991, thousands of women were galvanized by the Clarence Thomas hearings for the U.S. Supreme Court, in which Anita Hill's testimony of sexual harassment went unheeded by an all-male Senate Judiciary Committee. In the fall of 1992 an unprecedented number of women ran for office and won election. But by the mid-1990s the momentum for change appeared to have slowed. Although President Bill Clinton signed the Family and Medical Leave Act into law in 1993, there was continuing concern about the fragility and isolation of American families. Even though the Equal Rights Amendment had been defeated, no-fault divorce had made the family an alliance of individuals. Susan Faludi's book *Backlash* (1991) documented a tide of resistance to feminist gains. In *Fire with Fire* (1993), Naomi Wolf urged feminists to exert their power rather than succumb to claims that they are "special" and thereby consign themselves to victimization and defeat.[1]

To those who might be discouraged at such slow progress, the history of the women's movement since 1920 is a reminder that much has been accomplished that lays a solid foundation for current reform. As Theda Skocpol shows in *Protecting Soldiers and Mothers* (1992), American women's groups, in contrast with the pattern in most European social states, played a key role in launching a broad program of provision for families and children.[2] Temperance groups, women's clubs, and settlement house social workers helped to establish standards and provisions for maternal and child health and worked for mother's pensions.[3] Concurrently, the equal rights stream of American feminism gave rise to the Woman's Party, the League of Women Voters, and modern groups such as the National Organization for Women. Together they pressed for equal rights in employment, education, political office, jury service, and reproductive choice.

To enjoy these gains fully, however, the women's movement of the 1990s has yet to consolidate its support among the mass of American women. The suffragists lifted themselves out of the doldrums with new methods and a broader message to win the wider support necessary for a constitutional amendment.[4] Similarly, today the feminists who have focused on abortion rights and the election of women to public office need to reach out to the cultural right, who believe in traditional family values and who see woman's rights as a threat to women's caregiving.

This chapter raises the question of how contemporary feminists can embrace the traditional family and community concerns of women without compromising the goal of equality. The analysis begins with a review of the dramatic changes that have occurred in women's roles since 1920, then takes up the two major forms of feminist response. The more visible has been equal rights activity focused on women's public roles (work, education, politics). Less apparent, but becoming more important, are change-oriented policies aimed at women's private roles (family and caregiving). This chapter suggests that the coalition strategy behind the suffrage victory should be replicated today. A century ago, equal rights to the vote were legitimated by arguing the importance of women's family and community interests that needed to be represented at the highest levels of government. Today, the analogous argument is that women's equal rights in public life simply *are not possible* without the family and children's policy supports that ensure equality of the sexes in the home.

Women's Changing Roles, 1920–1990

Fueling the resurgence of the modern women's movement of the 1960s and 1970s was a massive change in women's roles that had continued beyond the suffrage watershed of 1920. In the 1830s and 1840s the woman's rights movement was a response to the beginning of industrialization and urbanization. A century later the whole society was on its way to becoming urban. Women's and men's spheres were no longer so distinct. More women entered the workplace and stayed there longer, even as their numbers who married rose to historic highs. Yet the institutional arrangements that would facilitate the crossovers between home and work were not yet in place. The nineteenth-century women's goal of access to the public sphere may have been accomplished. But the goal of equal opportunity for responsibility and authority in the world outside the home—government, the professions, and ordinary jobs—had yet to be realized.

The momentous changes in women's lives created role strain that sparked a new women's movement to address the problem. Modern feminism took root especially among those who felt the tension between their rising education and high aspirations and the traditional expectations of wives, mothers, and community volunteers. In the process of forging an ideology and goals appropriate to the times, a new generation of leaders rediscovered the two main themes of the early feminists—equal rights and continuing responsibility for the welfare of others—but now in the context of women's supposed liberation from the home and from traditional stereotypes.

Combining work and family life.   By 1970, when the new feminism reached full strength, women's lives had changed in three major respects—in education, employment, and family arrangements. Women responded by developing a more complex form of the life course, especially during their middle years, when they combined work and family life and sometimes further education and community service.

Before the turn of the century the majority of females died before reaching adulthood. Others spent much of their life in childbearing. By the 1950s, however, life expectancy for women stood at 73, and women's "child-free" years had increased to between 30 and 40 years, giving them time to pursue further education or a paid job.[5] Along with improved health, a key factor in this demographic transition was a change in sexual behavior and the growth of contraception.

Educational improvements were evident in the increasing proportion of all women finishing high school, college, and graduate degrees. By 1980, one-fifth of 25-year-old women had completed four years of college. Women's share of the college-educated population also increased; in 1980, they were receiving half of all bachelor's degrees. More women also entered traditionally male professions as their medical and law school admissions tripled between 1960 and 1990 (from less than 10 percent to 30 percent).[6] These rising educational levels were linked to increased participation in the labor force. By 1952 more than half of college-educated women aged 45–64 were employed compared with only 39 percent of high school graduates. Between 1960 and 1980, the proportion of women college graduates aged 25–34 in paid work rose from 42 to 75 percent, and with five years of college or more, from 59 to 80 percent.

As family life moved off the farms, the proportion of rural population dropped from 54 percent in 1910 to 41 percent in 1950 and stood at only 27 percent in 1970. Jobs in sales, communications, service, and government (which tended to be more hospitable to women), grew from just over half of all jobs in 1920 to more than three-quarters of all jobs by 1990. Only one-fifth of all women were in the paid labor force in 1900 and 26 percent in 1940. But after World War II women's employment rates soared to 34 percent by 1950, 43 percent in 1970, and 56 percent in 1990. As the security of many men's jobs was threatened by globalization and economic restructuring, a woman's capacity to tide a family over difficult economic times gained even further recognition and legitimacy in the 1980s than during the Great

Depression. A decline in average family income, which set in after 1973, also encouraged women to enter or remain in the labor force to maintain the family's standard of living.[7]

Add to this mix the changing structure of the family. No longer was it so important to have large families with lots of children to do the farm labor or supplement family income. The removal of the family from its productive base at the same time made it more subject to splitting for emotional reasons. The divorce rate rose steadily; by the 1970s an estimated 40 percent of current marriages would end in divorce. Single-parent families and single-person households also increased after 1950. Only 73 percent of all households were made up of families in 1980 (defined as persons related by blood, marriage, or adoption) compared with about 90 percent in 1940. Mothers of even very young children became much more likely to enter or remain in the workforce. In 1970, the labor force participation rate of married women with children under six was 30 percent. By 1988, that rate had almost doubled to 56 percent, and beginning in 1987 even the majority of mothers with infants a year old and under were employed at least part-time or for part of a year. Family day-care homes and child-care centers multiplied to fill a growing need; by 1989 more than 60 percent of infants and more than 80 percent of other preschool children were receiving some care outside their homes.[8]

All these changes led to a reorganization of women's typical life course, especially among the college educated. Women born during the first two decades of the century and early 1920s generally made paid employment an add-on to their homemaking roles. Among these early cohorts, it was fairly unusual for women to combine work and family roles simultaneously. Older women born before 1931 mostly followed a "long interrupted" pattern with time out of the labor force until their youngest child was six or older. Women born during the 1930s and 1940s, however, were a transitional group. Although they grew up expecting to follow the traditional role as homemakers and volunteers, they in fact established a new multiple-role pattern that combined marriage, motherhood, paid work, and sometimes continuing education while they were still in their middle to late 30s. While they usually held expectations that they would follow the older pattern, they in many instances differed from their predecessors by not dropping out of the labor force completely when they married and had children. Whereas earlier cohorts showed a brief dip in labor force participation around age 30, the women born between 1936 and 1945 were the first to show ever higher employment rates from age 20 onward.[9]

By the 1960s, when they were just 29 or 30 years old, a remarkable number of college-educated women were combining motherhood with employment and graduate school. In 1968, the National Opinion Research Center surveyed the college class of 1961 (born 1939). At that time, of the 62 percent who were mothers, about one-third were working or in graduate school or both. My own surveys of 3,000 alumnae from three colleges in 1982 showed comparable results for the class of 1959 (born in 1937). But by the class of 1964 (born 1942) half of the mothers were in the labor force, in school, or both seven years after their graduation (in 1971). A 1981 survey of Bryn Mawr alumnae also found that among women born after 1941, more than two-thirds worked between births of their children or took less than six months out of the labor force for the birth of each child.[10]

Statements by Mills College alumnae who graduated in 1958 and 1960 reveal that only a fifth had scheduled their lives as they had expected. They did conform to the social clock in getting married within a few months of graduation. But more of them were working or were enrolled in graduate education than had been expected, and fewer of them had married or had as many children as they thought they would. Gifted women in the class of 1961 at the University of California at Los Angeles similarly grew up with expectations that they would follow the traditional wife-mother-homemaker role, yet in fact 54 percent had a continuous career path or one with only minor breaks, and 57 percent received advanced degrees. Only two of the 35 who were surveyed in 1990 were full-time homemakers during their prime childbearing years.[11]

Women born during the 1940s had similar expectations that they would adopt a traditional feminine role, but they departed from that expectation in even greater numbers. Although two-thirds of the Radcliffe class of 1964 (born in 1942) had married within two years of graduation, only a quarter were home full-time as mothers. In 1986, at the age of 43, 90 percent had married and 78 percent had had at least one child, yet 72 percent had also pursued a graduate degree and 85 percent were in the labor force. Data from the University of Michigan, Carnegie-Mellon, and Radcliffe classes of the late 1960s tell a similar story. Roughly twice as many had no children fifteen years after graduation as had expected to when they were in college. Less than a fifth had more than two children, compared with more than half who had expected to when they graduated. But on the other hand, twice as many got a Ph.D. or professional degree (28 versus 14 percent) and twice as many experienced some degree of family-career conflict (50 versus 25 percent) as had thought they would when they were college seniors.[12]

In sum, among women born in the 1930s and 1940s, the integration of work and family roles was more than an isolated occurrence. Mary Catherine Bateson, the daughter of Margaret Mead who was born in 1939, expressed the philosophy of this age group in the title of her 1989 book *Composing a Life*. Although married early, Bateson gained a graduate education, had a child, and worked continuously in the academic world throughout her young and middle adulthood. The challenge of her life and that of her age group was to integrate family and career to achieve in both worlds without having to sacrifice one for the other.[13]

The new feminist movement.   Ultimately these changes in women's lives caused considerable strain in the traditional culture of femininity. In response, a new women's movement brought forth two types of feminist groups that developed a more nearly egalitarian ideology of gender roles. The formal branch included the National Organization for Women (NOW), the Women's Equity Action League (WEAL), and the National Women's Political Caucus (NWPC) and worked for changes in legislation and enforcement of equal rights laws, such as the Equal Pay Act of 1963, Title VII of the Civil Rights Act of 1964 banning sex discrimination, and Title IX of the Higher Education Acts of 1969 and 1972, which prohibited sex discrimination in such matters as school sports programs.[14]

The informal branch of the new feminist movement developed small consciousness-raising groups that attacked sexism and discrimination in everyday life. *The Feminine Mystique* (1963) by Betty Friedan became the most famous attack on the traditional division of labor between male and female. Sociologist Alice S. Rossi pressed the feminist critique even further and suggested not only that women be treated equally at work and in the public sphere but that men be expected to perform an equal share of caregiving, parenting, and domestic work in the home.[15]

Where did this new women's movement come from? Earlier chapters of this book have shown that strains in the traditional feminine role gave rise to efforts by leaders to create a social order more in line with their own ideals and experience. Something similar occurred among the women born in the 1920s and 1930s who found their life experience at odds with that of their mothers. They began to envision laws against discrimination, supports for divorced and working mothers, and other changes in the social order that would make their lives better. They then used their energy and vision to mobilize other like-minded women for change.

The leaders of the new feminist movement that surfaced in the 1960s were women like Betty Friedan, generally considered its founder, who was born in 1921. Friedan graduated from Smith College summa cum laude in 1942, married in 1947, and divorced in 1969. Alice Rossi, born in 1922, first married at the age of 19 in 1941, finished college in 1947, divorced and remarried in 1951, earned a Ph.D. in 1957, held a number of minor research positions, and did not become a professor until 1969. Significantly, these women born in the 1920s were members of a transitional age group. Their life patterns were quite unlike those of their age mates, who followed the dictates of the feminine mystique. Truly leaders, they had early come upon the new role patterns that would become more common later. In their 40s in the 1960s, they helped to found NOW and forge an ideology for the rebirth of feminism.[16]

The rank and file of the new women's movement were generally younger, born after 1930, and came of age in the 1950s and 1960s. These younger women who reached 40 in the 1970s had already been living the dual roles that the older women helped to discover. Their paychecks reinforced their sense of independence and their power in the family.[17] Their entry into adulthood and middle life thus fueled the second wave of feminism after 1970. Together the leaders and their younger following breathed new life into the Equal Rights Amendment and helped to implement the new equal rights legislation.

The primary thrust of these new feminists was to extend the rules of equal opportunity to women in the workplace and to mothers in the home. Why should women be kept out of Yale or Princeton because they were women? Why should female teachers receive lower pay than male teachers, or female sales clerks less than their male counterparts? Earlier restrictions against the vote for women had been addressed by changing the laws. But suffrage rules did not cover the marketplace or the family. As all jobs became more differentiated and specialized and less bound to the home, and as women were increasingly having to meet the same demands as men, it became clear that the rules had to change on other issues besides the vote. Women had to be included in all aspects of citizenship—social and economic as well as political. And to effect this change, women had to discover a way of showing that their new cause of "liberation" was an expression of American values, not a negation.

Feminism thus exemplifies a dynamic of specialization and "adaptive upgrading" that sociologist Talcott Parsons found characteristic of modern societies.[18] First, jobs such as that of housewife or paid worker become more "specialized" than their precursors in the farm home or family-owned business and introduce more variety into the types of work that women are expected perform. But then women workers in these new occupations discover that they require more training, autonomy, and pay than had traditionally been considered necessary or appropriate for women. A second process of "upgrading" refers to efforts to increase woman's rights and capacities to meet their new responsibilities. Resulting improvements occur along with a third step of "inclusion" whereby it is recognized that women are just as intelligent, hardworking, and innovative as men and that the same opportunities should be extended to them as to men. Finally, these changes all have to be reconciled with existing cultural beliefs in a process of "value generalization." Thus women struggle with the question of how they can embrace the new opportunities in education and the workplace (by being equal and the *same* as men), yet keep their femininity and identity as wives, mothers, and daughters (by being equal and *different* from men).

This process of generalizing American values to cover the feminist goal of equality has been more successful in the realm of individual rights than of responsibility for others. Maren Carden explains the asymmetry by the distinction between "role equity" and "role change." Role equity is much easier to accomplish because individual rights focus on the similar capacities or obligations of men and women—to get an education, to have children, be self-supporting, and take part in public life.[19] But the issue of responsibility for others has been handled very differently by men and women. Men "care" for their families by supporting them economically through paid work outside the home. Women "care" for their families through child care, cooking, and being present in the home. Thus feminists have usually hit a snag when they work for equality of family responsibility and caregiving because parity would mean that women do less at home and men do more. Yet it is clear that unless women can escape the disproportionate burden of family work that is added to paid work, the feminist enterprise will have only partially succeeded.

Extending Equal Rights

Of the two streams of modern feminism, the individual rights branch has been the stronger. But even it has met with slow progress. In 1961–62, the President's Commission on the Status of Women found that despite a widespread feeling that suffrage had accomplished equal rights, inequality still abounded. Weight-lifting restrictions excluded women from high-paying but physically demanding jobs. In many states, women were not expected to serve on juries. The laws did not prohibit pay discrimination.[20]

The feminist response to these difficulties has gone through three phases and is about to embark on a fourth. The first was a critique of the earlier suffrage movement for not having been broad or radical enough. Then came redoubled efforts to pass new laws and attack discrimination. When the ERA was finally consigned to defeat in 1982, proponents attributed the loss to conservatives who did not want women's roles to change. A new phase is now in the wings that will recast equality as a principle that applies to responsibilities for others as well as rights and privileges for the self. A number of years ago historian Jill Conway astutely observed that there are two general varieties of feminism and that historians have primarily given their attention to the equal rights branch and have ignored the social basis and intellectual justification for opposition to equal rights.[21] Here I review the course of the equal rights stream of feminism since 1920 to appreciate both its accomplishments and the extent to which it has failed.

Critique of the suffrage movement.　After 1920 and before the new feminist movement surfaced in the 1960s, there was a tendency to feel that suffragists had already fought the biggest battles for equality and had won. I myself remember, as a graduate student in sociology at Harvard in the late 1950s, a tendency to think that the suffragists had gotten somehow over-excited about a reform that was so obvious it would have happened anyway. In this climate of opinion, the temperance women were also regarded as over-excited about prohibition; but that reform movement was even more suspect because prohibition was repealed.[22]

As the findings of President Kennedy's Commission on the Status of Women chaired by Eleanor Roosevelt turned up one more uncomfortable inequality after another, and Betty Friedan's book published in 1963 made women begin to realize they weren't so well off after all, the next reaction was to question why there was so much reform still left to do. Into this climate came the historians Kraditor and O'Neill, who laid much of the problem at the feet of the younger generation of suffrage leaders. O'Neill argued that the movement had narrowed its sights on suffrage to the exclusion of all other feminist issues:

[W]ell before 1917, the woman movement, while not altogether bankrupt intellectually, had lost its original verve and openness to new ideas. . . . But what in the long run would be fatal to the movement was . . . its inability to ask fundamental questions about itself. Hard-core feminists, having firmly rejected their own radical origins, were, by the turn of the century, too respectable and too certain that women's rights was a simple political matter. . . . Woman suffrage thus became a substitute for all the things feminists were unwilling to do or consider [such as challenge the structure of marriage and sexual practice]. As their vision narrowed, the emotional weight they invested in the ballot became all the greater, and their need to exaggerate its value all the more urgent. After the 1890s, therefore, ardent feminists became increasingly obsessed with the suffrage question, and to understand the dead end into which this led them we must examine in more detail what they expected from the vote.[23]

Aileen Kraditor suggested that suffragists subordinated the higher ideal of equality and justice to an "expedient" argument that the vote was needed to get other reforms. She discovered two arguments for suffrage.[24] The *natural rights* argument predominated among the earliest suffragists, like Stanton and Anthony. It held that women deserved to vote because of their equal right with men to share in self-government. The *expediency* argument adopted by the WCTU and the later suffragists claimed the vote for women not as an end in itself but as a means to rid the society of vice and corruption and to make it a good place for families, women, and children. By implication, the expediency argument concerned not only women's use of the ballot as a means for social reform but also quelled fears that women would desert the family for the world of public affairs. This argument subordinated the vote as an expression of equal rights to its use as protection of family interests. Thus both Kraditor and O'Neill implied that the lesser good of serving private family life replaced the nobler view of public citizenship and that the suffragists should have held true to their original ideals and been less naive about what the vote could accomplish.

Two other authors, however, rejected the arguments that suffragists lost their way. Historian Ellen DuBois noted that "Nineteenth-century feminists and anti-feminists alike perceived the demand for the vote as the most radical element in women's protest against their oppression and we are obligated to honor the perception of the historical actors in question. . . . [T]he demand for the vote was the most radical program for women's emancipation possible in the nineteenth century."[25]

William Leach in *True Love and Perfect Union* found that even the natural rights proponent Elizabeth Cady Stanton referred to "social problems" as "the more vital questions of this reform." According to Leach, "It was in the realm of civil society, the area of political struggle that we ordinarily think of as private, that feminists sought, and in some degree captured, power. It was in this sphere that they established the strongest alliance with other reformist intellectuals of their own class. In this sphere they attacked the possessive individualism embedded within the democratic liberal tradition."[26]

Viewed in this positive light, the 1920 suffrage victory was instrumental in eventually winning a larger feminist end—representation of female interests in the public sphere—what Stanton seems to have said was the primary goal of the suffrage struggle. Thus the "natural rights" (justice) arguments of Stanton and Anthony for seeking entry into and self-governing membership in the polity were inherently no more radical or more appropriate than the use of the vote for social reform.[27] While the justice argument focused on solidarity of all women and identified their condition with that of all men, the social reform arguments distinguished women's interests from men's. These use-oriented appeals for the vote as a means to social reform could be understood as conservative, because they sounded a bit like the conservatives' old arguments for men's and women's separate "spheres." In fact, however, the suffrage movement was changing the definition of sex roles by the very process of showing that values of equality could apply to women as well as men.[28] The so-called expediency argument was actually raising claims about male and female difference to a broader level of society, the political world, where participation by women in public affairs did not threaten the family or ignore social problems but gave them new importance.

Kraditor recognized that bureaucracy, industrialism, and greater complexity in government and society were in part responsible for the shift toward expediency: "In a day when government was allegedly becoming more and more housekeeping on a large scale, women's demand for the vote could and did change from a claim based on abstract principle to a very practical demand to participate in governmental activities that had theretofore been considered the special province of women both in their separate homes and in their volunteer aid societies."[29]

Kraditor mentions a favorite suffrage metaphor in which the doctor (male voters) is permitted to treat the causes of disease and the nurse (disenfranchised women) can only patch and bandage after damage is done. She concludes that "The suffragists were not simply overestimating the power of women; they were overestimating the power of the vote to cure the ills of society."[30] I think one could as well interpret this metaphor to mean that those who have access to control of the state (the doctor or voters) can influence the structure of society and prevent some of its ills. The vote, for the suffragists, meant more than just a literal casting of the ballot. The franchise was instead symbolic of all the power inherent in citizenship and self-government, and these rights transcended the constraining boundaries of women's separate sphere (that of the nurse or the disenfranchised).

Because the vote was regarded by some as primarily a tool, many observers looked for some observable effects after 1920. The chroniclers found almost none in the candidates elected or the legislation passed. In fact, during the 1920s about half as many women as men even voted at all.[31] Degler concluded that "though the suffrage cause in the nineteenth century became increasingly central to the feminist cause, suffrage, once achieved, had almost no observable effect upon the position of women."[32]

Equal rights after 1920.   What then was the accomplishment of the equal rights feminists? Descendants of the suffragists, such as the League of Women Voters, worked to obliterate sex distinctions by making possible women's political representation and by focusing on equality rather than difference between the sexes.[33] American women's attainment of suffrage in 1920 brought them to the threshold of political equality with men. What had yet to be accomplished was the full exercise of their civil rights through informed voting, readiness to stand for office, and the shaping of legislation and policy. In 1920 there was immense enthusiasm for women's involvement in this whole range of activity. Then disappointment set in at women's low voting turnout and slow entry into politics.[34] Now, after three-quarters of a century, it is possible to see that women at first had to undergo a socialization process to become involved. As they did so their voting turnout increased; they gained delegates to the Republican and Democratic National Conventions; their numbers in elective office also grew; and they learned better how to act as a pressure group to promote their own interests.

Turnout among women voting after the suffrage victory was smaller than had been expected or hoped, but steadily rose. The proportion gradually increased from as low as 18 percent in Louisiana in 1920 to more than 40 percent in some of the eastern and New England states by 1930 and to 48 percent in Vermont and Chicago by 1940. By the 1980 elections, the Bureau of the Census estimated that 59 percent of each sex voted.[35] Professional working women over age 30 were the most likely to vote. By 1985, when the difference in men's and women's voting turnout had diminished to zero, experts predicted that women's continued employment would eventually result in a higher percentage of women voting than of men. This actually occurred in the 1992 presidential election, with 62.3 percent of females reporting they had voted as compared with 60.2 percent of males.[36]

Party membership and activity revealed a notable increase in women's representation at the national Republican and Democratic conventions. Although the Republican party was historically more supportive of the ERA, women's representation among convention delegates was noticeably higher among the Democrats. Between 1920 and 1932 women delegates to the Republican National Convention rose from 27 to 87, while for the Democrats the increase was from 93 to 208. In 1980 the Democratic National Convention made history with equal numbers of women and men as delegates.[37]

Women's elections to public office grew remarkably. In 1921, some 37 women held seats in state legislatures compared with 146 a decade later. The numbers elected to local office were even more striking, doubling or tripling over the decade in states such as Connecticut (to 178), Michigan (to 590), Minnesota (to 245), and Wisconsin (to 158). The number of women in state legislatures nationwide (a total of 29 in 1920, 610 in 1975) has always been higher than representation in Congress, which was zero in 1920 and only 19 by 1975.[38] The rise of women in political office paralleled a growing willingness on the part of the electorate to vote for a woman as president. When asked, "If your party nominated a woman for President, would you vote for her if she seemed qualified for the job?" only 55 percent of men and women said yes in 1958 compared with 78 percent by 1979.[39] Between 1971 and 1992, the proportion of women in Congress doubled (from 3 to 10 percent); their representation in state legislatures more than tripled (from 5 to 18 percent); and the number of women mayors multiplied from 1 percent in 1971 to almost 10 percent in 1985. The first woman governor to run in her own right was Ella Grasso in Connecticut in 1975. In 1994 there were four women governors in office: Joan Finney (Kansas), Barbara Roberts (Oregon), Ann Richards (Texas), and Christine Todd Whitman (New Jersey).[40] This marked and steady increase is attributable to such factors as higher general involvement by women and more women running for local boards and state legislatures who can then realistically run for higher office.[41]

Accompanying women's growing political involvement was the emergence of a new women's movement in the late 1960s that helped to transform equal rights feminism into a classical political interest group. Sociologists Ferree and Hess note that a social movement succeeds when it becomes transformed into an interest group that participates in the regular political process.[42] By 1973, the National Organization for Women, the Women's Equity Action League, and the National Women's Political Caucus all had Washington offices. They built alliances with such established mainstream groups as the Business and Professional Women, the League of Women Voters, the American Association of University Women, the National Council of Jewish Women, and United Methodist Women. The new organizations learned from the old the art of lobbying and together they formed a coalition to win a number of feminist causes during the 1970s: a minimum wage for domestic workers, educational equity, access to credit, admission to military academies, job protection for pregnant workers, and funds for observance of International Women's Year. Membership of NOW grew impressively from 1,122 members in 14 chapters in 1967 to 220,000 members in more than 700 chapters in 1982. By 1985 the combined membership of five new feminist groups with headquarters in Washington was 350,000 and the older feminist organizations of the League of Women Voters and Business and Professional Women together counted more than 2.5 million members.[43]

Political effects of women's increasing political activity have been seen in a voting pattern known as the gender gap. Ever since a 1977 study by the Rutgers Center on Women and Politics, it had been known that regardless of liberal or conservative identification, women legislators of both parties took more feminist positions on issues such as abortion, the ERA, child care, and Social Security for homemakers than their male counterparts.[44] With the presidential election of 1980 and the congressional elections of 1982, it became evident that the male and female electorate also voted differently. A higher proportion of women voted Democratic than men; women were 8 percent more likely to vote for Jimmy Carter than Ronald Reagan and to support detente and to oppose defense spending. By the time of the 1988 election between George Bush and Michael Dukakis, the Republicans exploited the gender gap to their advantage. The Bush campaign deliberately emphasized the dangers of rape and crime going unpunished and played to women's compassion and interest in child care and families with an emphasis on a "kinder, gentler nation." Dukakis's defeat in the polls between August and November was largely due to a loss of 10 percent from the original 17 or 18 percent advantage that he had among women voters earlier in his campaign.[45]

Rise and fall of the ERA.   Besides encouraging women to hold office and vote their interests, the new feminist movement further institutionalized the gains of the suffrage movement by reshaping sex-role ideology.[46] Nancy Cott has pinpointed the distinctive ideology of equal rights feminists: "The more that science, religion, or politics baroquely specified how women still did differ from men, the more that women leaders, with few exceptions, emphasized equality of opportunity and 'disregard' of sex."[47] As a result, Cott argues, the debate over what was truly in the interests of women was new. Equal rights feminists could take credit not only for framing the terms of this debate but winning a growing segment of public opinion to their cause. Their accomplishment appears in changing attitudes about women's roles and in changing public policies concerning discrimination in the workplace and reproductive freedom. Support grew for the Equal Rights Amendment that had first been proposed by the Woman's Party in 1923, but at the same time equal rights were rejected by a significant proportion of the population.

Perhaps because the second wave of feminism accompanied a dramatic contemporary change in women's roles, the public showed a growing willingness to endorse the aims of the women's liberation movement. Between 1972 and 1976, all groups' feelings toward the women's movement grew considerably warmer. Among men, there was a gain of 6 points (from 47 to 53) on a "feeling thermometer" developed at the University of Michigan and used on systematic panel surveys. Among employed women, there was a gain of 7 points (from 48 to 55); and the greatest gain, 11 points, was among housewives (from 39 to 50).[48] A 1989 New York Times–CBS poll found that 68 percent of men and 75 percent of women thought the women's movement had made both work and personal relationships between women and men "more honest and open" than three decades earlier. The overwhelming majority of women were supportive of a women's movement (85 percent of African-American, 76 percent of Hispanic, and 64 percent of white women).[49]

In addition, there was a growing belief that women should have equal opportunity in the workplace and that men should help in the home. All parts of the population moved toward more egalitarian attitudes. An overwhelming 98 percent of a national sample of the high school class of 1980, when polled in 1986, said that women should have exactly the same educational opportunities as men and that women should be considered for executive jobs as seriously as men. Moreover, a surprising majority (73 percent of men and 82 percent of women) agreed with the statement that "a working mother of preschool children can be just as good a mother as a woman who does not work." But mothers and fathers disagreed on how much fathers actually helped with child care; 51 percent of the men but only 24 percent of the women thought that fathers helped equally.[50]

After 1960 women scored a number of legislative victories against discrimination in the workplace. But these gains were preceded by several decades of internal division among feminists over the issue of protective labor laws. The National Woman's Party proposed the Equal Rights Amendment in 1923 and thereafter opposed any form of protective legislation (special hours for women, exclusion from dangerous jobs, etc). Mainstream social feminists, however, represented by the League of Women Voters, the Consumers' League, trade union women, and the Women's Bureau were in favor of protection. When the U.S. Supreme Court in *Adkins v. Children's Hospital* declared the minimum wage unconstitutional, the Woman's Party, to the horror of all the social feminists, hailed the decision as "a great triumph for equal rights."[51] Many of the resources of the Women's Bureau during the next few years went to collection of data from 11 states and more than 1,500 factories to demonstrate that protective legislation raised labor standards not only for women but men.

Until the 1950s the overwhelming norm was that married women did not and should not work. Poll data from the 1930s reveal that 80 percent of the public thought a wife should not work if she had a husband to support her.[52] Work discrimination was taken for granted and was embodied in such legislation as Section 213 of the National Economy Act of 1932, which until 1937 prohibited more than one member of a family (typically the wife) from being employed by the civil service at any one time.[53] Demobilization of wartime women workers proceeded without protest, and young women coming of age in the 1950s were caught up in the "feminine mystique."

Yet sentiment simultaneously grew in favor of equal rights for women. Support for the ERA increased among the Business and Professional Women from the 1930s on. The labor force participation of married employed women more than doubled from over 20 percent in 1950 to over 40 percent in 1970. The President's Commission on the Status of Women, established in 1961, and numerous subsequent state commissions discovered a wide range of women's civil and legal disabilities—not only the protective labor laws that kept women out of selected well-paid jobs but also exclusion from jury service and inequities in marital rights and property. After the passage of the Equal Pay Act of 1963 and Title VII of the Civil Rights Act of 1964, which prohibited sex discrimination, various protective labor laws and occupational qualifications not directly required by the job (such as weight lifting in the case of *Weeks v. Southern Bell*) were struck down or called into question. Sentiment shifted in favor of the Equal Rights Amendment, which by 1972 had the approval of 34 out of the 38 states required for ratification. A spate of equal rights laws followed over the next decade: the Educational Amendments of 1972, the Equal Credit Opportunity Act of 1974, the Pregnancy Disability Act of 1978, and the Retirement Equity Act of 1984.[54] In matters of work it was clear that most Americans had come to believe in equal rights for women and men.

Protection of equal rights in women's reproductive and family roles was more difficult. Women's capacity for pregnancy and childbirth was incontrovertible evidence of sex difference, so how could equal rights be claimed? Only if birth control and parenthood for women and men were similar in the balance of individual control and state interest. Equal rights feminists held that women should have the right to

March for the Equal Rights Amendment, Fifth Avenue, New York City, 26 August 1970, the fiftieth anniversary of the suffrage amendment. Bettye-Lane Studio.

control their bodies just as do men. This ideology evolved through Margaret Sanger's valiant attempts to publicize and legalize contraception—a mission that gradually gained more acceptance during the Depression because of the economic need to control family size and that culminated with the establishment of Planned Parenthood in 1942.[55]

During the 1960s, with pressure from NOW and with the tragic birth defects resulting from the use of thalidomide and from the contraction of German measles during pregnancy, the policy frontier moved from the right of contraception to the right of abortion. In January 1973, in *Roe v. Wade,* the U.S. Supreme Court declared a woman's right to choose abortion during the first 12 weeks of pregnancy as protected by the constitutional right of privacy under the Fourteenth Amendment. Since that historic decision, right-to-life groups have sought to overturn the decision on the grounds that human life begins at conception and that a woman in choosing abortion is wantonly taking the life of her unborn infant. In 1983 funding was denied for abortion under Medicaid. In the early 1990s feminists expressed great consternation about the new appointments to the Supreme Court that might reverse the right to choose abortion. A number of efforts have been made to limit the grounds for abortion (to rape, incest, etc.) or the number of weeks into pregnancy during which an abortion can be performed. As of 1987, the comparative legal scholar Mary Ann Glendon concluded that "Today, abortion is subject to less regulation in the United States than in any other country in the Western world."[56] Ironically, however, in women's broader reproductive roles as family members caring for children, or daughters caring for frail elders, they were likely to feel that they had been left all too much to fend for themselves, when greater outside support of the kind found in other Western societies would be to their own and their families' advantage.[57]

It is instructive to examine why the ERA met with defeat. There was an initial euphoria in 1972 when ratification by the required three-fourths of the states appeared quick and sure. A campaign by the supporters seemed unnecessary, as did a concerted strategy to win unratified states. But as early as 1973, with the growth of Phyllis Schlafly's campaign to STOP ERA and the consequent slowing of the ratification process, passage was in trouble.

Deeper than these issues of political organization and strategy, however, were the substantive questions about the amendment itself.

Was it really needed? What would be its unintended and long-term effects?

From the vantage of hindsight it now appears that the Equal Rights Amendment did not sufficiently account for the consequences of equality in a society that was deeply gendered in its private life. The amendment aroused fears that it would undercut the informal and implicit safeguards by which traditional families were supposed to protect women against economic and sexual vulnerability. The famous symbolic issues used by STOP ERA to mobilize opponents were the threat of integrated public rest rooms, lack of women's legal recourse in case of rape, compulsory military service (which might take mothers from their children), and loss of economic support after a divorce.[58] Even though 63 percent of the American people at one point supported the ERA, and this support actually grew during the early 1980s before the deadline ran out, the amendment went down to defeat because the opposition had been so successful in raising fears among those few states yet needed to ratify.

There are two major lessons in this defeat, one about social movements, the other about feminism. The first lesson is that focus on change at the system level without adequate attention to its implementation in subsystems will result in social "short-circuiting," which like its electrical analog sends more uncontrolled energy through the system than it can handle. Social movements, particularly at the outset, develop general ideologies or blueprints for change but do not spell out the day-to-day mechanisms that actually institutionalize the reforms they seek.[59] Thus, the ERA won support for its ideology of equal rights for women. But its failure to specify what equal rights would entail in private life allowed fantastic images to be conjured up of all the change it *might* produce, even changes that were not intended and were quite unlikely.

The second lesson of the ERA is that feminist theory and ideology must address questions of sex difference along with gender equality. Otherwise they will not be believed. A number of contemporary observers (Degler, Elshtain, Hewlett, and others) have noted that many equal rights advocates seemed to think of women as men and so skipped the problem of the family.[60] But the family cannot be skipped, because one of the main reasons women lack equal education, employment, and pay is that they have unequal (and greater) responsibilities for families and children. The ERA did not address the question of the deeply gendered and unequal division of labor in the family, in part because family arrangements are more the result of tradition, socialization, and informal arrangements than of domestic or civil law. The conclusion of the doubtful voters—and legislators in the unratified states—was that the amendment could not be trusted.[61]

As the new women's movement became more familiar and accepted during the 1970s, the nature of feminist struggle subtly changed from contention over ideology to engagement in the political mainstream. While feminist organizations became in some ways less visible, their message began to permeate many groups and institutions. According to sociologist Carol Mueller, "Women's causes and women's language for talking about their concerns are now closer to the mainstream of electoral politics than ever before."[62] What has gradually emerged is a local, state, and national policy network made up of various feminist organizations such as NOW, NWPC, and the Congressional Women's Caucus. Together these organizations have tried to implement equal rights policies at the grass roots by working with state and municipal governments. In 1985, a Council of Presidents brought together the heads of 17 member groups. The council now represents more than 40 women's groups and 10 million members and periodically produces a consensual multi-issue platform known as the Women's Agenda.[63]

Several observers believe that the future of the feminist movement now rests at the state and local level.[64] A policy network based on grass roots participation is sufficiently complex and locally based so that it is more resistant to opposition than if it stems from a national, top-down policy.[65] In 1990 there were 36 active State Commissions on the Status of Women (SCSWs) and more than 200 local women's policy networks made up of municipal and county organizations (where women now hold 16 percent of the positions available). By 1987, 16 states had enacted their own ERAs. States have often been the leaders in efforts to reform marriage and divorce laws, to gain fairer laws governing sexual assault, and to aid displaced homemakers. In the face of federal cutbacks, states and localities have continued to support work on domestic violence, maternal and child health projects, affirmative action, and comparable worth.[66]

Another possibility for the future is that social concerns will begin to gain precedence over individual rights. A NOW survey in the summer of 1991 asked its members to rank 15 issues in order of priority for the 1992 elections. The content of the items is revealing: seven concerned health, reproduction, and family issues; six involved equal rights, such as affirmative action and pension security; only one focused on political action (forming a new feminist party); and one on violence against women.[67] The trend is in keeping with a new emphasis in feminism on *rights in relationship,* an awareness that equality of the individual woman can be realized only in the context of larger institutional structures that support and encourage the development and autonomy of the person. The new relational language for addressing women's equality suggests a coming convergence between the two streams of feminism.

Feminist Caregiving

To some, "feminist caregiving" would seem a contradiction in terms, because feminism connotes women who are looking out for themselves whereas caregiving means looking out for others. I have intentionally created this juxtaposition to highlight the most pressing issue of the modern women's movement. For most of this century feminist consciousness has been associated with woman's rights. Equality and caregiving have been construed as opposites. Now the challenge is to break apart this simple dichotomy and replace it with a more comprehensive understanding of feminism. The key to the new understanding is a recognition that working women who are not confined to the traditional homemaker role are still interested in and capable of concern for families, children, aging parents, neighborhood, and community.

In this discussion of feminist caregiving, I first recount the tension between equal rights and social feminists over protective legislation and then show the actual contributions of women to the formation of the welfare state. Recent developments in family policy, which have emerged since 1970, carry forward the maternalistic or domestic side of feminism. At the same time a new school of feminist thought has begun to reframe the old opposition between rights and care. The synthesis now emerging sees the rights of the individual and the needs of the society as inextricably intertwined.

Equal rights versus protective legislation for women.   Winifred Wandersee, in summing up the history of the women's movement between the wars, concluded that feminism during that period had failed "because it did not recognize the most essential characteristic of the great majority of American women, their commitment to a traditional pattern of family life."[68] In a similar vein, Jill Conway, after an extensive historical review of the many strands of American feminism, concluded that the social basis and justification for opposition to equal rights was not well understood, largely because women's special expertise and authority in the home and community were not fully appreciated by those feminists who were focused on equality in the public sphere.[69]

Looking back on the accomplishments of the Progressive Era, it is clear that feminists were divided over whether women should receive special consideration or protection in their jobs because they were women. The Woman's Party and other equal rights supporters were at odds with social feminists in the Women's Bureau, the Children's Bureau, and the mainstream women's organizations such as the League of Women Voters or the General Federation of Women's Clubs. Both of these mainstream groups favored protective labor legislation that would bar women from working nights and from working more than 9 hours a day or 54 hours a week. In 1908, Louis Dembitz Brandeis in his brief for *Muller v. Oregon* argued that women should be protected from long hours and unhealthy workplace conditions. The focus of that era was on the mother, and the Sheppard-Towner Act of 1921 institutionalized concern for both maternal and child health in local provisions for pre- and postnatal care, federal aid for medical help, hospital care, and visiting nurses.[70] Women's rights as workers were submerged in an overwhelming concern for child health.[71]

But from the standpoint of the equal rights feminists, efforts to "protect" working women threatened to perpetuate old inequalities with men. In addition, women's expression of maternal concerns for needy families and children appeared retrograde to those emancipated women who no longer took motherhood and family life as their principal source of identity.[72]

This greater emphasis on equal rights obscured the alternative tradition that focused on family and community, even though an important use of the woman's vote was on behalf of women's and children's interests. Ellen DuBois described woman suffrage as radical just because "it bypassed women's oppression in the family, or private sphere, and demanded instead her admission to citizenship, and through it admission to the public arena."[73] According to William Leach, suffragists' interests were from the very beginning social, not political: "They directed their political attention to schools, asylums, libraries, hospitals, and prisons, to the professions and to the home. They did not employ the language of power, faction, or conflict, nor did they make significant use of political parties or attempt to create a new genuine political alternative to the established party system. In these terms, suffrage . . . was above all a 'social question.'"[74]

Do women's interests in social welfare really qualify as feminist? Nancy Cott explains that "feminism" was a new term that entered the language only after 1910 and came to signify not just one movement but several, and among these was a notion of equality applied to women even though they were different. "Feminism," according to Cott, "asks for sex equality that includes sexual difference." Thus the advent of feminism "marked the end of the *woman* movement," which assumed that all women had the same interests, as expressed in the collective *woman,* and created a diverse agenda for many *women* that embraces feminist caregiving as well as equal rights.[75]

Elaboration of the welfare state.   Because there was division among feminists, women's contributions to social welfare have until recently been ignored or underrated.[76] New scholarship, however, has begun to recover the accomplishments of the suffragists that were related to family support and social welfare. Historians Kathryn Kish Sklar and Anne Firor Scott found that the same women's volunteer organizations that sponsored the suffrage campaign also lobbied for mothers' pensions, improved maternal and child health measures, and reform of municipal government. Women appealed in a number of states for subsidies to widowed mothers and establishment of visiting nurses and well-baby clinics.[77] Now in place of the earlier critique a remarkable new claim is being made: it was precisely these volunteer women, temperance, suffragist, and club women who were "present at the birth of the welfare state".[78]

By the 1950s and 1960s young women like me who had become the supporters of a new feminism had "forgotten" or never really learned what enormous contributions the social and maternal feminists had made to American social reform. To us the temperance and club women represented an outmoded gentility that seemed at odds with careers and achievements we admired. Yet as early as the 1970s, David Gil had resurrected the record of mother's pensions. A decade later, Anne Firor Scott had begun *Natural Allies* to document the contributions of women to volunteer groups all over the nation. Kathryn Kish Sklar was reconstructing Florence Kelley's contribution to settlement houses and the Children's Bureau as well as to the women's trade union movement. Finally, Theda Skocpol was unearthing the long-forgotten contributions of women's organizations to welfare for widowed mothers, immunizations for children, the growth of the Children's Bureau, and, ultimately, the shaping of the U.S. Social Security system.[79] The swing of the pendulum from an almost exclusive preoccupation with equal rights was bringing feminism back to a concern with social welfare and the needs of the community.

After 1920 the "domestic" or "social" stream of feminism fed into the elaboration of government-sponsored social programs. Before 1910 temperance women, settlement house workers, and working women were those principally devoted to keeping social questions at the forefront of feminism. But after 1910 many suffragists also took the part of the less fortunate.[80] Between 1920 and 1960, as a result of war and depression, social welfare issues found an increasingly important place in the national consciousness along with traditional governmental concerns such as defense, natural resources, the economy, and the budget.

Did the granting of woman suffrage have anything to do with this enlargement of the state? The temperance and suffrage movements first socialized women to the role of citizens, then they actively helped to shape social policy. Even before suffrage was finally achieved, the various elements of the woman's movement were active in support of new measures to promote social welfare. For example, the Children's Bureau, founded in 1912 but sparsely funded, relied on a whole network of voluntarism to advance its programs. Local women's clubs and chapters of the National Congress of Mothers distributed leaflets and publicized its services. Thousands of personal letters poured into the bureau from all over the country requesting copies of *Infant Care* or seeking advice on everything from infant formula to birth control.[81]

Passage of the Sheppard-Towner Maternity and Infancy Protection Act in 1921 was largely due to the development of a vast network of women who had earlier been mobilized by the Children's Bureau in its baby-saving campaign. By 1918, there were 11 million women who served on 17,000 committees as part of the drive to lower infant mortality. After Sheppard-Towner was enacted, many of the same volunteer organizations helped to implement it. The Mothers and Parent-Teacher Associations were involved in 42 states and the women's clubs in 30; also involved were the League of Women Voters, Daughters of the American Revolution, State Federation of Colored

Women's Clubs, and the American Legion auxiliaries. As a result of this vast grass roots effort, infant mortality rates actually dropped sharply, from 76 per 1,000 live births to 69 per 1,000 births in a matter of just three years.[82]

After 1920, there developed a number of broad state coalitions of women and a wide range of activities in state government. Rather than perpetuating lady bountiful philanthropy, these women were learning how to use the instruments of government on behalf of the interests of women and children. In Texas the "petticoat lobby" succeeded in its appeal to the 1923 Texas state legislature to establish a prison survey and plan for reform, to accept the Sheppard-Towner Maternity and Infancy Protection Act, to institute an educational survey, to pass two prohibition bills, and to make a special appropriation for the public schools.[83] In New Jersey, the League of Women Voters joined with an impressive coalition of mainstream women's organizations—the General Federation of Women's Clubs (with 26,000 members), the Consumers' League, two peace organizations, the WCTU, and others to advance women's political and legal status (by jury service, political office, or active membership in political parties). They also worked for protective labor legislation to shorten women's legal work day from ten to nine hours, ban women's night work in manufacturing, laundries, bakeries, and sales work, and prohibit children's work in agriculture during the school year.[84]

At the national level, a similar pattern evolved. A broad coalition of 10 women's groups under the aegis of the Women's Joint Congressional Committee combined to push for social reform legislation. By 1925 they could claim an impressive array of successes: the Sheppard-Towner Maternity and Infancy Protection Act of 1921, the Packers and Stockyard Act of 1921, the Cable Act of 1922 according married women independent citizenship, the Lehlbach Act of 1923 upgrading the Civil Service merit system, the Child Labor Amendment to the Constitution of 1924, and the Federal Prison for Women Act of 1924. The organizations behind the coalition represented 10 million women and included the National League of Women Voters, the General Federation of Women's Clubs, the National Council of Jewish Women, the WCTU, the National Trade Union League, the National Consumers' League, the National Congress of Mothers and Parent-Teacher Associations, the Association of Collegiate Alumnae, the American Home Economics Association, and the National Federation of Business and Professional Women's Clubs.

Such widespread support from so many quarters showed that the citizen role for women was in fact becoming institutionalized.[85]

Even among the WCTU, which like the women's clubs, might well be thought distinctly less political than the League of Women Voters, there was similar commitment to social reform and legislative involvement. The 1924 Jubilee Convention was not a requiem at all for the end of an era but a celebration of prohibition. The convention also noted other accomplishments: the drafting of the child labor amendment, the founding of the Committee on the Causes and Cure of War, appropriations for the Women's Bureau and Children's Bureau, the Sheppard-Towner Act, and the organization of a new WCTU department of women and industry. In short, temperance women's activities were much like that of the League of Women Voters or the General Federation of Women's Clubs in supporting broad social policies in the interest of social welfare.[86]

Before 1915 the suffragists stood for the equal rights branch of the women's movement whereas temperance and the women's clubs were mostly social feminists. By the 1920s these old boundaries had shifted and the vast majority of the League of Women Voters and the coalitions of other women's organizations were working to bring women's voice into the public sphere. A statement of the New Jersey League expressed this sentiment: "Most women care more about babies and homes and happy human conditions than do most men." They were therefore "willing to work with other women to help improve conditions."[87]

Two of the "conditions" that feminists then addressed—as they do now—were the needs of mothers and children. By and large the protective stance of the social feminists persisted through the 1950s. Since that time, however, such remarkable changes have occurred in women's lives that mainstream women's organizations have modified their emphasis. Rather than focus on home and family concerns in the manner of the old-fashioned "woman's sphere," they are now more likely to touch on matters of concern to both sexes, such as parenting and working, and on issues that cross boundaries of class, race, and family type.

Emergence of family policy.   When modern feminists first became interested in how to extend justice and equal rights to caregiving and the family, they encountered ignorance and what seemed like lack of interest. Economist and former Barnard professor Sylvia Ann

Hewlett has described her search for new ideas on child care and parental leave among feminist leaders and female candidates. When she attended a NOW meeting with 1984 Democratic vice presidential nominee Geraldine Ferraro as the featured speaker, she found detailed positions on abortion rights and antidiscrimination but virtually nothing on matters of family concern.[88]

Gradually over the ensuing decade, however, women and men trying to combine work and family life began to develop an agenda for public policy that would address their issues. The changes in their actual lives—more two-parent families with mother and father in the labor force and young children to care for, and more single-mother families with children—had outrun available institutional support. They sought more affordable preschool and after-school care, as well as flexible hours and parental leaves for working parents. At present "family policy" appears to be the most concrete mechanism available for implementing justice in the family. Only by means of such practical policies as more flexible working hours for parents, more widely available child care, and greater societal investment in children does it seem possible to extend equality into the private and gendered sphere of the home.[89] The two best understood items on this emerging family policy agenda have been parental leave and child care, and the key breakthrough in both has been a shift from treating these problems as *women's* problems to treating them as *parents'* problems. With the Clinton presidency, two other family policy issues have emerged— how to treat welfare mothers and nontraditional families. On these there is less consensus and as yet no clear "feminist" position.

Parental leave. The concept of protective legislation for women and children has today been replaced by the concept of parental leave. A major breakthrough in protectionist thinking occurred with the Pregnancy Disability Act of 1978, which treated pregnancy as a medical disability in no way different from men's need to take time away from work if they were sick or disabled. The focus shifted to the job-related aspects of pregnancy and helped women mobilize the benefits and schedule of the workplace for a distinctly female physical condition. According to political scientist Margaret Stetson, the act became the first U.S. national policy on employment and motherhood. "The triumph of the feminists in the 1970s was to find a way to relate pregnancy and childbirth to something that happened to men—namely, job-related disability."[90]

In the 1980s working mothers began to propose maternity and parental leave as the best way to handle conflicting claims of work and family. These ideas of reconciling "women's two roles, at home and at work, without sacrificing one or the other,"[91] had first been put forward in Klein and Myrdal's 1956 book *Women's Two Roles* and had been revived with Betty Friedan's *The Second Stage* (1981). Conflict between work and family was becoming less of a woman's issue and more of a family or labor policy issue. Montana's promising Maternity Leave Act and the 1987 Cal Fed case (*California Federal Savings and Loan v. Guerra*) allowed pregnancy to be taken into account and women as well as men to have families without losing their jobs. The new Family and Medical Leave Act, which passed Congress in 1990 but was vetoed by President Bush (before being passed in the Clinton administration in 1993), also brought many kinds of feminists together to accommodate women's two roles by recognizing two roles for men as well.[92]

Child care. Feminist involvement with child-care policy took a course similar to that of parental leave. It began with protection. From the 1880s through the 1920s, day nurseries were philanthropic efforts set up in conjunction with the settlement houses and the schools to supervise young children who would otherwise have been left alone while their mothers worked. The fee was as low as 5 cents a day. But conditions were usually crowded, and only about 25 percent of those enrolled were present on any given day.[93]

Between the wars publicly funded day care had two brief spurts of development. During the Depression, for the first time government-funded day-care centers were available to working mothers and were administered by the WPA. They were generally located in basements of public schools and employed women teachers who had been let go by the school boards. During World War II, beginning in February 1944, government-sponsored day care was again made available to support the war effort by caring for young children of mothers employed in the war industries. Even with 66,000 places available, however, capacity was thought to be only 10 percent of the need. These centers were quickly dismantled after the war, and their use was discredited even when a mother had to work. A mother's work was still primarily attributed to her desire for a career rather than the necessity of supporting a family.[94]

"Women Demand Day Care," a feminist plea for public support for families and caregiving. Bettye-Lane Studio.

In the late 1960s, however, the United States began to develop a fragmentary child-care system. The establishment of Head Start centers in 1965 coincided with the dramatic rise in mothers' labor force participation. The National Council of Jewish Women documented the scandalous conditions in unlicensed facilities.[95] A children's lobby made up of child development experts, feminists, and minority groups proposed the Comprehensive Child Development Act, which was passed by Congress in 1971 and vetoed by President Nixon; efforts to revive it in 1975 and 1979 failed. Because much of their effort was going into campaigns for the ERA and reproductive rights, feminists' support during this period was rather simple and mainly rhetorical: that universal child care should be available to help liberate women.[96]

But by the late 1980s there was a new consensus shared by feminists and the New Right that laid the foundation for support of A Better Child Care Act (ABC), which was passed in 1990. In Houston in 1977 at the convention for International Women's Year, there had been a softening of the New Right position on child care. In 1980 pro-family forces at the White House Conference on Families did not oppose a resolution to support the importance of child care as an aid to working parents.[97] The work incentive, or WIN, program and Title XX of the Social Security Amendments had provided federal funding for day care of welfare mothers and linked it with "workfare" to get mothers off welfare.[98] In the meantime, the number of mothers of young children in the work force rose steadily, so that by 1987 half the mothers of infants under a year old were employed at least part-time. Actual availability and use of child care was changing. In 1964, one-quarter of all three-to-five-year-old children were in nursery school or kindergarten, compared with 45 percent just 10 years later.[99] Child-care places had grown from less than 200,000 in 1960 to a million by 1974.[100] By 1984–85, less than a third of children between the ages of one and two were being cared for in their own homes, compared with 42 percent in another home and 17 percent in an organized child-care facility.[101]

Thus the child-care question, like protective legislation and parental leave, has reached acceptance in national public policy. Social feminists thought primarily of what kind of child care was good for children. Equal rights feminists tended to focus on how child care would help working women. Public support of child care became legitimate when it was seen as necessary not only to poor children but most children and not only to working women who were once in the minority but to working parents.

Welfare mothers. While middle-class career women have pressed for child care and parental leave, another population of nonworking mothers receives Aid to Families of Dependent Children (AFDC). The majority of voters in both political parties is interested in getting these women off welfare and into positions where they can support themselves. The overall goal, in the words of President Clinton, is "to end welfare as we know it."

The Family Support Act of 1988 calls for a combination of training and child care to help welfare mothers go to work. Cultural conservatives have called for measures such as aggressive media campaigns comparable to antismoking to prevent out-of-wedlock pregnancy and tougher divorce laws to prevent family breakups. Others, like Mary Jo Bane and David Ellwood, would set up a more varied menu of policy alternatives to help the unemployed and working poor—programs ranging from raising the minimum wage to providing job training, child care, and public service employment for those who cannot find work otherwise.[102]

Up to now feminists have generally ignored the welfare problem, but recently a few local NOW chapter meetings have begun to discuss the question with an eye toward helping other, less fortunate women.[103] Feminist scholars have also begun to study the question. Economist Hilda Kahne asks whether greater availability of part-time work could serve the double purpose of helping welfare mothers to care for children while at the same time providing valuable on-the-job training. Policy analyst Sherry Wexler contrasts the Family Support Act of 1988 with the Family and Medical Leave Act of 1993 and finds much less sympathetic and supportive attitudes toward combining work and family obligation in the case of welfare mothers than in the case of middle-class parents whose needs are served by parental and medical leave.[104]

The welfare issue is also linked to whether absent fathers comply with court orders to make their child-support payments. When AFDC was instituted in the 1930s, it served primarily widowed mothers and their children. This is no longer the case as separation, divorce, and unwed parenthood have become the main reasons for single-parent families. Over the same period, the welfare population became increasingly black and Hispanic. Such families are much more likely to be poor, with an average income in 1991 of less than $20,000 compared with more than twice that for white two-parent families.[105] But the fact that it is *women* who are so disadvantaged when they are sole heads of families makes poverty and welfare issues that feminists no longer can ignore.

Nontraditional families. Closely related to disadvantage among women is the question of family form. During its first 150 years, feminism in America was primarily concerned with assuring the equal rights of married and unmarried women. But after 1950, the divorce rate increased so rapidly that one-third of all married women will now likely experience a dissolution of their marriage.[106] No-fault divorce, the equal rights stance toward families in the 1970s, turned out to have quite negative consequences for women and children. Lenore Weitzman demonstrated that the income of a divorced woman and her children fell sharply while that of the husband rose.[107] Many drew the lesson that equality for women, when construed as treating them exactly the same as men, winds up doing them harm.

What should be the stance of the women's movement toward separated and divorced women, women who bear children out of wedlock, lesbians, and others who do not live in a traditional family? The issues are so new that feminists are still wrestling with how they should respond.

Those who hold to a traditional but egalitarian model of family life particularly emphasize the need to increase the father's participation in the home through parental leaves, greater involvement in child care, and continued monetary support if there is a divorce. They would also restore greater value to child care by the mother or compensate a working woman so that she can take time out from work to care for her children while they are young.[108]

Some others, however, consider the traditional family a straitjacket of patriarchal control and therefore welcome the variety of new family forms. To them the key challenge is to provide societal supports for children in these new types of families.[109] They ask why the United States is the only developed nation without universal child allowances. They argue that children should not be made to suffer for their parents' life choices. To the claim that women will have children to get on welfare and live off the child allowances, they respond that out-of-wedlock pregnancy originates in other causes, such as blocked educational and career opportunities or lack of hope. Their answer is not to punish children for conditions they did not create but to stimulate better work prospects for their parents, who will then be dissuaded from starting their families so early.[110]

Where is this debate on family form likely to end? If past experience can be counted as a guide, it seems likely that American underlying suspicion of the helping role of government will combine with equal rights individualism to squelch support for child rearing in nontraditional families. The greatest likely development in the near term is an elaboration of supports to women who wish to combine work and family care. Even support for lesbians or unmarried welfare mothers will likely occur in this guise rather than as the right of children to be well cared for regardless of family form.

Well-being of children. In formulating these various provisions of a family policy, the national consciousness has begun to shift toward recognizing the importance of *children's* welfare to the future of the nation, as well as that of their families. High numbers of children in poverty are a direct consequence of the poverty of single-parent families, which are usually headed by women. Children who are inadequately cared for or are poor are more likely to become substance abusers, drop out of school, be unemployed, or die as a result of violence. They fall into protective custody or the criminal justice system, where the costs for their care are far greater than would have been the case for ensuring adequate income to their parents or needed child care, training, and job opportunities in the community.[111] Most people realize that children's conditions are intimately related to the resources and availability of their parents. Except for adherents of the New Right, who might think the problem could be solved by putting women back into the home, most policy makers are searching for a new way to institutionalize the community's responsibility for all of its children. Suggestions range from a "parental bill of rights" patterned after the GI bill of rights to stemming the tide of unwed parenthood and providing more flexible work, education, and training opportunities for working parents.[112] What is helpful about this focus on children is a reframing of women's equality as being beneficial not only to self-interested feminists but to the family and the future of children.

Joining public and private feminism.   As the twentieth century draws to a close, the lessons of the new feminist movement are about to repeat the lessons of the old: only when the equal rights and caregiving streams are joined can the goal of equality of the sexes be attained. History records defeat in every instance where one branch failed to recognize the valid arguments of the other. In the 1870s, temperance women made little progress until Frances Willard called for the home protection ballot. In the 1920s, social feminists lost gains in maternal and child health because they were at odds with equal rights feminists in the Woman's Party. In 1982 the ERA went down to defeat because its proponents did not address the concerns of homemakers who felt threatened by so-called equal rights for working and professional women.

Conversely, reformers have made a winning combination when they joined together in recognizing the dual reality of women's lives: that they desire equality of opportunity and power, and yet that men and women do differ in their everyday roles. The WCTU was at its peak when it combined recognition of women's vulnerability in the family with a call for justice and the home protection ballot. During World War II, the mobilization of women for the war effort showed that it was possible to combine equal rights (nontraditional jobs) with maternal feminism (public day care for children of working mothers). In the 1990s, as working mothers have become the norm, a new interest in family policy holds promise for again joining the issues of justice and care.

The next steps in the elaboration of social and equal rights feminism are already visible. A new accommodation is developing that integrates the themes of difference and equality. Such long-time adversaries as conservative Republican Phyllis Schlafly and Democratic Congresswoman Patricia Schroeder in 1991 joined together in calling for social policies that provide more government protection for families and children.[113] At the grass roots, ordinary women are combining work and family obligations in multiple simultaneous roles. Women's changing lives are thus the next developments to watch as the values of the feminist movement become more widely shared and institutionalized.

Political theorist Susan Moller Okin has shown why equality is just as necessary in the private as the public sphere. Women's vulnerability to inequality in marriage is likely to be perpetuated outside the home.[114] Okin argues for justice in the family in two ways. First, women cannot come to the public sphere equipped for equality if they have been vulnerable to an unjust burden of work and division of power in the private sphere. To think otherwise is to commit the error of all the classic political philosophers by assuming that women exercise their citizenship with the same mindset and freedom as men. Second, women's participation in public life is both limited by and predicated on their expertise in bringing up children; mothers make possible the very existence of morally responsible adult citizens on whom a democracy depends, and presumably they should be able to share in that public life themselves.

To remedy women's disadvantage, it is necessary to incorporate the differences between women and men into the theory of justice and equality. Fairness should be used as a standard for the everyday arrangements of family life, the division of working hours between men and women so that they can share parenting equally, and, in a more traditional family, compensatory treatment for a woman who is the primary parent while her husband is the breadwinner. These ideas about family justice add up to an implicit "family policy," namely, programs for child care, work-family flexibility, child support, and other government and corporate means to support family life. In fact, such programs have recently gained support from feminists, developmental psychologists, and social welfare workers concerned with helping poor women and children.[115]

Okin's ideas contribute answers to what law school professor Martha Minow has termed the "dilemma of difference." Some proponents of equality focus on difference in order to appreciate and include women's "different voice" and give it a value equal with men's. Others argue that such attention to difference actually hurts women and keeps them down. As Nancy Cott observes, women leaders have often maintained, "I am not a feminist" precisely because the feminist legacy is a feminist paradox: how to be human beings and women too. The danger has been that "an articulation of sexual differences" risks "reconfirming rather than subverting gender hierarchy."[116]

These patterns of conflict or integration in the two types of feminism appear to suggest an underlying dynamic that is characteristic of all social movements. The maternal feminists, by focusing on gender difference, spoke for the needs of women, men, and children in the private family, a *subsystem* of the larger society. The equal rights feminists claimed irrelevance of gender to citizenship and thereby put a greater emphasis on membership in the *larger system,* society as a whole. System and subsystem can be in conflict or work together. The failure of the ERA was a case study in the conflict between the two. The coming interest in family policy promises to reconcile the forces committed to gender equality and gender difference.[117]

Such a reconciliation between the equality and difference branches of feminism would realize what political philosophers and legal theorists have begun to call for—the recognition that no rights are possible without consideration of the matrix of social relationships that either hold back or encourage each individual's expression of the self. Susan Okin documented women's vulnerability to inequality and lack of public voice because they bore an unjust burden of work and division in the power at home. Martha Minow shows that people will be dealt with unfairly if treated the same when situated differently. Thus, it is necessary to take women's different family obligations and role histories into account or they will be the losers in such seemingly "equal" solutions as no-fault divorce.[118] Mary Ann Glendon calls for new attention to the missing dimension of social connection. Social policies should acknowledge not just the rights of the individual but the needs of the family and the community. Along with assuring women equal rights, society must at the same time see to it that children are not neglected, that both parents have time for their children, and that the community recognizes and supports their efforts.[119]

Combining rights and responsibilities could unite liberal and conservative women. To the extent that the socially conservative women of the New Right have captured women's concern for families and children and argued the need for women's traditional roles, they have seemed like enemies to the equal rights feminists.[120] But if the goal of equality can be reframed as requiring women's rights *and* the well-being of families, there is the possibility of a women's juggernaut that will move forward the feminist agenda on both the individual and family fronts.

Where Do Women's Movements Go?

In this final chapter we have seen how the double strands of the first feminist movement have continued right up to the present. Attaining the vote in 1920 did make a difference. Women's access to broader rights of citizenship allowed them to vote, hold office, and lobby for their causes. Equal rights feminists gradually gained the support of working and professional women throughout the 1930s and 1940s. By the 1960s their issues were poised for take-off and gained legitimacy in the Equal Pay Act of 1963, Title VII of the 1964 Civil Rights Act prohibiting sex discrimination, the founding of the National Organization for Women in 1966, and the resurrection of the ERA.[121] The social feminists experienced both victory and defeat during the 1920s in what happened to protective labor legislation and maternal and child health, and their work for mothers' pensions and for poor children had a formative influence on the provisions of the modern welfare state. In the 1990s, social feminism could bring to fruition some of the rudimentary family policies that will support working parents in their community and child-care responsibilities.

This book began with the question, "Where do women's movements come from?" The answer to this question both for the historical temperance and suffrage movements and for modern equal rights and family feminists is the same. Women's movements arise out of strain in the feminine role between what women are supposed to do and what they actually do. The strain sets in motion a collective reaction that casts up leaders who form a coherent ideology of change. These leaders construct organizations that reach out to other like-minded followers and together shape an agenda for legal and social change. That is where women's movements come from.

Now at the close of this book, my parting question is, "Where do women's movements go?" Just as I placed this book's opening question in an international perspective, it seems appropriate to end on a similar note. As shown in the opening chapter, the onset of feminist protest was linked to a nation's political and economic development. Those states with democratic governments, Protestant religion, and industrializing economies were the first to spawn woman's rights protests. As these nations and their women's movements have matured, they have generally moved in the direction of seeking more public support for women's caregiving tasks in the family. At the close of the twentieth century, Americans, like several European nations somewhat earlier, are exploring family policies that will undergird caregiving by working parents, expand child care outside the home, and support poor and nontraditional families reproducing the next generation.

Variety among nations suggests, however, that no one nation's feminism is exactly like that of another. The cultural and social matrix is different; women's economic and family responsibilities vary with the national economy; and the histories of the women's movements themselves have laid out a different set of available options. Thus, for example, more generous social provisions for child care and parental leave exist in Sweden and France than in the United States or Great Britain. Even though Anglo-American feminism was stronger in the first decades of this century, the actual work histories of British and American women followed a traditional middle-class model of wives and mothers as homemakers. In France and Scandinavia, however, during the critical formative decades of social policy earlier in the century, many more women combined work and family life in agricultural and service occupations and therefore shaped the kind of child-care provisions and family allowance system that would accommodate the needs of working mothers.[122]

Despite such national variation, however, the feminist agendas appear to be converging because the trends in women's lives are converging in the direction of increased paid work outside the home. Their jobs are especially valued in an uncertain global economy where men's jobs are fast changing and in danger of being cut because of corporate downsizing or loss of a manufacturing base.[123] Yet this trend occurs against a backdrop in which men traditionally had greater authority and responsibility for family support and in which women's paid work was clearly secondary to their caregiving role in the family. The equality stream of feminism will continue to the extent that women's emerging and more autonomous life patterns are at odds with past subordination. We can expect that new women's movements will explore the next frontiers and extend the rules of antidiscrimination and equal rights.

On the side of women's continuing concern for families and caregiving, there may also be an international convergence. Whether one is thinking of the Mothers of the Plaza de Mayo in Argentina, who protested the disappearance and murder of their family members, or the women in Yugoslavia who early demonstrated to stop the civil war, or mothers in the United States who want to take guns away from children, there is a common thread of concern for the future, for social reproduction. Temperance women, suffragists who used the vote for social questions, and modern social feminists have all shown an interest in the interdependence of the community and in the need to preserve a sense of mutual regard. Just as women's new multiple roles set forth new frontiers for extending equality, so the threats to families, children, and neighborhood raise new challenges to women's sense of common humanity and their capacity to bind persons together in a shared community.

The women's movements of the future will thus likely push forward the frontiers of both equality and care. The equality principle will be extended to cover more of the "special" situation of women and more of the private sphere. The ethic of care will be used to judge men as well as women and will serve as a standard in an ever widening circle in the community and the nation.

Appendix A: Content Analysis of Newspapers

The content analysis for the comparison of temperance and suffrage materials was originally done in the summer of 1960. Using materials located primarily at the Radcliffe Women's Archives (now the Schlesinger Library) at Radcliffe College, I developed the category codes first by reading through a number of stories and articles in the newspapers of each group. I then codified these categories into major headings that had to do with the current issues and reforms of the day as well as the implicit images of men and women.

In the summer of 1963, after I had become a faculty member at Wellesley College, I had the help of Wellesley alumna Helen Lefkowitz Horowitz, who also read over a sampling of the materials to see what level of reliability could be achieved between readers. Our agreement was never perfect, but there was sufficient overlap to believe that we were capturing some real differences in the materials put out by the temperance and suffrage women. In the following account, I describe the original sampling and selection of materials and the way the themes were scored.

In the early 1960s the development of content analysis was not very far advanced. I relied heavily on an article entitled "Content Analysis" by Bernard Berelson as well as the ideas behind a scheme for the scoring of interaction in groups that had been developed by Robert F. Bales.[1] In 1988, I returned to these materials and read over those articles that were scored on major themes in order to illustrate them in this book with direct quotations. In general, I found that the original coding categories still made sense and had stood up well over 30 years.

Sampling and Selection of Material

All materials for the content analysis were taken from the *Woman's Journal* and the *Union Signal*. The suffrage paper the *Woman's Journal* began publication in January 1870 in Boston. The *Union Signal* was first published in Chicago in 1882 as the result of a merger of *Our Union* and the *Signal*. It would have been ideal to compare the two papers for every five years, beginning in 1875 and ending in 1915, thus getting as wide a spread as possible over the span of years that the two papers were running. (*Woman's Temperance Union,* one of the forerunners of the *Union Signal,* had begun publication in 1875). It turned out, however, that such precursors to the *Union Signal* were unavailable to me. For that reason, the first year for which I have a content analysis of temperance material is 1885. The actual years from which newspapers were selected are 1885, 1890, 1895, 1900, 1905, 1910, and 1915. Within each of these years, I selected the first issue of each quarter in January, April, July, and October.

Selection within issues.   The following rules guided selection of material to be coded. *Excluded* were editorial correspondence, unless on page 1; anecdotal material, "Notes and News," literary reviews; poetry, serials, stories (unless specific satire, or story related to suffrage or temperance); news from abroad, local chapter news, personal eulogies, "What the Press Thinks of Us," children's section; editorial notes on page 1 unless they bore a heading; "Women's Clubs and Club Women"; anything that could not be scored meaningfully. *Included* were all else with any kind of implied editorial comment consistent with goals of the paper—if quick scanning indicated that the story was direct reportage of detail or concerned some news so remote from suffrage or temperance that it was impossible to assess editorial attitude, the article was omitted; regular columns of the type "Women Physicians," "Women Lawyers," "Women of the Press," "Women in Churches," "Women and Colleges," even if the story was about only one woman; any story directly relevant to suffrage or temperance.

Scoring of themes.   The *context unit* could be as large as the whole article or as small as a few phrases that together expressed the theme. The main danger was that a theme might be scored too easily. To avoid this, the code was to make sure that there was some *direct* evidence of the theme in the article—a phrase, a sentence, a paragraph. A single word or an implied statement was not enough. *The theme was not to be arrived at purely by inference.*

A single article might be scored for more than one *theme.* A theme could exist in several subparts. When that occurred, the codes were to record all the subparts. If an article was largely concerned with reporting the views of the opposition, then the code was to record what seemed to be the view of the paper. If it was unclear exactly what was the view of the paper toward a speech or an event, the article was not to be scored at all.

Total articles analyzed. The total number of suffrage articles analyzed was 200; the total number of temperance articles, 301. These totals were not always the same as those used for the chi-square test. Articles were always assigned to one or another category in order to achieve discrete groups. If no decision was possible because an article had been scored equally in each category, it was excluded from the groups being compared.

Categories of the Content Analysis

The content analysis categories were developed with both theoretical and empirical considerations in mind. Chapters 3 and 4 on the temperance and suffrage movements use the content analysis to illustrate themes in the ideology of each movement. At the time of analysis, an article was scored on as many categories (or themes) as appeared within it. The five main headings of the coding scheme were as follows: image of woman, image of man; arguments for equality; reform proposals for equality; other reform proposals.

I. Image of woman.

Category 1: Bad new
1. unsexed, feminine, anti-man
2. feminine, but not principled, petty coquette
3. recognizes 1 as view of opposition
4. recognizes 2 as view of opposition
5. combination of 1 and 3, "grain of truth"
6. combination of 2 and 4, "grain of truth"

Category 2: Good new
1. principled, moral, intelligent, strong-minded, alert, free, competent—in all these, equal to men
2. warm, loving, tactful, but not servile, protective, affectionate
3. combination of 1 and 2, motherly, etc.
4. aesthetic, neat, clean, methodical in household affairs, equal to man's technical competence but in household

Category 3: Bad traditional
1. a. narrow, rigid, bigot
   b. morally submissive, ignorant, cloistered
   c. gossipy, trivial
2. a. overly affectionate, swamps child or others in tyranny of love
   b. weak, feminine, soft, husband rules
   c. wheedles money, etc.
3. selfish, narcissistic, concerned with self-adornment
4. bogged down in technical duties, a "Martha"

Category 4: Good traditional
1. courageous, moral, loyal, upright
2. feminine, warm, soft, submissive, typically married
3. combination of 1 and 2, good mother, loyal daughter
4. aesthetic, neat, clean, household technician, fastidious in all things

II. Image of man.

Category 5: Bad new
1. tempted, evil habits
2. bad husband, father
3. immoral in public life

Category 6: Good new
1. virtuous if not tempted by lack of laws, strong personal moral code, abstainer, no bad language, principled
2. good husband, father, some feminine traits, equal partner with wife
3. responsible as citizen in politics and business

Category 7: Bad traditional
1. tempted by lack of laws, pledge, or personal religion
2. harms family or self in his temptation to:
   a. drink
   b. take money
   c. not work hard
   d. take children or treat them cruelly
   e. rob women of their virtue, or treat them cruelly
3. unprincipled in public life—politics and business
   a. inelegant, spits tobacco juice in public halls, etc.

Category 8: Good traditional
1. Puritan ideals, etc., limit temptation, upright
2. trustworthy husband, father, master of his house, rules with justice
3. responsible in community affairs, Puritan, Yankee tradition

III. Arguments for equality—assertions about the equality of women and men.

Category 9: Moral and spiritual equality
1. women are as responsible as men
2. women are superior to men in character and moral responsibility

Category 10: Intellectual equality
1. in capacity and potential
2. in actual achievement

Category 11: Equality in competence and performance
1. women work as hard as men
2. women's physical endurance is equal to that of men
3. women are equally skillful and efficient

Category 12: Implicit civil equality
1. women are citizens
2. women are taxed as property holders
3. single women and widows are not represented through their husbands

Categories 13, 14, 15 (not used)

IV. Proposal for reforms—involving status of women.

Category 16: Political equality suffrage
Universalistic reasons
1. ballot for uplift of women—to make them at least equal to the drunkards, Negroes, etc., who vote, and able to defend political and economical interests
2. ballot in order to implement general political responsibility of women

Particularistic reasons
3. to implement particular responsibility of women
   a. as mother-wife interested in family, community welfare
   b. to bring about general moral reform
   c. to increase elegance, decency of politics

Tactics
4. ballot as first goal, other reforms secondary
5. ballot primarily as a means to other reforms—secondary in importance as a goal in itself

Category 17: Equality of status of women in family
Universalistic Reasons
1. household as a specialized enterprise where women equal to men
   a. regarding children
   b. money
   c. specialization and technical knowledge—they have some life outside the home too
2. civil rights and property rights of women should be protected
   a. if married
   b. if single
   c. if marital status not designated
3. entrance of women into public life will not disrupt the family, lower birth rate, etc. (recognition of view popular among the opposition)

Particularistic reasons
   4. equal moral purity for men and women—fallen women are no more at fault than men
      a. need to raise age of protection of girls
   5. need to protect women in marriage and divorce laws, and anti-polygamy measures, etc.

Category 18: Educational equality
   1. need equal educational opportunity, to enter colleges, etc.
   2. need same standards of achievement for boys and girls—same levels of expectation
      a. coeducation desirable
      b. same standards in home
   3. need higher levels of expectation, higher standards in women's work — nursing, cooking, domestic science, kindergarten, pure food, pure air

Category 19: Professional occupational equality
   1. need equal job opportunities (though may be different from men's)
   2. need equal wages, hours, working conditions
   3. need to expect higher things of women regarding the work they enter—women are needed for important positions

Category 20 (not used)

Category 21: Equality of women in moral, spiritual realm
   1. need for equal positions of responsibility and authority in churches—as lay participants or pastors
   2. need for general respect for women's behavior in moral and ethical matters—honesty of a woman's word, etc.
   3. need for higher levels of expectation of women—ability to abstain from questionable luxuries—alcohol, cookery, candy, gum, reading novels, etc.

V. Proposal for reforms—not necessarily involving the status of women.

Category 22: Temperance—attitude toward issue
   1. just a positive mention of prohibition or temperance without pointed advocacy
   2. temperance cause and its adherents will help get woman's ballot
   3. opponents of woman suffrage backed by those opposed to prohibition, the liquor interests
   4. unequivocal support of prohibition—state or national
      a. local option
      b. other methods
   5. personal restraint advocated
      a. temperance
      b. abstinence

Category 23: Temperance—reasons for reform
1. effect on individual
   a. will increase the well-being and effectiveness of the individual family member; will make the individual worker more productive
   b. will make the individual a better citizen
   c. will improve the general moral character of the individual
2. effect on society
   a. waste of economic energy, money, etc.
   b. corruption of politics
   c. crime, poverty, and other harmful side effects on general morals

Category 24: Humanitarian welfare reforms—charity, civic improvement
1. peace crusade
2. anticruelty to animals, to children; antiboxing, anticapital punishment, antigambling, etc.
3. healing, therapy arts—prison reform, juvenile courts, etc.
   a. police matrons
4. charity, aid to poor—aid to dependent children, minimum wage laws and improved working conditions
   a. child labor laws
5. educational improvement, better schools, etc.
6. civic improvement, municipal progress in playgrounds, streets, sewers, etc.

Category 25: General moral reform, need for
1. activation of moral responsibility in individuals—truth, courage, etc.
2. higher levels of responsibility in business, pure food and drug, compulsory arbitration, antimonopoly, etc.
3. higher levels of responsibility in government—civil service, fair elections, fair taxes, good candidates

Category 26: Concern for breakdown of revered American traditions, alarm at
1. the foreign vote; prevalence of aliens, immigrants, of diversity of culture that is not Anglo-Saxon
2. Catholic vote; Catholic power or belief, etc.
3. desertion of the country; evils of the city
4. Sabbath desecration

Reliability of Scoring

When in the spring of 1961 another person (Susan Sagoff) independently coded a sample of articles by reading all articles in the *Woman's Journal* and *Union Signal* of 1885 that were scored for this study, there was 94 percent agreement with my scoring if counting agreement on the blanks as well as the hits, but only a 52 percent agreement if agreement on blanks was ignored and only agreement on hits counted. That is, out of 47 articles ¥ 21 categories for a total of 987 possible ratings, there was agreement on 927, or 927 by 987 = 94 percent. But of the total of 125 codes actually assigned to these 47 articles, there was agreement on only 65, or 65 by 125 = 52 percent.

Closer examination of the coding discrepancies gave reassurance, however, that the general themes that differentiated the two movements were not obscured by differences in coding. Most of the coding disagreements were the result of categorizing a theme under general images or principles found in parts I, II, or III of the coding scheme rather than under specific reforms listed under parts IV and V. But the nature of the themes themselves (for example, the "new good woman" in category 2 or "woman suffrage" in category 16) were consistent with a larger theme common to both, and it was these more general themes that were the focus of my analysis.

Appendix B: Biographical Comparison of Temperance and Suffrage Leaders

My objective in selecting prominent leaders in the temperance and suffrage movement groups was to compare the social characteristics of women who were active in each group. I was looking not only for differences and similarities among leaders but a way to characterize the general membership of each group. My assumption was that successful leaders were effective largely because their followers could identify with them. If such identification was possible, I reasoned that the social characteristics and beliefs of the leaders would tell me something about their followers.

There was the possibility, of course, that leaders of the two groups, because they were leaders, would be more similar to each other than to their followers. If that were the case, there would still be no error in interpreting the membership as being different in the ways that leaders were different. As is shown in chapters 3 and 4, the leaders were significantly different in a number of ways. It is fortunate to have such information on the leaders, for there is virtually no other way to compare characteristics of the ordinary rank and file; biographical data for them is either nonexistent or very difficult to find.

Criterion of Selection: General Prominence

Because I wanted to compare and illuminate the difference in motivations and social characteristics of temperance and suffrage women, I wanted to select leaders for comparison who were similar in as many other respects as possible. A number of different selection strategies were conceivable. Leaders of the two groups could be paired by region of primary activity, type of office in the organization, period of prominence, etc. The best single independent variable for my purposes was the criterion of general prominence. I reasoned that if it were possible to find with some degree of certainty the most prominent women of each group, then I would have confidence that the two groups of women could be appropriately compared on a wide range of other variables.

One of the crucial factors in my decision to use the prominence criterion was the availability of lists of the most important temperance and suffrage leaders. These lists had been developed by Edward T. James, senior editor of the biographical dictionary *Notable American Women, 1607–1950*, that in 1959–60 (when I was doing this work) was being prepared under the sponsorship of Radcliffe College.

The list of WCTU leaders included roughly 75 names; the list of suffrage women totaled more than 150 names. Each of these lists had been constructed from a general card file of information on prominent women.[1] Those women who were noted as being active in the WCTU or suffrage had been included on the appropriate list. Then each list had been sent by the editors of *NAW* to major scholars who had special acquaintance with the history and leadership of the WCTU or the suffrage movement.[2] Each expert rated the leaders on their overall importance. When I received the lists I used a combination of criteria to arrive at a list of about 50 names of prominent leaders in both the WCTU and the suffrage groups.

For the WCTU, virtually no other criterion was necessary in order to make a decision on which ones to include. The list was small enough to begin with, and the ratings clear enough to make an immediate selection possible. To the WCTU list I added only the names of Ella Boole (who died after 1950 and was therefore not in the *NAW* list) and Katherine Lent Stevenson.

For the suffrage group I relied on the overall ratings of the leaders made by the experts and the numbers of entries under any given name in the index of volumes 4 and 5 of the *History of Woman Suffrage*. To the suffrage list I added the names of Lillie Devereux Blake, Jane Addams, Julia Ward Howe, M. Carey Thomas, Antoinette Brown Blackwell, Ruth Hanna McCormick, Elizabeth Upham Yates, Gertrude Foster Brown, and Helen Hamilton Gardener. These women were added because they were not listed under "suffrage" in *NAW* but were included under other rubrics of activity.

Characteristics of Prominent WCTU and Suffrage Leaders

I made an attempt to secure the following information on each of the WCTU and suffrage leaders[3]:

1. Date and place of birth; date of death.
2. When active in the WCTU or suffrage; and *where* active.
3. Occupation; major activities in club work, philanthropy, church work, etc.; major offices held in temperance or suffrage and other facts related to reason for prominent position in those reforms.

4. Father's occupation and general economic status; and mother's, if mentioned.
5. Ancestral background (nationality) and geographical background; important family migrations, if any.
6. Education: schools, colleges, universities, and degrees.
7. Religious affiliation.
8. Marital status: date of marriage, husband's name and occupation, number of children.

From the information that was obtained, I summarized general characteristics of the two groups related to age, time of prominence, socioeconomic background, and so on. The prominent leaders of the WCTU were most often active in the period before 1895. The number of WCTU leaders prominent before 1895 was 40; the number prominent after 1895 was 9. The number of suffrage women who were prominent before the turn of the century was about equal to the number who were prominent after; before 1895, 25, and after 1895, 24.

Yet among the women who were prominent, whether in the early or later periods, there was remarkable comparability between the two groups in age of birth. The average date of birth for WCTU leaders prominent before 1895 was 1835; of suffragists who were prominent before 1895, it was 1830. For the later period, the average date of birth for temperance women was 1855; for suffragists, it was 1856. The average date of birth for all WCTU leaders (1837) and for all suffragists (1838) was almost exactly the same. Such comparability of age ensures that comparison of the two groups on other variables, such as education or marital status, was also legitimate.

Finally, one other characteristic of the samples of leaders should be noted. Although they were independently drawn, three women ended up on both lists—Mary Garrett Hay, Mary Livermore, and Zerelda Wallace. I still felt justified, however, in using the chi-square test for two independent samples. The samples had been independently drawn and the simultaneous representation of three women in each of the samples could lead only to a more conservative value of chi-square rather than an illegitimate inflation of it.

Names of Prominent WCTU and Suffrage Leaders

An asterisk next to a name on the following list indicates that the woman was most prominent in the period after 1895. The year 1895 was chosen as the cutting point because it coincided with the waning involvement of Frances Willard in the WCTU and with the increase in broad-scale organization efforts in the suffrage movement. That year seemed to be a meaningful turning point in both movements. The decision as to whether a woman was more prominent in the early or late period was based on the facts of her life. For the suffrage group, it was also possible to check the indexes of *History of Woman Suffrage,* volumes 4 and 5, for additional information as to period of prominence. Earlier or later prominence is used in several tables to contrast the characteristics of each group.

Prominent WCTU leaders.

1. *Ackerman, Jessie A.
2. *Allen, Martha Meir
3. Bailey, Hannah Johnston
4. Barney, Susan Hammond
5. Bateham, Josephine Penfield Cushman
6. Bittenbender, Ada M. Cole
7. Blackall, Emily Lucas
8. *Boole, Ella A.
9. Brown, Martha McClellan
10. Buell, Caroline Brown
11. Bushnell, Kate
12. Burt, Mary Towne
13. Carse, Matilda Bradley
14. Chapin, Sallie F. Moore
15. Colman, Julia
16. *Ellis, Margaret Dye
17. Foster, J. Ellen Horton
18. *Gordon, Anna Adams
19. Hay, Mary Garrett
20. Henry, Josephine Kirby Williamson
21. Henry, Serepta M. Irish
22. Hunt, Mary Hannah Hanchett
23. Ingham, Mary Bigelow
24. *Kearney, Belle
25. Kinney, Narcissa Edith White
26. Lathrap, Mary Torrans
27. Leavitt, Mary Greenleaf Clement
28. Livermore, Mary Ashton Rice
29. Lovell, Mary Frances Whitechurch
30. McCabe, Harriet Calista Clark
31. Merrick, Caroline Elizabeth Thomas
32. Miller, Emily Huntington
33. Newman, Angelica French Thurston Kilgore
34. Pugh, Esther
35. *Stevens, Lillian M. N. Ames
36. *Stevenson, Katherine Lent
37. Stewart, Eliza Daniel

38. *Stoddard, Cora Frances
39. Thompson, Eliza Jane Trimble
40. Wallace, Zerelda Gray Saunders
41. Watson, Ellen Robb Murdoch
42. Way, Amanda M.
43. West, Marry Allen
44. Wheeler, Mary Sparkes
45. Willard, Frances Elizabeth Caroline
46. Willard, Mary Bannister
47. Willing, Jane (Jennie) Fowler
48. Wittenmyer, Annie Turner
49. Woodbridge, Mary Ann Brayton

Prominent suffrage leaders.
1. *Addams, Jane
2. Anthony, Susan B.
3. Avery, Rachel Foster
4. *Belmont, Alva Ertskin Smith Vanderbilt
5. *Blackwell, Alice Stone
6. Blackwell, Antoinette Brown
7. Blake, Lillie Devereux
8. *Blatch, Harriot Eaton Stanton
9. *Breckinridge, Madeline McDowell (Mrs. Desha)
10. *Brown, Gertrude Foster (Mrs. Raymond)
11. Brown, Olympia
12. *Catt, Carrie Lane Chapman
13. Cheney, Ednah Dow Littlehale
14. *Clay, Laura
15. Colby, Clara D. Bewick
16. Couzins, Phoebe
17. Dall, Caroline Wells Healey
18. *Dennett, Mary Ware
19. *De Voe, Emma
20. Duniway, Abigail Scott
21. Foster, Abigail Kelley
22. Gage, Matilda Joslyn
23. *Gardener, Helen Hamilton
24. *Gordon, Kate M.
25. Gougar, Helen Mar Jackson
26. Harbert, Elizabeth Morrison Boynton
27. *Hay, Mary Garrett
28. Hazard, Rebecca
29. Hooker, Isabelle Beecher

30. Howe, Julia Ward
31. *Howland, Emily
32. *Jacobs, Pattie Ruffner (Mrs. Solon J.)
33. Johns, Laura Mitchell
34. Livermore, Mary Ashton Rice
35. Lockwood, Belva Ann Bennett
36. *McCormick, Ruth Hanna (Mrs. Medill)
37. *McCulloch, Catherine Waugh
38. *Miller, Elizabeth Smith
39. Phelps, Elizabeth B.
40. *Sewall, May Wright
41. *Shaw, Anna Howard
42. *Shuler, Antoinette (Nettie) Rogers
43. Stanton, Elizabeth Cady
44. Stone, Lucy
45. *Thomas, Martha Carey
46. *Upton, Harriet Taylor
47. Wallace, Zerelda Gray Saunders
48. Yates, Elizabeth Upham
49. *Youmans, Theodora Winton

Further Analysis of Leader Biographies

In 1989–90, while revising my earlier work on the temperance and suffrage movement, I undertook further qualitative analysis of the leaders' biographies. With the help of Doreen Shulman, I returned to *Notable American Women,* now published, which at the time of my earlier work in 1959 and 1960 was still only in the planning stages. This three-volume work had the advantage over earlier biographical collections of being much more complete and objective in its accounts. Each biographical entry ranged from 750 to 1,500 words and permitted a review of the "flavor" of a woman's life. It was possible to test several new hypotheses about the contrasts between women in each movement and to retest hypotheses borne out by the earlier analysis.

Selection of cases. For this analysis of leader biographies published in *Notable American Women,* the comparison groups to be roughly equal in size, were limited to those 17 temperance and 18 suffrage women who were born before 1840. (If we had taken all the leaders in *NAW,* the numbers would have been quite different; the total for temperance only 23 as compared to a total for suffrage of 41.) From the two lists of 49 leaders that appear above, we selected the following:

Prominent WCTU leaders.
1. Bailey, Hannah Johnston
2. Bateham, Josephine Penfield Cushman
3. Brown, Martha McClellan
4. Carse, Matilda Bradley
5. Foster, J. Ellen Horton
6. Hunt, Mary Hannah Hanchett
7. Leavitt, Mary Greenleaf Clement
8. Merrick, Caroline Elizabeth Thomas
9. Miller, Emily Huntington
10. Newman, Angelica French Thurston Kilgore
11. Stewart, Eliza Daniel
12. Thompson, Eliza Jane Trimble
13. Wallace, Zerelda Gray Saunders
14. Way, Amanda M.
15. Willard, Frances Elizabeth Caroline
16. Willing, Jane (Jennie) Fowler
17. Wittenmyer, Annie Turner

Prominent suffrage leaders.
1. Anthony, Susan B.
2. Blackwell, Antoinette Brown
3. Blake, Lillie Devereux
4. Brown, Olympia
5. Cheney, Ednah Dow Littlehale
6. Couzins, Phoebe
7. Dall, Caroline Wells Healey
8. Duniway, Abigail Scott
9. Foster, Abigail Kelley
10. Gage, Matilda Joslyn
11. Hooker, Isabelle Beecher
12. Howe, Julia Ward
13. Howland, Emily
14. Livermore, Mary Ashton Rice
15. Lockwood, Belva Ann Bennett
16. Miller, Elizabeth Smith
17. Stanton, Elizabeth Cady
18. Stone, Lucy

Characteristics for the leader comparison.   Using a spread sheet program, my assistant Doreen Shulman then coded the biographies according to the following list of characteristics:

Column A: Identification (name or number)
Column B: Movement
    1-Suffrage
    2-Temperance
Column C: Date of birth (year)
Column D: Date of death (year)
Column E: Place of birth (early childhood)
    1-East
    2-South
    3-Border South
    4-Midwest
    5-West
    6-Unknown/other
Column F: Type of hometown
    1-Rural
    2-Small town
    3-Urban/large town (now a city, i.e. Pittsburgh)
    4-Unknown
Column G: Parents' (primary) job
    0-Farmer (small farm)
    1-Farmer (large farm, plantation)
    2-Business (merchant, banker, editor, manufacturer, school director, laborer)
    3-Professional (doctor, lawyer)
    4-Clergy
    5-Unknown
Column H: Economic status
    0-Poverty
    1-Lower middle class
    2-Middle class
    3-Upper class (wealthy)
    4-Unknown
Column I: Religion (from birth)
    1-Unitarian/Universalist
    2-Quaker
    3-Baptist
    4-Episcopal
    5-Methodist
    6-Presbyterian
    7-Congregationalist
    8-Other Protestant
    9-Catholic
    0-Other

Column J: Health—self
- 0-No problems
- 1-Physical problems
- 2-Mental problems

Column K: Health—husband
- 0-No Problems
- 1-Ill
- 2-Other problems (including early death, marriage fewer than 10 years)

Column L: Health—parent
- 0-No problems
- 1-Mother ill
- 2-Mother, early death (daughter less than 19 years old)
- 3-Father ill
- 4-Father, early death (daughter less than 19 years old)
- 5-Parents divorced
- 6-Orphaned (daughter less than 19 years old)

Column M: Health—other relative
- 0-No problems
- 1-Physical problems
- 2-Mental problems
- 3-Early (untimely) death

Column N: Marital status
- 1-Never married
- 2-Married
- 3-Widowed early (marriage fewer than 10 years)/no remarriage
- 4-Widowed early (marriage fewer than 10 years)/remarriage
- 5-Divorced/no remarriage
- 6-Divorced/remarriage
- 7-Other

Column O: Innovation—public speaking
- 0-No
- 1-Yes

Column P: Innovation—writing
- 0-No
- 1-Yes

Column Q: Innovation—organization/leadership (president, vice president) of conventions, organizations
- 0-No
- 1-Yes

Column R: Innovation—religion (novel ideas, ministry as a profession)
- 0-No
- 1-Innovative ideas, profession, missionary

2-Changed denominations (as an adult)
3-Combination
Column S: Innovation—dress
    0-No
    1-Yes
Column T: Innovation—use of maiden name or change of name
    0-No
    1-Yes
Column U: Innovation—higher education
    0-No
    1-Yes
Column V: Innovation—profession (lawyer, physician, professor, etc.)
    0-No
    1-Yes
Column W: Social activism—parental
    0-No
    1-Abolition/women's movement
    2-Politics
    3-Religion
    4-Combination
    5-Temperance
    6-Other
Column X: Social activism—husband
    0-No
    1-Abolition/women's movement
    2-Politics
    3-Religion
    4-Combination
    5-Temperance
    6-Other
Column Y: Innovation—other
    0-No
    1-Yes
Column Z: Barrier—public speaking
    0-No
    1-Yes
Column AA: Barrier—school (denied admittance, denied degree, etc.)
    0-No
    1-Yes
Column AB: Barrier—career (unable to practice profession)
    0-No
    1-Yes

Column AC: Family opposition to education or career
    0-No
    1-Parental, siblings
    2-Husband
    3-Combination
Column AD: Barrier—association/organization (denied admittance, attendance)
    0-No
    1-Yes
Column AE: Barrier—civil/legal (loss of citizenship upon marriage to non-American, not permitted to vote when legal)
    0-No
    1-Yes
Column AF: Frustration—economic (struggle for self and/or family support, women having to work, etc.)
    0-No
    1-Yes
Column AG: Barrier/frustration—other
    0-No
    1-Yes

Analysis. Following coding of the biographies, we then compared the temperance and suffrage groups to see if they were significantly different by using the Fisher Exact Test of Probability. Results generally confirmed the earlier findings for the two groups of 49 leaders. In addition, it was possible to compare innovative behavior and experience of barriers to achievement as reported in table 4.5 in chapter 4.

Comparisons confirmed that the two groups were similar in marital status and economic level. They differed significantly, however, in the following characteristics:

1. *Birthplace.* Suffragists were more often born in the East (T = 8, S = 14, p = .050). Temperance women were much more likely to live in a small town (T = 15, S = 6, p = .001).

2. *Religious denomination.* Temperance women were much more likely to be Methodists, Baptists, or Presbyterians (T = 12, S = 6, p = .025).

3. *Family opposition.* Suffragists were much more likely to have faced family opposition to their activities (T = 1, S = 7, p = .023).

4. *Innovation—other.* In such matters as cremation, adoption, revision of their marriage vows, and other types of innovations not captured by columns O through V, the suffragists were more numerous (T = 2, S = 8, p = .032).

5. *Experiences of opposition to public speaking.* None of the 17 temperance leaders reported barriers to public speaking, but 5 of the 18 suffrage women did—a highly significant difference (p = .026).

Notes

Complete bibliographic information on periodical articles, books, and parts of books can be found in the References.

Preface

1. Because this book covers almost two centuries of women's activism, it also spans changes in terminology that refer to "woman's" and "women's" organizations. Nancy Cott, in *Grounding of Modern Feminism* (1987), explains why the usage changed. Typical practice before 1910 was to refer to female interests or activities as "woman's," as in woman's rights, woman's temperance, woman suffrage; after 1910, it seemed more natural to say "women's." Cott explains the change as reflecting a profound shift from a belief that all women had fundamentally the same nature and interests to a realization that their cause was pluralistic. As the movement divided over purposes and means, a new term, "feminist," entered the lexicon to express the wide variety of policies, practices, and advocacy that would promote women's interests and equality.

2. MacGregor (1955, 48).

3. For the new scholarship on benevolence and moral reform, see Cott (1977), Berg (1978), Smith-Rosenberg (1971), Boylan (1984), and Melder (1977). See Brumberg (1980) and Bass (1979) on missionary societies. Bordin (1981, 1986) gives the best single modern overview of woman's temperance activities. Flexner (1959), Kraditor (1965), Scott and Scott (1975), and DuBois (1975, 1978) are the modern classics on the suffrage movement. Anne Firor Scott's *Natural Allies* (1991) gives an overview of women's clubs and the whole range of nineteenth-century women's voluntarism. The importance of the women's club movement to social policy is documented by Skocpol (1992).

4. Mary Beth Norton (1980), Linda Kerber (1980), and Mary Ryan

(1981) have all illuminated what happened to women's roles during and after the American Revolution.

5. Carol Gilligan's *In a Different Voice* (1982) is the most famous statement of the difference perspective. Cynthia Epstein (1988) focuses on the dangers of emphasizing differences between the sexes and represents the contrasting equality perspective.

6. Two recent anthologies link the political activities of women to the emergence of social policy; see Linda Gordon (1990) and Louise Tilly and Patricia Gurin (1990). Political scientist Susan Okin (1989) has framed a political theory for extending justice to the family. Psychologist Joseph Pleck (1992) has documented the recent emergence of work-family policies for child care and parental leave in the United States, which he also links to the modern women's movement.

7. Two examples of the literature that portrayed social movements as deviant were written by psychologists and social psychologists. See Hadley Cantril's *Psychology of Social Movements* (1941) and the description of a cult by Festinger, Riecken, and Schachter (1956).

8. Key examples of this new literature on social movements are to be found in Smelser (1963), Gamson (1975), Charles Tilly (1978), McCarthy and Zald (1973, 1977), and Snow, Rochford, Worden, and Benford (1986).

9. For a basic description of the "new" feminism, see Carden (1974).

10. Antler (1981).

11. Parsons and Bales (1955) characterized the male role as "instrumental" in representing the family to the outside world through the father's breadwinner role. The female role was "expressive" in that the mother was the expressive and emotional manager for the family.

12. See, for example, Dorothy M. Brown's *Setting a Course: American Women in the 1920s* (1987) and others in the series: for the 1930s, Ware (1982); for the 1940s, Hartmann (1982); for the 1950s, Kaledin (1984); for the 1960s, Linden-Ward and Green (1993); and for the 1970s, Wandersee (1988).

13. Ferree and Hess (1985).

Chapter 1

1. Elizabeth Cady Stanton, Susan B. Anthony, and Matilda Joslyn Gage, *History of Woman Suffrage* (1881, 1:70–71). The early volumes of the six-volume set (hereafter cited as *HWS*) contain the basic documents of the American woman suffrage movement. Volumes 1 and 2 were published in New York by Fowler and Wells in 1881 and 1882. Volume 3 was published in Rochester, New York, by Susan B. Anthony in 1886. Volume 4, edited by Susan B. Anthony and Ida Husted Harper, was published in Rochester by Anthony in 1902. Volumes 5 and 6, edited by Ida Husted Harper, were published by the National American Woman Suffrage Association in 1922.

2. Since British historian O. R. MacGregor commented in 1955 that the emancipation of women has been neglected in scholarly writing, new analyses of the women's movement have emerged. In political science see Marilley (1985); in sociology see Buechler (1986) and Rosenthal et al. (1985).

3. Ruth Bordin (1981) persuasively argues that the Woman's Christian Temperance Union (WCTU) contribution was overshadowed by suffrage because it was linked more closely with a cause (prohibition) that ultimately failed, whereas suffrage, even though less popular at the time, was associated with a successful movement. Between 1910 and 1920, however, suffragists were frequently linked with the prohibition cause, despite their efforts to differentiate themselves from the temperance women. See Catt and Shuler (1926).

4. Evans (1977, 216).

5. Evans (1977, 69). Women in Finland gained the vote in 1906; women in Norway in 1913.

6. Evans (1977, 240).

7. Principal comparative theories of women's status have been developed over the past three decades. Lenski (1966) developed a general theory to show that class inequality is greater in peasant agricultural societies than in either simpler horticultural or more advanced industrial economies. Giele (1977), Blumberg (1979), and Chafetz (1984) extended and elaborated Lenski's general argument to show that inequality between the sexes also tended to be greatest in the societies at an intermediate stage of technological development.

8. Evidence for the nuclear or "symmetrical" family comes from several sources. Smelser (1959) describes the change in authority within the family that occurred with the industrial revolution in England. Goode (1963) sees a trend toward nuclear families and equality between the sexes across various cultures as they modernize. Within current Western societies, Young and Willmott (1973) show how the trend plays out in modern British families, and Lopata (1971) describes the "couple-companionate" norms of contemporary Chicago families.

9. For a general picture of this period as seen through the letters of 100 women, see Cott (1977).

10. Cott (1977, 3).

11. Koyama (1961, 56).

12. Koyama (1961, 55).

13. Koyama (1962, 67–68).

14. Pharr (1981, 12–13).

15. Banks (1981) chaps. 2, 3, 4.

16. Cott (1977, 132). Mary Ryan (1981, 79), in her detailed study of the revivals in Oneida County, New York, found that the proportion of converts who were women ranged from 52 percent in the Whitestown Baptist revival

of 1814 to almost 72 percent in that church's awakening of 1838. She goes on to document the widespread establishment of female charitable and missionary societies that followed in the wake of the revivals.

17. Paulson (1973, 102–21) particularly documents the alliance between suffrage and temperance in Scandinavia, Australia, New Zealand, Great Britain, and the United States. Evans (1977, 60–63) refers primarily to Australia, New Zealand, and the United States.

18. Mill ([1869] 1909, 75).

19. See Stites (1978, 233–42); also Lapidus (1978), chap. 1.

20. See Salaff and Merkle (1973).

21. Coffin (1987) and Hause and Kenney (1984) attribute the slowness of France in establishing female suffrage to the failure of both the church and the class structure to support female autonomy. Lacking was a political and philanthropic culture that legitimated female independence. According to Hause and Kenney (1984, 281), "The emancipation of women threatened the collectivist visions of Catholics, socialists, and radicals alike. To Catholics it threatened the family; to socialists, it impeded the revolution; to radicals it implied the clerical dismantling of the republic."

22. See Pharr (1981, 174–76) for a thoughtful historical analysis of why suffrage was accepted at different times in different countries. Also compare Giele (1977, 16–18).

23. Both Prelinger (1987) and Koonz (1987) outline the cultural, religious, and political barriers to women's participation in public life that persisted from mid-1800s through World War I.

24. Ragin (1987).

25. For an excellent sampling of contemporary sociological thought about social movements, see particularly the volumes in the series *Research in Social Movements* edited by Louis Kriesberg and his introduction to volume 2 (1979).

26. Kraditor (1965, 43–74), Sinclair (1965, 339).

27. O'Neill (1969, vii–viii). O'Neill goes on to describe his book as "first of all an inquiry into the failure of feminism."

28. Buechler (1986), Phillips (1986a, 1986b).

29. McCarthy and Zald (1973) offered a major new theoretical alternative to the social psychological emphasis on internal motivations of protestors and to the sociological emphasis on structural strain. For examples of the earlier social psychological theories, see Cantril (1941), Festinger, Riecken, and Schachter (1956), and Inkeles and Levinson (1954). For two well-known treatments of structural strain, see Smelser's study of the industrial revolution in England (1959) and his *Theory of Collective Behavior* (1963).

30. Turner (1981), a leading theorist of collective behavior, traces the historical development of these two major intellectual currents by grouping

them under the categories of collective behavior theory and resource mobilization theory. For examples of the collective behavior school of social movement theory, see Park and Burgess (1921), Blumer ([1937] 1951), Turner and Killian (1972). For examples of resource mobilization theory, see McCarthy and Zald (1977) and Olson (1968). Other excellent discussions of the same distinction can be found in Zurcher and Snow (1981), who describe both motivational and organizational emphases, and Buechler (1986, 31–36), who contrasts "internalist" and "externalist" perspectives.

31. Gusfield (1963), Rosenthal et al. (1985), Lance (1983), Buechler (1986).

32. See Skocpol (1992).

33. Morris (1984).

34. I have used here a sociological theory developed by Talcott Parsons known as functionalism. Although currently out of fashion, a functionalist framework allows one to treat such entities as social movements as actual or potential social systems with recognizable and universal parts. These parts (structures and functions) can then be compared despite obvious differences among specific historical cases. The four dimensions of social movements listed here roughly correspond with Talcott Parsons's (1966, 28–29) four-function paradigm for analysis of social systems: pattern maintenance, goal attainment, integration, and adaptation.

35. Marilley (1985).

36. See Carden (1974, 1977, 1978) and Ferree and Hess (1985).

37. There is a long tradition in sociological theory that relates education, socioeconomic status, and other background characteristics to membership in political, social, and religious movements. See, for example, Mannheim ([1929] 1936).

38. McCarthy (1986), Blocker (1985).

39. Tilly (1978) develops a conceptual framework for analyzing social movements in nineteenth-century France wherein *larger system demands* (imposition of new taxes by the state) ultimately foment *collective action* (tax rebellions). Necessary to the final result are both the aroused *interests* (of local landowners) and the *organization* of those interests (through use of established community institutions).

40. The structure of society at the end stage of a social movement may also affect its outcome. This factor has only recently become an explicit topic for extended discussion. The Tillys (1975) show that in the case of revolutionary movements in France, the nature of the surrounding society and the opposition also affected the movements' success. A number of other social scientists also recognize the powerful impact of the larger society and its agents of social control on the outcome of any social movement. See Zurcher and Snow (1981), Jenkins (1983), and Snow, Rochford, Worden, and Benford

(1986). More specifically, with regard to the contemporary women's movement, Katzenstein (1984) notes that success depends in part on election or appointment of sympathetic law makers and government officials.

41. "Dr. Harris on Women's Education," *Woman's Journal,* 6 October 1900, 313.

42. Ellen H. Richards, "Value of Science to Women," *Woman's Journal,* 7 July 1900, 212–13. Ellen Richards studied sciences at Vassar, then did graduate work in chemistry at MIT. For a description of her many contributions to sanitary engineering and domestic science, see the entry by Janet Wilson James in *Notable American Women,* 3:143–46 (hereafter cited as *NAW*).

43. Gilligan (1982).

Chapter 2

1. Banks (1981), Giele (1990).
2. Norton (1980, 190), Rossi (1973b, 7–15).
3. Norton (1980, 178–87).
4. Norton (1980, 188–94).
5. Rossi (1973b, 7–85).
6. Kerber (1980, 282–84).
7. Norton (1980, 288–89).
8. A. F. Scott (1984a, 64–88).
9. Norton (1980, 273–94); Kerber (1980, 189–231). For biographies, see Frederick Randolph, "Willard, Emma Hart," *NAW,* 3:610–13; Barbara M. Cross, "Beecher, Catherine Esther," *NAW,* 1:121–24; and Sidney R. MacLean, "Lyon, Mary," *NAW,* 2:443–47.
10. Quoted in Kerber (1980, 278) from "The Humble Address of Ten Thousand Federal Maids."
11. Norton (1980, 242).
12. Bacon (1986, 1).
13. Galatians 3:28.
14. Ryan (1981, 75–77).
15. Cross (1950).
16. Ryan (1981, 85). Ryan's profile of the Utica women recalls the dissatisfaction of Japanese housewives (described in chapter 1) who were surveyed in the 1950s and were less happy than farm women or production workers, presumably because they did not find their roles fully absorbing. The Utica women were also in the early phases of industrialization.
17. Cott (1977, 138).
18. Quoted in Rossi (1973b, 178–79).
19. Giele (1978, 147).
20. Yet in 1870, the first year for which a breakdown by sex is available, only 15 percent of these paid workers were women and the great majority of

them were probably domestics. See U.S. Bureau of the Census (1975, 1:134, 138, 49) and Tilly and Scott (1978) for the importance of domestic occupations during industrialization in Great Britain and France from 1850 to 1900.

21. See Degler (1980, 6, and all of chap. 1) for a clear and concise summary of modern historical scholarship on the changing nature of family structure in Europe and America after 1600.

22. Welter (1976, 21–41).

23. Norton (1980, 242) describes how the public sphere gradually became relevant to women as they were taught that the nation would not survive unless its citizens were virtuous. Martin (1985, 127) notes the changing conception of women's educative function as reaching "beyond the formation of the character of individuals to the formation of the character of the nation itself."

24. Beecher (1841), Sklar (1973).

25. Sklar (1973, 174).

26. Beecher (1835, 19–20).

27. Irene Brown (1986) develops an original and penetrating analysis of American women in the early nineteenth century as challenged by secularization. Their concern with death and friendship can be understood as a kind of "spiritual kinkeeping" in the face of the powerful cultural forces of modernization. By drawing on the resources of the religious Enlightenment and "the domesticity *culture*—not cult—of antebellum America," which was connected to the Reformation and the High Anglican Royalists of the English Civil War (119), women between 1800 and 1850 could link their continuing religious faith to rational domesticity and friendship that extended beyond the family. Even though they resigned themselves to changes in the secular world, women "sought to live according to the imperatives of the spiritual world . . . where friendship served a crucial mediating role" and where "private life had not only individual or familial meaning but also communal religious significance" (123). According to the typical pattern of structural differentiation of women's roles, outlined in chapter 1 of this volume, this focus during the first half of the nineteenth century on the spiritual meaning of friendship is consistent with a lack of clear differentiation between the public and the private world of women. The public-private distinction appeared sometime after 1835 and by 1850 had become the catalyst for the emergence of feminism.

28. Epstein (1981, 2, 76) notes women's greater economic dependence and their development of a distinct set of values that extended the activities of motherhood into the community. This description of the conditions that produced women's activism is congruent with my analysis of the structural differentiation of the family from the economy in the early stages of urbanization, which caused strain in women's traditional roles and led them to seek a change in the way their roles were defined.

29. Karen J. Blair (1980, 4–5), in her study of women's nineteenth-

century literary clubs and philanthropic activities, builds on the work of Daniel Scott Smith (1974), Carroll Smith-Rosenberg (1971), and Nancy Cott (1977) to define club women as feminists, albeit in that branch of the movement known as "Domestic Feminism." What is characteristic of the domestic feminists as compared with the equal rights feminists is that they use their "ladylike," or distinctly womanly, traits as a basis of strength for entering and transforming the public world. Blair contends, "Despite public criticism, thousands of nineteenth-century women effectively employed the lady's traits to justify their departure from the home to exert special influence on the male sphere. By invoking their supposed natural talents, women took the ideology of the home with them, ending their confinement and winning influence in the public realm. Domestic Feminism resulted when women redefined the ideal lady." Domestic feminists "found themselves arriving at public influence when they contested the double standard inherent in widespread prostitution" or reasoned that "improving women's minds 'was founded on, not opposed to, women's domestic occupation and material destiny.' . . . [C]lubwomen transformed ladydom by providing an intellectual and social self-improvement program outside the realm of the household . . . to demand reforms for women and for all people in a society that relegated them to the sidelines." Their activity was able "to render obsolete the nineteenth-century cliché, 'Woman's place is in the home.'"

30. Both Hewitt (1984) and Boylan (1984) reject the prevailing historical opinion expressed in Smith-Rosenberg's (1971) work on moral reform societies, which suggests that the earlier type of benevolent society *did* evolve into moral reform. By careful analysis of the membership of such groups, Boylan demonstrates for Boston, New York, and Philadelphia, and Hewitt for Rochester, that benevolent and moral reform societies were distinct in character and coexisted alongside one another.

31. Mary S. Benson, "Graham, Isabella Marshall," *NAW*, 2:71–72.

32. For listing of the great variety of these benevolent associations, see Berg (1978, 156–57) and Scott (1991, 13–18).

33. Scott (1991, 14).

34. Boylan (1981, 17).

35. Quoted in Brumberg (1980, 82).

36. Beaver (1980, 38) provides a number of organizational details about the early missionary societies. Cott (1977, 134) found scores of women's religious associations in New Hampshire between 1804 and 1814, and 138 towns in which there were affiliates of the New Hampshire Bible Society between 1820 and 1828. The same picture held in Connecticut and Massachusetts. Dorothy Bass (1979, 281) concludes that as a result of the Second Great Awakening, membership in religious reform groups became the most important extrafamilial activity of middle-class women from 1795 to 1835. Ryan (1981, 83–93, 108–9) found in Whitestown, New York, that one-fifth of the

conversions in the Finney revivals of 1814 and 1825–26 were of children whose mothers belonged to the women's missionary societies. Other associations, such as the Bible Society, Sunday School Union, Tract Society, and Female Missionary Society, were by-products of the revivals.

37. Welter (1978, 111–25).

38. For an extensive discussion of women's missionary activities, see Beaver (1980) and Brumberg (1980, 86–93).

39. Brumberg (1980, 105).

40. Cott (1977, 149–50), Beaver (1980, 46), Ryan (1981, 91–92).

41. Ryan (1981, 89–92, 105–9). In Utica in 1832, more than a third of the more than 26 religious and charitable associations were exclusively for women members. The members were chiefly wives of the business class who took a rather condescending attitude toward helping widows and poor mothers through such programs as infant schools.

42. Epstein (1981, 82–83).

43. Berg (1978, 166) describes the Boston Seaman's Society. Susan Porter Benson (1976) provides a fine-grained account of the membership and activities of the Providence Employment Society.

44. Smith-Rosenberg (1971, 575), Belyea (1976).

45. Berg (1978, 172–73) recounts a story of one woman who after childbirth was cruelly beaten by her husband then abandoned with only two sticks of wood, a pail of water, and a piece of ship's bread.

46. Belyea (1976) and Scott (1991, 46) both describe the various laws and practical measures (such as shelters for women) that resulted from the efforts of the moral reform societies.

47. Smith-Rosenberg (1971), Boylan (1984).

48. Blair (1980, 8).

49. Cherrington (1920, 36–60).

50. Ryan (1981, 133). Hewitt (1984, 99) reports that during the revivals of the early 1830s, signing the temperance pledge became "the most widely acknowledged symbol of spiritual rebirth, a virtual prerequisite for salvation."

51. Dannenbaum (1984, 49–51).

52. See Dannenbaum (1984, 203). During the late 1850s praying bands of women regularly converged on local saloons to advance the cause of temperance reform. According to Epstein (1981, 94), Dr. Dio Lewis (whose own mother had used such a method in the 1830s to curb the excesses of her alcoholic husband) in 1858 counseled women in Dixon, Illinois, to adopt such a method. Others, however, like women in Greenfield, Ohio, in 1865, engaged in physical assault and wrecked saloons with axes and mallets—a technique later associated primarily with Carry Nation.

53. Dannenbaum (1984, 3).

54. Martineau (1837, 3:159–60).

55. Wittenmyer (1878); Stewart (1888).

56. Ryan (1981, 135).

57. *HWS* ([1881], 1:481–82).

58. According to historian Ellen DuBois (1975, 63), the great significance of the suffrage movement rested in helping the woman to skirt "opposition within the family, a private sphere," and demand "instead her admission to citizenship, and through it admission to the public arena." I am suggesting that even prior to the suffrage movement, the progress of women in entering higher education, the professions, and public speaking also helped them to escape restriction to the private sphere.

59. Jill Ker Conway, "Sill, Anna Peck," *NAW,* 3:290–91. For biographies of this interlocking group of leaders who themselves or whose mothers were educated at Rockford and who were connected with social reform and social welfare in the first half of the twentieth century, see Jill Ker Conway, "Abbot, Grace, *NAW* 1:2–4, and Louise C. Wade, "Lathrop, Julia Clifford," *NAW* 2:370–72.

60. Newcomer (1959, 12–13), Notestein ([1937] 1971, 38).

61. Alice Felt Tyler, "Hunt, Harriot Kezia," *NAW,* 2:235–37; Elizabeth H. Thomson, "Blackwell, Elizabeth," *NAW,* 1:161–65; John B. Blake, "Zakrewska, Marie Elizabeth," *NAW,* 1:702–704.

62. C. I. Nichols, Second National Woman's Rights Convention, Worcester, 1851, *Report,* 76. Matilda Joslyn Gage, Woman's Rights Convention, Syracuse, 1852, *Proceedings,* 39–40. See also Wendell Phillips, Second National Woman's Rights Convention, Worcester, 1851, *Report,* 57.

63. Paulina Wright Davis, Woman's Rights Convention, New York, 1853, *Proceedings,* 29.

64. Paulina Wright Davis, Woman's Rights Convention, New York, 1853, *Proceedings,* 29.

65. David Baldwin, "Larcom, Lucy," *NAW,* 2:368–69.

66. Kessler-Harris (1982), chap. 3, and Foner (1979), chap. 2.

67. Foner (1979, 129–37).

68. Quoted in Grimké (1838, 18).

69. B. M. Solomon (1985, 28–29).

70. Second National Woman's Rights Convention, Worcester, 1851, *Report,* 37.

71. Porter ([1918], 1969, 138), Beard (1946), Kerber (1980, 159–84), Salmon (1986, 14, 193), Melder (1977, 6). British law had provided two major methods for resolving domestic disputes. *Equity,* which relied on the courts and special decrees, had long been used by the wealthy to protect a daughter's right to her property even after marriage. In the late eighteenth century, however, the Revolution weakened this tradition in America, and *common law,* as based on Blackstone's *Commentaries* (1765–69), gained ascendancy.

72. Kessler-Harris (1982, 20–72).

73. Warbasse (1960), Flexner (1959, 65).

74. Alice Felt Tyler, "Rose, Ernestine," *NAW,* 3:195–96. *History of Woman Suffrage* (1:64–67) credits Judge Fine of St. Lawrence as the originator of the New York Property Bill of 1848, which he first proposed in 1836. Flexner (1959, 65).

75. Warbasse (1960, 179–81). The earliest property laws had the effect of safeguarding the property of landlords who were speculators. These laws were accepted earliest in the South, where women's status was less advanced but where the laws appealed to the self-interest of speculators and yet protected women according to the chivalrous ideal.

76. Flexner (1959, 85–86).

77. Warbasse (1960, 272–74).

78. The woman's rights arguments that were worked out in the 1830s–50s were then carried into the organized temperance and suffrage movements that emerged after the Civil War. My content analysis for 1900, for example (described in appendix A), identified several stories containing images of woman's domestic vulnerability so long as she lacked equal rights to her earnings and the vote. See the temperance paper, the *Union Signal,* "A Retrospect," 4 January 1900, p. 4, col. 3, or the suffrage paper, the *Woman's Journal,* "Shall the Men Wash the Dishes?" 7 July 1900, p. 210, cols. 1–3, and "The National Legislative League," 7 April 1900, p. 108, cols. 1–2, for arguments about how the ballot is necessary to protect a woman's rights in the home.

79. DuBois (1978, 41), Morgan ([1937] 1972, 40), Chused (1985).

80. Trollope (1832, 226–27, 131).

81. Martineau (1837, 1:199–207; 2:149).

82. Grimké (1838, 46, 47).

83. *HWS,* 2:189–90; *Revolution,* 29 January 1868, 57. Although a number of feminist women found bloomers convenient and comfortable to wear, especially in comparison with trailing long skirts up and down stairs while carrying infants, they eventually gave them up because of ridicule.

84. B. M. Solomon (1985, 37–38). Patricia Spain, "Longshore, Hannah E. Myers," *NAW,* 2:426–28. Clifton J. Phillips, "Thomas, Mary Frame Myers," *NAW,* 3:450–51.

85. Quoted in B. M. Solomon (1985, 39). See also *HWS,* 1:322.

86. Melder (1967, 246). Also cited by Marilley (1993b). Eleanor Flexner, "Stewart, Maria W. Miller," *NAW,* 3:377–78.

87. Marilley (1993b, 11); Flexner (1959, 51); Kerber (1980, 85–99).

88. DuBois (1979, 31).

89. DuBois (1979, 23).

90. Grimké (1838, 16, 18).

91. DuBois (1979).

92. *HWS,* 1:116.

93. *HWS,* 1:67–73.

94. Elizabeth Cady Stanton's letter to the First National Woman's Rights Convention, Worcester, 1850 (*Woman's Rights Tracts,* no. 10, Syracuse, 1853).
95. Woman's Rights Convention, Syracuse, 1852, *Proceedings,* 30–34.
96. Woman's Rights Convention, New York, 1853, *Proceedings,* 57–58.
97. Woman's Rights Convention, New York, 1853, *Proceedings,* 60.
98. Porter ([1918] 1969, 3–46).
99. *HWS,* 1:247–54.
100. *HWS,* 1:634. Quoted in DuBois (1978, 41).
101. DuBois (1978:42–46).
102. Catt and Shuler (1926, 98), Flexner (1959, 143–44). Note that the Fourteenth Amendment, by basing representation on the number of *male* inhabitants in each state, introduced the word "male" into the U.S. Constitution. Some suffragists were nonetheless convinced that the Fourteenth Amendment did give the vote to women, and so in 1871–72 they tested it by registering and trying to vote, but their claims were denied. See Catt and Shuler (1926, 92).
103. Flexner (1959, 145–47).
104. DuBois (1978, 19, 52).
105. Epstein (1981, 61).
106. This language was used by Ernestine Rose at the Second National Woman's Rights Convention, Worcester, 1851, *Report,* 42.
107. Berg (1978, 152–53) describes the crisis of clergy opposition to women's activism in religious groups; Dannenbaum (1984, 190–91) documents the same problem in temperance.
108. Bass (1979), Cott (1977, 154–55), Berg (1978, 162–63).

Chapter 3

1. *NWCTU Minutes,* 1885, 122–23, *NWCTU Minutes,* 1895, 160ff. My figures are based on the listings of the state and national corresponding secretaries who frequently cautioned that their figures were incomplete. Bordin (1981, 3) places the WCTU membership in 1892 at around 200,000 if one counts the young women's auxiliaries as well as the nearly 150,000 dues-paying members.
2. This is Gusfield's thesis in *Symbolic Crusade* (1963). My own dissertation (Giele, 1961) comparing the temperance and suffrage women also reflects the sentiment common in the 1950s and 1960s that the WCTU was a rather narrow and moralistic organization; I gave it less credit then than I do now for its broad-ranging innovations in social reform on behalf of women.
3. Bordin (1981, 9, 116) places the WCTU squarely within the tradition of what Sochen (1973, 8–9, 65–66) terms "pragmatic feminism" or what O'Neill (1969, 51) calls "social feminism." Also related is "domestic feminism," women's increasing insistence on control of their own sphere and

their own bodies; see Bordin (1981, 202n113) and Daniel Scott Smith (1974, 119–36).

4. Hampel (1982, 1–59).

5. Wittenmyer (1878, 112).

6. Blocker (1985, 24–25).

7. An illustrious example was the New York woman's temperance society, founded by Susan B. Anthony in 1852 when she was denied the right to speak at a temperance convention in New York. See Bordin (1981, 5).

8. *NWCTU Minutes,* 1874.

9. Bordin (1981, 152).

10. Giele (1961, 196).

11. For the methods of the content analysis, see appendix A. In all succeeding notes on the categories of the content analysis, I will give several references to the *Union Signal* as examples of the kind of themes scored in a given category. The references cited will in general be from the years 1895, 1900, or 1905, simply as an arbitrary criterion for choice of examples from the many that were collected. They will also be chosen to represent the different subparts of the category. For category 25, for example,see *Union Signal,* 4 January 1900, p. 2, col. 3; 6 April 1905, p. 2, cols. 1–2, p. 9, cols. 1–2.

12. Interview with Arthur Schlesinger, Sr., in 1959 or 1960. Schlesinger (1922, 1950) had done much to revive interest in the reform movements of the turn of the century, including temperance and suffrage, but he doubted that I would find any major difference between the two groups. Among nineteenth-century feminists themselves there was disagreement as to the amount of identification between temperance and suffrage. Many WCTU members, such as Mary Livermore of Massachusetts, were part of the leadership of both movements. Others, such as suffragist Abigail Scott Duniway of Oregon, resented the intrusion of temperance advocates into the suffrage issue. On Duniway see Moynihan (1983, 131–32).

13. For example, in "A True Story for Today," *Union Signal* (1885, vol. 11, no. 38, pp. 7–8), a newly married young minister goes to the church where his wife's father is pastor, but does not join in the celebration of communion. The young wife is surprised but learns that her husband promised his mother he would never touch a drop of alcohol because his own father's thirst for strong drink was each time reawakened by communion wine such that he would stay away from home for several days afterward and died when the pastor was only a small boy. The young pastor asks his wife to understand and tells her his church has given up fermented wine, a reform that the story clearly implies should be adopted by other churches as well.

14. See "Mothering," *Union Signal,* 2 October 1890, 7. This essay presents a charming review of how mothers feel about bringing up boys when their sons "treat custard pie with disdain," want to rush out to be with their friends, or think they can bring themselves up. Then all at once they may

acknowledge that they are wrong and mother is right. It is not discipline but love that brings about this reversal. So it is with the ballot; love is the great moral agent that somehow saves men. The mother knows that her boy will never be a robber or make any woman a slave. (An example of category 4.3 in appendix A).

15. "Missionary Work in the Logging Regions." Two articles by the Reverend Albert C. Derr, Ph.D., D.D., *Union Signal*, 6 January 1910, 1–2; 13 January 1910, 1–2.

16. Laura J. Rittenhouse (of Cairo, Illinois), "Joab Robinson's Conviction," *Union Signal*, 2 October 1890, 2.

17. Proverbs 31:20.

18. *Union Signal*, 4 October 1900, p. 9, col. 2; 6 July 1905, p. 2, cols. 1–3; 5 October 1905, p. 1, cols. 1–3, p. 4, col. 1.

19. This pattern was in sharp contrast to the suffrage newspaper, *Woman's Journal*, which devoted more than 80 percent of its articles during the same period to discussion of educational, employment, religious, or political equality (categories 16, 18, 19, 21.1, 21.2).

20. *Union Signal*, 4 October 1900, 8; 7 July 1910, 8; 1 January 1915, 8.

21. *Union Signal*, 6 April 1905, p. 2, cols. 1–3; 4 April 1895, p. 6, col. 1.

22. For the reasons tied to a particular use of the ballot, see *Union Signal*, 4 October 1900, p. 4, cols. 1–2; 5 July 1900, p. 8, cols. 1–2. Frances Willard expressed these sentiments in an address in London in 1895: "Organized motherhood is a force the most deeply rooted, the most steadily enduring that this planet knows, among all the beneficent forces that the ages have developed. . . . The ballot for women is part and parcel of our prohibition cause; the two sink or rise together." See "Frances Willard and Woman Suffrage," *Union Signal*, 7 October 1915, p. 5; see also 10 January 1895, 8.

23. Mrs. M. Curry Stretch, "The Mayor's Economy," *Union Signal*, 5 January 1905, 6.

24. The "culture-and-personality" school of social psychology during the 1950s documented connections between inner conflicts and participation in social movements. See Erikson (1950) for an analysis of Hitler's youth, Inkeles and Levinson (1954) for a theoretical framework, Hoffer (1951) for a description of the "true believer," and House (1981) and Zurcher and Snow (1981) for recent formulations.

25. Frank L. Byrne, "Wittenmyer, Annie Turner," *NAW* 3: 636–38.

26. Mary Earhart Dillon, "Willard, Frances Elizabeth Caroline," *NAW*, 3:613–19.

27. Frank L. Byrne, "Stevens, Lillian Marion Norton Ames," *NAW*, 3:370–71.

28. "Willard," *NAW*, 3:613–19. It was both an intriguing and painful irony that many years after breaking off her engagement in 1861 to Charles Fowler, Frances Willard was frustrated in her efforts to achieve equality for women by

this very man. In 1873–74, as president of Northwestern University, Fowler rebuffed her efforts as head of the Evanston College for Ladies to establish women's education on an equal footing with men's. Again in 1889, as a bishop of the Methodist Church, he refused to seat five women delegates at the Church Convention (of whom Frances Willard was one).

29. "Stevens," *NAW*, 3:370.

30. "Willard," *NAW*, 3:615.

31. U.S. Deptartment of the Interior, *Compendium of the 11th Census, 1890* (Washington: Government Printing Office, 1897), 3:117.

32. Woody (1929, 2:323).

33. Janet Z. Giele, "Leavitt, Mary Clement Greenleaf," *NAW*, 2:383–85. It has recently been discovered that more leaders than were once thought struggled privately with the tragedy of alcoholism because of its impact on some of their closest relatives. Examples are the brother (Oliver) of Frances Willard and the son of Eliza Thompson (Thompson was daughter of an Ohio governor and the leader of the most famous 1873 crusade at Washington Courthouse). See Bordin (1986), Blocker (1985).

34. Niebuhr (1957, 143–45).

35. In her biography of Frances Willard, Mary Earhart (1944) emphasizes that in their attitudes toward the ballot, WCTU women from the Midwest were more progressive and women of the East more conservative. In light of this observation, it is not immediately clear why the conservative temperance women as a group were more frequently from the Midwest whereas the progressive suffragists were concentrated in the East.

36. "Willard," *NAW*, 3:615.

37. Paul S. Boyer, "Wallace, Zerelda Gray Sanders," *NAW*, 3:535–36.

38. Robert K. Riegel, "Livermore, Mary Ashton Rice," *NAW*, 2:420–23.

39. Frank L. Byrne, "Bailey, Hannah Clark Johnston," *NAW*, 1:83–84. Lesser-known leaders also crossed back and forth over the boundaries between temperance and suffrage work. Mary Garrett Hay of Indiana first became politically active in the WCTU at the state and national level, then went into lecturing and organizing in the suffrage organization, serving brilliantly in the 1896 California campaign and then as head of the New York campaigns of 1915 and 1917. See James P. Louis, "Hay, Mary Garrett," *NAW*, 2:163–65.

40. Gusfield (1955; 1963).

41. Sewall (1894).

42. McCulloch Papers, Schlesinger Library.

43. Unger (1933, 34–49), *NWCTU Minutes*, 1885, 132–33.

44. Everett C. Hughes to Janet Z. Giele, 5 December 1960.

45. Clara Hoffman, president of the Missouri WCTU in 1890, in reply to the state suffrage president's accusation that the WCTU was opposed to suffrage, commented that WCTU organizations reached throughout the state

and publicized and discussed suffrage, whereas there was only one suffrage organization, in St. Louis. *Woman's Journal,* 15 March 1890, 82. (Eight years later there were 11 more suffrage clubs; see National American Woman Suffrage Association (NAWSA), *Proceedings,* 1898, 101.)

46. *Union Signal,* 8 May 1890, 10–11.

47. Mary A. Livermore to Alice Stone Blackwell, 15 January 1894. Blackwell Papers, Schlesinger Library.

48. For a rough count of the departments, I relied on the superintendents' reports listed in the index to the *Minutes* of the annual conventions for 1880, 1895, and 1910.

49. Bordin (1981, 73).

50. "Leavitt," *NAW,* 2:383–85.

51. *Union Signal,* 19 July 1890, 10.

52. Bordin (1981, 47–48, 90).

53. Missouri suffragist Phoebe Couzins and Hannah J. Bailey of the Maine WCTU were each appointed to the National Board of Charities and Corrections. Susan Hammond Barney carried the police matron movement to the WCTU. Mary Torrans Lathrap of Michigan was instrumental in getting a state appropriation for a girls reformatory in 1878. See Willard and Livermore (1893, 44, 56, 449–50).

54. The early identification of the WCTU with organized religion should not be understated. At the first convention in 1874, the temporary chairman, Jennie F. Willing of Illinois, prominent in women's missionary society work, told the assembly, "You have no need to be reminded that this is simply and only a religious movement . . . Many are praying and praying for us" (*Minutes,* 1874, 6).

55. *NWCTU Minutes,* 1877, 172. There had been various versions of the pledge, which at the Fourth Annual Convention were reconciled to produce a single official WCTU version.

56. *NWCTU Minutes,* 1874, 25.

57. Consistent with what might be interpreted as a nativist purpose was the establishment in 1884 of the WCTU department for suppression of Sabbath desecration, with one of its better-known leaders, Josephine Bateham, at its head.

58. One *Union Signal* story described the winning essay in one school temperance contest: Elsie Brown wrote on how a woman should never marry a man who uses liquor; then she will never be the wife of a drunkard. "Safety First," *Union Signal,* 7 October 1915, 4, 6.

59. Mrs. C. G. Cooper of Mt. Vernon, Ohio, argues that the physical effect of certain articles used as food makes it reasonable to think "that parents can do more in their homes to weaken the power of the saloon than all that can be done outside." "More Home Talks—No. 1," *Union Signal,* 2 April 1885, 7.

60. "Secretary Bryan's 'Dry' Dinners Popular with Foreign Envoys," *Union Signal,* 1 January 1915, 4.

61. Stebbins (1876).

62. Bordin (1981, 48–49).

63. Earhart (1944, 194).

64. "Faithful Are the Wounds of a Friend," *Union Signal,* 3 January 1895, 8.

65. After the turn of the century, Martha Meir Allen of the WCTU lobbied in Washington to press for the control of patent medicine claims. She played an important role in publicizing frauds and health hazards, which led to the enactment of the pure food and drug law.

66. Mezvinsky (1959, 247–48).

67. "Lizzy's Divorce," *Union Signal,* 4 January 1900, 3, recounts the story of a woman who has gone to a lawyer because her husband hit both her and her seven-year-old daughter. She returns home to find her husband, who promises to stop drinking before he goes to work that afternoon. Lizzy makes a good supper and waits for him. At 9:30 he returns, closes the door, stares at Lizzy, and with a drunken leer throws a brick that kills her. The article concludes: "Lizzy had her divorce and she had not taken the children." Gilfus (1988) and Herman (1981) provide evidence on contemporary connections between alcoholism, physical and sexual abuse of women and children, and the backgrounds of prostitutes and women prisoners.

68. There is an interesting sidelight on the request of Methodist women missionaries to be ordained. Their hope was that they might then be able to administer communion to heathen women. Their request was not granted.

69. Mormon marriage practices continued to be of concern. For example, the *Union Signal,* 4 January 1900, 2, reported on "The Roberts Case" with clear disapproval. Brigham H. Roberts, a congressman from Utah, had been charged with polygamy, having three wives and three sets of children by them. For a description of Mormon work, see the biographical sketch of Angie Newman, in Willard and Livermore (1893, 534).

70. Mezvinsky (1959, 236).

71. See the White Cross pledge of purity in Frances Willard, *Do Everything* (Chicago: Woman's Temperance Publishing Assoc., 1895), 48. Mezvinsky (1959, chap. 9) has an extended treatment of the social purity theme in the WCTU.

72. Mezvinsky (1959, 245).

73. *HWS,* 5:225.

74. Helen Campbell, *Prisoners of Poverty* (Boston: Little, Brown, 1900); Mrs. John Van Vorst and Marie Van Vorst, *The Woman Who Toils* (New York: Doubleday, Page, 1903); and U.S. Bureau of Labor, *Fourth Annual Report,* "Working Women in Large Cities," (1889).

75. It was in this period that Frances Willard strongly praised the

Knights of Labor for their contribution in elevating women industrially to their rightful place by claiming equal pay for equal work. Frances E. Willard, *Glimpses of Fifty Years* (Evanston, Ill.: NWCTU, 1889). The WCTU in its convention of 1886 resolved that Willard's speech to the Knights be broadly distributed; Tyler (1949, 91–92).

76. "A White Life for Two," *Union Signal*, 6 April 1905, 9.

77. Mezvinsky (1959, 147).

78. Unger (1933, 176–77, 180) observes that during the 1880s the WCTU developed several departments related to health, hygiene, heredity, and dress reform. In addition, their opposition to patent medicine, tobacco, and narcotics strengthened over the years. For a well-developed argument against all kinds of addictive substances, see "Tobacco as a Physician Sees It," *Union Signal*, 7 July 1910, 5.

79. *NWCTU Minutes,* Third Annual Convention, 1876, 99–100.

80. Mezvinsky (1971, 137–39).

81. Mezvinsky (1959, 148–52).

82. Mezvinsky (1959, 153–54; 1971, 237–39), Bordin (1981, 89).

83. Mezvinsky (1959, 159–88).

84. Mezvinsky (1959, 188).

85. Bordin (1981, 56).

86. *HWS,* 3:500, records this negative suffrage sentiment about the crusade. Abigail Scott Duniway, peppery suffrage leader in Oregon, had a similar reaction but expressed the hope that the crusaders' inevitable frustration with getting real change would open their "eyes to the *power of the ballot.*" Clark (1951) quotes several of Duniway's 1874 editorials in the *New Northwest.*

87. Blocker (1985, 171–72).

88. Kraditor (1965, 44n1), Giele (1961, 143).

89. See, for example, "Governor Clarke Signs Iowa's Prohibition Bill," *Union Signal*, 1 April 1915, 3; "The Challenge of Today," *Union Signal*, 1 January 1915, 15.

90. *NWCTU Minutes,* Second Annual Convention, 1875, 65. The WCTU also gave oblique support to a limited form of woman suffrage when it passed a resolution that the "question of a prohibition of the liquor traffic should be submitted to all adult citizens regardless of race, color, or sex"; see Unger (1933, 100), and *Minutes,* 1875, 61.

91. *NWCTU Minutes,* Fourth Annual Convention 1877, 176.

92. Bordin (1981, 79) says that no comparable grass roots organization existed to promote the woman's ballot. See also Marilley (1985, 331, 343–44) and Unger (1933, 81, 103, 110, 118–19).

93. Gusfield's dissertation (1954, 1) argues that the repeal of the Eighteenth Amendment "reduced the WCTU from a position of relative prestige and acceptance in American middle class groups to a position of

relative ridicule, ostracism, and alienation." My own thesis (Giele, 1961) carries some of this disparaging tone, which was pervasive in the years in which I wrote it.

94. Wittenmyer (1878, 6) said, "The liquor traffic of this country is mainly in the hands of a low class of foreigners, and they are responsible for all the mobs, and nearly all the insults offered to the Christian women engaged in the Crusade." As in many other campaigns, the defeat of suffrage in 1890 in South Dakota was alleged to be the result of prejudice and "the foreign vote." See *Union Signal,* 25 December 1890, 9.

95. Ella Boole, "President's Annual Address," *Forty-First Annual Report of the New York WCTU,* 1900, 38–39. B. M. Solomon (1985, 122).

96. *Union Signal,* 7 October 1915, 3.

97. Jessie Ozias Donahue of Illinois is a case in point. When Jessie was a senior at the University of Michigan, she heard Susan B. Anthony speak. "Returning to her home, she found no suffrage organizations down state, so she went to work in the suffrage department of the WCTU. . . . She had served as state and national superintendent of suffrage in the WCTU. When she moved to Chicago in 1900, she became identified with regular suffrage organizations." Ella S. Stewart, *Scrapbook,* vol. 1, Dillon Collection, Schlesinger Library.

98. Ella S. Stewart to Catherine Waugh McCulloch, Harrisburg, Pennsylvania, 19 October 1915; Carrie Chapman Catt to Ella Harrison, New York, 13 July 1896; Ella S. Stewart to Catherine Waugh McCulloch, Cedar Rapids, Iowa, 14 February [1916?]; Perle Penfield to Ella S. Stewart, 11 May 1910. McCulloch Papers, Schlesinger Library. Ella Harrison to Pa (D. A. Harrison), Charles City, Iowa, 8 May 1898: "I wrote Dr. Adams that they knew the W.C.T.U. had seen its best days & now it was going to pieces it sought a cause, someone to blame." Harrison had been the victim of WCTU suspicions in her activity as a suffrage organizer. See Harrison Papers, Schlesinger Library.

99. After Willard's death the nonpartisan group was reunited with the WCTU. See Mezvinsky (1959, chap. 6).

100. "An Address to the Ohio W.C.T.U.," *Union Signal,* 2 July 1885, 4. Willard believed that the WCTU could heal sectional hatred between the North and the South by supporting the Prohibition party instead of either of the old parties.

101. "An Address to the Ohio W.C.T.U.," *Union Signal,* 2 July 1885, 4.

102. "The Prohibition Party of Kansas . . ." *Union Signal,* 1 January 1885, 3.

103. "On the Friends," *Union Signal,* 2 April 1885, 3.

104. "The Prohibition Convention," *Union Signal,* 5 July 1900, 9.

105. Catt and Shuler (1926, 147). On the involvement of the WCTU in prohibition and suffrage campaigns, see also Colvin (1926, 214) and Unger (1933, 83).

106. *HWS,* 4:141–42.

107. Marilley (1985, 331).

108. Mary A. Livermore to Lucy Stone, 17 September 1891, Blackwell Family Papers, Schlesinger Library. See also note 47 for reference to a similar but later letter to Stone's daughter, Alice Stone Blackwell.

109. A. F. Scott (1970, 145, 150, 144).

110. "West Virginia's Glad Days; Prohibition Laws Well Enforced and Suffrage Sentiment on the Increase," *Union Signal,* 1 April 1915, 5. After 1900 the annual addresses of the national and state presidents consistently included some comment on women's professional advancement and the suffrage movement. See *Union Signal,* 29 March 1906; 10 December 1908; 30 May 1912, 3; NWCTU, *Annual Address of the President,* Thirty-Fourth Annual Convention, Nashville, Tennessee, November 1907, 42; WCTU of Wisconsin, *Forty-First Annual Report,* 1914, 45.

Chapter 4

1. For example, Noun (1969, 27–32) describes the extensive and sometimes competing work of Annie Wittenmyer and Mary Livermore in mobilizing support for the Sanitary Commission in Iowa.

2. Catt and Shuler (1926, 107–8).

3. DuBois (1975, 63).

4. DuBois (1978, 96, 102–3, 126, 164).

5. DuBois (1978), 79–104.

6. Flexner (1959, 164–67); Brown (1965, 153–65); Allen and Welles (1950, 24).

7. *HWS,* 2:286, 272; Brown (1965); Allen and Welles (1950, 31).

8. McDonagh (1987, 1990) found that 96 percent of the members of the House of Representatives who came from states with suffrage at the state level voted for the federal woman suffrage amendment in 1915, compared with only 37 percent of those from states without woman suffrage.

9. See also table 10 in Giele (1961, 141). For reforms outside the home, see appendix A, categories 16, 18, 19, 21.1, 21.2, 22.4, 23.2a, b, c. For reforms inside the home, see appendix A, categories 21.3, 22.5, 23.1a, b, c.

10. Howe (1913, 100–101). In the same vein of maternal sentiment, Anna Howard Shaw told the story of visiting a boy's state reformatory in Pontiac, Illinois. A year later a boy recognized her on a train and came up to say that the boys had liked her lecture because she didn't assume they were all bad. See Shaw (1915, 165).

11. See table 3.1 in chapter 3.

12. "Two Girls Save Six Hundred Lives," *Woman's Journal,* 7 July 1900, 209.

13. "Women in Science," *Woman's Journal,* 7 July 1900, 210; "College

and Alumnae," *Woman's Journal,* 7 April 1900, 106; "Women in the Churches," *Woman's Journal,* 6 January 1900, 8; 6 October 1900, 316.

14. Suffragists were more likely than temperance women to note faults in traditional women. See category 3, "bad traditional woman," in appendix A and examples: Phoebe W. Couzins, "Shall the Men Wash the Dishes?" *Woman's Journal,* 7 July 1900, p. 210, cols. 1–3; "A Silver Vase," *Woman's Journal,* 7 April 1900, p. 105, cols. 2–3. On the other hand, suffragists found many merits in "good traditional women" (category 4), as outlined in "Dr. Harris on Women's Education," *Woman's Journal,* 6 October 1900, 313. They especially recognized the existence of the "good new woman" capable of public service and scientific thought. See Charlotte Perkins Stetson, "Superfluous Women," *Woman's Journal,* 7 April 1900, 105, or Ellen H. Richards, "Value of Science to Women," *Woman's Journal,* 7 July 1900, p. 212, col. 5.

15. Analysis of the traditional versus new images of women in the *Union Signal* and *Woman's Journal* between 1885 and 1915 showed the temperance paper heavily weighted toward representation of good traditional women (27 out of 37 articles), whereas the suffrage paper emphasized the good new woman (28 out of 39 articles). The difference is statistically very significant: Chi-square with Yates's correction = 13.483; $p < .001$.

16. Talcott Parsons and R. F. Bales (1955) used the distinction between instrumental and expressive orientation to characterize men and women. I use that dichotomy here not for gender role differentiation but to describe two types of feminine role orientation.

17. Richards, "Value of Science to Women," *Woman's Journal.*

18. Couzins, "Shall the Men Wash the Dishes?" *Woman's Journal.*

19. In *Woman's Journal:* "The National American Memorial," 7 July 1900, p. 213, cols. 2–3; "Women of the Press," 6 October 1900, p. 316, cols. 2–3; "College and Alumnae," 7 April 1900, p. 106, cols. 1–2; 6 October 1900, p. 320, cols. 2–4.

20. "Women in the Churches," *Woman's Journal.* See note 13.

21. Nearly a third of all suffrage articles compared with only about 3 percent of temperance articles between 1885 and 1915 concerned the theme of women's equality in performance, intellectual competence, and citizenship (categories 10, 11, 12 in appendix A). Another 10 percent of suffrage articles asserted women's equality in moral and spiritual matters, compared with 3 percent in the temperance paper (category 9 in appendix A).

22. "Editors of Famous Papers Declare for Suffrage," *Woman's Journal,* 3 April 1915, 110.

23. "Women in the Churches," *Woman's Journal.* See note 13.

24. "A Social Museum," *Woman's Journal,* 6 January 1900, 1.

25. Suffragists tended to argue for the ballot more as an extension of the instrumental rather than the expressive side of the woman's role. Parsons and Bales (1955, 151–52) recognize that the mother's role is instrumental

rather than expressive when she is representing the interests of her children, thus making her orientation similar to that of the father when he is representing the family to the outside world. The feminists similarly argued that women needed the vote in order to represent not only their own interests but those of children and the poor. See two editorials by Alice Stone Blackwell in the *Woman's Journal*, 5 October 1895: "Inseparable Interests," p. 316, cols. 2–4, and "Sex Antagonism," p. 316, cols. 4–5.

26. "Superfluous Women," *Woman's Journal.* See also the following in *Woman's Journal:* "Editorial Notes," 7 July 1900, p. 209, col. 3; "Growth of the General Federation," 7 July 1900, p. 210, cols. 4–5; "Dr. Harris on Women's Education," 6 October 1900, p. 313, cols. 3–4.

27. See category 18, appendix A. "College and Alumnae," *Woman's Journal.* See also Howe (1913, 113, 152–72) and Meyer (1891, 99).

28. "Letter from Ohio," *Woman's Journal,* 7 April 1883, 108–9.

29. "Mr. Shearman's Advice to Women," *Woman's Journal,* July 7, 1900, 215.

30. "Superfluous Women," *Woman's Journal.*

31. Dall (1868), especially the section entitled "Death or Dishonor."

32. An article on the front page of the first issue of *Revolution* hints at the relationship between the woman's ballot and the power to eliminate prostitution. See "The Ballot—Bread, Virtue, Power," *Revolution,* 8 January 1868, 1. Schlesinger (1927–37, 156).

33. Smuts (1959, 73), U.S. Bureau of Labor (1889, 20–21), Calhoun (1945, 3:90).

34. Breckinridge (1933, 93–95, 181). See also Flexner (1959, 208–9) for a description of efforts by the Consumers' League to arouse public sentiment against the working conditions of sales clerks.

35. "A Modern Declaration of Independence," *Woman's Journal,* 3 July 1915, 214.

36. See categories 19 and 21, appendix A. *Woman's Journal:* "Superfluous Women," "Women in Science," "Mr. Shearman's Advice to Women."

37. Wood (1914, 78–87).

38. Addams (1914, 2). The WCTU Home Protection Petition expressed the need for the ballot in terms of men's failure to listen to their requests: "men, while claiming to represent our wishes and our interests, have signally failed to give us prohibitory laws." Quoted in Tyler (1949, 42).

39. "Inseparable Interests," *Woman's Journal.*

40. "The Experiment at New Ephesus," *Woman's Journal,* 20 June 1885, 198.

41. "The Mean-Spirited Side of the Suffrage Question." *Woman's Journal,* 4 April 1885, 108–9.

42. "The Mean-Spirited Side of the Suffrage Question," *Woman's Journal.*

"Mrs. Stansbury on Mr. Dana" [effects of woman suffrage in Colorado], *Woman's Journal,* 7 April 1900, 108–9. Sen. Frances Willard Mund [note the name], "Election Day in Arizona" *Woman's Journal,* 2 January 1915, 7.

43. "The National Legislative League," *Woman's Journal,* 7 April 1900, 108.

44. "Women Unionists Ask Working Men for Vote," *Woman's Journal,* 3 July 1915, 208.

45. "A Social Museum," *Woman's Journal.*

46. "Kansas Women Save Babies; Cut Death Rate by One Thousand in Cooperation with Board of Health," *Woman's Journal,* 2 January 1915, 7.

47. Kraditor (1965, 44) makes a similar distinction between arguments based on justice and on expediency. For a spoof of traditional women's particularistic orientations and the presentation of the feminists' universalistic alternative, see "The Mean-Spirited Side of the Suffrage Question," *Woman's Journal.*

48. "The National American Memorial," *Woman's Journal.*

49. Thomas Wentworth Higginson, "Temperance Suffrage Once More," *Woman's Journal,* 10 July 1880, 217.

50. Lutz (1959, 251).

51. "Women in Science," *Woman's Journal,* 7 July 1900, 210.

52. Flexner (1959, 83) shows such a cartoon, entitled "Woman's Emancipation," from an issue of *Harper's Monthly* in 1857.

53. Gurko (1976, 56–69); Alma Lutz, "Stanton, Elizabeth Cady," *NAW,* 3:342–47; Alma Lutz, "Anthony, Susan Brownell," *NAW,* 1:51–57.

54. Louis Filler, "Stone, Lucinda Hinsdale," *NAW,* 3:387–91; Gurko (1976, 122–44).

55. Van Vorhis (1987, 7–8). Intensely private about her personal life, Catt systematically destroyed all diaries and letters that would provide a fuller understanding of her childhood and early adulthood. Yet it is still possible from the biographical stories she did allow into print to pinpoint several formative experiences.

56. Eleanor Flexner, "Catt, Carrie Lane Chapman," *NAW,* 1:309–13; Fowler (1986, 3–31).

57. Catherine Waugh McCulloch, a prominent suffrage and temperance leader, practiced law with her husband; she received a formal degree from Union College of Law in Chicago. Ada M. Bittenbender of Nebraska followed the more informal method; her husband was also a lawyer. See Willard and Livermore (1893, 87, 484).

58. Bacon (1986, chap. 2), "The Traveling Women Ministers, 1650–1800."

59. One of these rare examples may have been Ada Bittenbender, the first woman lawyer in Nebraska, who helped to form the Nebraska Woman's Suffrage Association in 1881, then in 1882 became active in the Nebraska

WCTU and served from 1883 to 1889 as its superintendent for temperance legislation. Frank L. Byrne, "Bittenbender, Ada Matilda Cole," *NAW,* 1:153–54. These events occurred in such quick succession, however, that they demonstrate simultaneous commitment rather than a clear case of suffrage coming before temperance.

60. *Woman's Journal,* 29 March 1890, 101.

61. H. Solomon (1946, 109).

62. *HWS,* 5:56–58. A woman of Table Rock, Nebraska, in 1900 described the Woman Suffrage Club as the "fashionable social club of town." *Woman's Journal,* "College and Alumnae," 7 April 1900, 106.

63. Three of these categories—goals, membership, and allies—roughly correspond with Marilley's (1993a) description of the key political skills of Frances Willard: (1) creation of an agenda to challenge the existing cultural authority that excluded women from politics; (2) mobilization of members and supporters; and (3) incorporation into the larger political scene. A fourth category, organizational structure, is associated with *integration,* which like the other three (*goal attainment, adaptation,* and *latent pattern maintenance*) corresponds with the four functional requirements of any social system. See Parsons (1961; 1982, 157–82).

64. Lunardini (1986, 84).

65. Lunardini (1986, 4); Phillip R. Shriver, "Upton, Harriet Taylor," *NAW,* 3:501.

66. Flexner (1959, 355). The major single source of suffrage records is still the Library of Congress Manuscript Division's (1975) microfilmed collection *The Blackwell Family, Carrie Chapman Catt and the National American Woman Suffrage Association* (which, however, contains only a hit-and-miss collection of the NAWSA records).

67. In Massachusetts, where the AWSA was strong, school suffrage and tax and bond suffrage were obtained in 1879, and in 1881 a drive was begun for municipal suffrage. In 1880, Thomas Wentworth Higginson, in an editorial in the *Woman's Journal,* the newspaper of the AWSA, strongly contended that the temperance ballot was not like school suffrage; it advocated a particular course and therefore drew opposition where suffrage alone did not. *Woman's Journal,* 26 June 1880, 201, and 10 July 1880, 217. The AWSA position against partisanship was reiterated in 1889 when Henry Blackwell pleaded with Frances Willard not to alienate Republicans in Kansas by supporting the Prohibition party solely. Earhart (1944, 225–26).

68. Anthony (1954, 391); compare Lutz (1959, 244). At the time of the merger of the AWSA and the NWSA, the Reverend Olympia Brown, Matilda Joslyn Gage, and others protested the unification on the grounds that the National had always been interested in working for federal suffrage rather than for school and municipal suffrage as the American had done. See the pamphlet "A Statement of Facts," in the Casement Collection, Sophia Smith

Collection, Smith College. For the developments in Massachusetts, see a paper by Lois B. Merk, Papers of the Radcliffe Seminars, vol. 1, no. 9, Schlesinger Library.

69. One of the key historians of state suffrage activity has been A. Elizabeth Taylor. See, for example, her history for Tennessee (1978), her collection of documents for Texas (1987), and numerous other accounts for southern states such as Georgia, Florida, North Carolina, Mississippi, and Arkansas, which are located in the state historical journals.

70. These figures were obtained in the answers to questionnaires that Catt sent to all the state organizations. In the New York Public Library. Cf. NAWSA, *Proceedings,* 1914.

71. New York State Woman Suffrage Association, *Annual Report: A Record of the Campaign, Woman Suffrage, and the Constitutional Convention,* 1894, 139–40; New York State Woman Suffrage Party, *Annual Report,* 1915, 94–95; *Annual Report of the New York State Woman Suffrage Party and Proceedings of the Forty-Ninth Annual Convention,* 1917, 170–71.

72. Cross (1950) links all these phenomena to the distinctive religious history of western New York as well as to the bustling commerce and rapid social change caused by the Erie Canal.

73. New York State Suffrage Association, *A Record of the Campaign,* 1894, 221.

74. Ella Harrison, a native of Missouri, was sent out to organize suffrage sentiment in Mississippi and Louisiana. In her letters one reads the discouragement and loneliness of the task; it was hard to organize meetings and, in some cases, to find any people at all who were interested. See Harrison Papers, Schlesinger Library.

75. Blair (1980, 3).

76. Paulson (1973, 134–35).

77. Fox (1918).

78. Wilson (1979, 96).

79. Scott (1970, 150).

80. Scott (1970, 177).

81. For a list of famous persons who endorsed woman suffrage see *HWS,* 4:1081–83.

82. "Editors of Farm Papers Declare for Woman Suffrage," *Woman's Journal,* 3 April 1915, 110. "Facts Worth Knowing" (New York, 1915), brochure in Sophia Smith Collection, Smith College.

83. NAWSA, *Proceedings,* 1909.

84. Mowry (1958, 34–36; 87–92).

85. Blocker (1989, 85) notes that in 1889 WCTU leader Jane Ellen Foster, an important leader in the Republican party in Iowa, led 200 of the 7,000 local unions of the WCTU in 11 states to form the Non-Partisan WCTU.

86. Methodist and Unitarian leaders in Massachusetts endorsed the

municipal suffrage bill that was before the state legislature in 1890. Also in 1890, in a commencement address at Notre Dame University, Catholic Bishop Spaulding of Peoria expressed approval of higher education for women, equal rights, and equal pay for women. *Woman's Journal,* 5 April 1890, 109; 5 July 1890, 213; 4 October 1890, 210; *HWS,* 4:1079, 1083. Jews—such as Hannah Greenbaum Solomon, president of the National Council of Jewish Women, and members of the Central Conference of American Rabbis—were on record for suffrage. NAWSA, *Proceedings,* 1914, 127–29; 1913, 43–56; *Woman's Journal,* 3 January 1914, 4; Suffrage Campaign Collection, New York Public Library.

87. Merk (1948); also Dreier papers, Sophia Smith Collection. *HWS* 6:468–69. Krone (1946) on Pennsylvania. College Equal Suffrage League of Northern California, 1913, 8, Schlesinger Library.

88. Buechler (1986, 117–30).

89. "Growth of the General Federation," *Woman's Journal,* 7 July 1900, 210.

90. "Wanted, Modern Tools," *Woman's Journal,* 3 July 1915, 210.

91. For a description of the Women's Trade Union League see Flexner (1959, 244–46). NAWSA, *Proceedings,* 1910, 29–30. Suffrage literature was sent out to the WCTU and the Women's Trade Union in each state for distribution.

92. Mowry (1958, 102–3).

93. Tax (1980, 164–201).

94. Tax (1980, 207, 174).

95. At the 1880 convention of the Illinois Suffrage Association an appeal to be seated by the working-class Illinois Woman's Alliance was not even accepted. Buechler (1986, 125).

96. Quoted in Tax (1980, 178).

97. *HWS,* vol. 4, chap. 5.

98. *Woman's Journal,* 4 January 1890, p. 420, cols. 2–3; "Editors of Farm Papers Declare for Woman Suffrage," 3 April 1915, 110; NAWSA, *Proceedings,* 1910, 42.

99. Kenneally (1967).

100. McCarthy and Zald (1977). For an overview of new developments in social movement research and theory see McAdam, McCarthy, and Zald (1988).

101. Snow, Rochford, Worden, and Benford (1986). Klandermans (1986).

102. Johnson (1989) bases her work on that of Talcott Parsons on "upgrading" as a key process of social change in modern societies. See also Smelser (1963) for a structural-functional perspective on social movements.

103. Klandermans (1986), in a masterful synthesis of social movement theory, notes that the current principal contenders omit "consensus mobilization," which he believes is a fundamental step that should be addressed. I

believe "consensus mobilization" relates to the same process Parsons and Johnson refer to as "inclusion."

104. Gusfield (1981, 28–54).

105. See Kraditor (1965) and O'Neill (1969). Buechler (1986, 99–100) gives an excellent reinterpretation by reframing the issue as one of why expediency arguments were selected from a wide variety of appeals (rights and justice as well as expediency) that had existed from the beginning.

106. Gamson (1989, 459)

107. Lunardini (1986).

108. The precinct method became common in later campaigns—in Washington in 1910, in California in 1911, and in New York in 1915 and 1917. In the New York campaign of 1917 Tammany Hall gave suffrage its last-minute support. The Woman Suffrage Party had organized down to the district and precinct levels, where some of its captains and assembly district leaders were wives of men in the Tammany Executive Committee, who persuaded their husbands to keep "hands off" the election. As a result the suffrage amendment passed by a majority of over 100,000 votes in the city. Outside the city it lost by a little more than a thousand votes. Catt and Shuler (1926, 298–99).

109. Flexner (1959, 281). For Catt's similar strategy in New York State, see Empire State Collections, New York Public Library. Also Flexner, "Catt, Carrie Clinton Lane Chapman," *NAW* 1:311.

110. Lunardini (1986, 149).

111. Catt and Shuler (1926). Recent work by political scientist Eileen McDonagh (1987, 1990) demonstrates how successful Catt's plan was. Members of Congress from states with woman suffrage were far more likely to support the suffrage amendment than those from states without.

112. Klandermans (1986, 26) remarks that "The mobilization potential of a social movement describes the limits within which a mobilization campaign can be successful."

113. "Third Time Luck Changes," *Woman's Journal,* 7 July 1900, 212.

114. Strom (1975, 301–3).

115. Strom (1975, 303–9), Merk (1948, 15). Other street meetings were held in Philadelphia in 1911 and 1912 (Krone 1946, 45) and in New York. Florence Allen and Mary Welles (1950) describe the activities in Ohio: suffragists spoke before labor groups, WCTU conventions, and church groups. They held hundreds of open-air meetings, distributed thousands of pamphlets, and served innumerable suppers and sandwiches.

116. Catt and Shuler (1926, 240–41, 290).

117. *HWS* 6:459–64, Catt and Shuler (1926, 287–90). One pamphlet used in the New York campaign of 1915 was labeled "good for distribution among clergymen, lawyers, scholarly people." Another entitled "The Housewife and

the Cost of Living" was described as mainly humorous—"good for conservative women." "Measures Advocated by Woman's Organizations" (California,
1910), pamphlet, Sophia Smith Collection, Smith College. Among the measures advocated were mother's pensions, a pure milk bill, and protection of
songbirds, some 27 in all. In her letters to clergymen in 1915, Mary E.
Craigie asked them to choose as their Mother's Day sermon topic "The Need
of the Mother's Influence in the State." Empire State Campaign Collection,
New York Public Library; NAWSA, *Proceedings,* 1910, 101–2.

118. *Woman's Journal,* 3 April 1875, 108.

119. For Colorado see Marilley (1985, 327–31, 384); for Illinois see
Buechler (1986, 117–90). For other examples see Bordin (1981, 134–35); concerning Michigan in 1908, see *HWS* 6:305.

120. Quoted in Catt and Shuler (1926, 154).

121. Duniway (1914, 187–207); Krone (1946, 6); Catt and Shuler (1926,
156–59). In 1913 the Illinois Suffrage Association was offered $1,000 for tak-
ing an ad from the Brewers Association. Some argued that the ad should be
accepted to show that the organization was "broad and politic." Ella S.
Stewart to Catherine Waugh McCulloch, Chicago, 6 August 1913, McCulloch
Papers, Schlesinger Library.

122. Carrie Chapman Catt, "The Suffrage Single Plank" (1915), New York
Public Library. Carrie Chapman Catt to Ella Harrison, New York, 15 May
1896, Harrison Papers, Schlesinger Library.

123. Ella S. Stewart, a leader in both suffrage and temperance, wrote the
editor of a midwestern newspaper in 1913: "As a voter as well as an educator,
I would attempt to lift that curse [the saloon]. But as a suffragist I concede
the right of any woman who believes that the saloon is a blessing to humanity
to vote her own convictions." In Stewart Papers, Dillon Collection,
Schlesinger Library. Further evidence of the broad view is apparent in several letters written by Mrs. Edward Dreier, the prominent New York social
leader, to speakers for and against prohibition who were to be present at a
suffrage meeting. In a third letter, to Ella A. Boole, president of the WCTU,
who was also to be present at the meeting, she began: "Since we are made up
of women who differ on everything except suffrage . . ." and concluded, ". . . I
personally hope that the result will be helpful to the cause of Prohibition."
Mrs. Edward Dreier to Ella A. Boole, Brooklyn, 1 May 1918, Dreier Papers,
Sophia Smith Collection, Smith College.

124. *HWS* 4:148–49. For other examples, see the *Woman's Journal,* 6
January 1900, p. 8, cols. 2–3; 1 April 1905, p. 49, cols. 2–3.

125. *Woman's Journal,* 5 January 1895, 1. Among suffragists it was particularly Stanton who advocated educated suffrage.

126. *HWS* 5: 82–83. Catt voiced such caution at the National American
Suffrage convention in 1903 in New Orleans where Belle Kearney of the

Louisiana WCTU spoke for the woman's ballot as a means to ensure white supremacy.

127. Scott and Scott (1982, 26).

128. Marshall (1986, 332); Camhi (1973, 1–5, 138 ff.)

129. See "Give the Women of California a Square Deal" (1911), pamphlet, Sophia Smith Collection, Smith College.

130. Degler (1980, 341).

131. Degler (1980, 181), Wilson (1979, 44, 187–89).

132. U.S. Bureau of Education, *Report of the Commissioner, 1898–99,* 1853.

133. U.S. Bureau of Census (1975, 385).

134. Wilson (1979, 112), Degler (1980, 389, 484).

135. Edwards (1943, 101).

136. Hill (1929, 19). U.S. Bureau of Census (1975, 382).

137. For example, prison reform was one of the activities that interested suffragists and temperance women alike, especially in the South. Louisiana suffragists were doing prison work of this kind at the turn of the century; see NAWSA, *Proceedings,* 1898, 95.

138. Degler (1980, 317, 325), Furer (1969, 297).

139. Jensen (1973, 271), in a study of notable American women, found suffrage support positively correlated with WCTU activity and memberships in women's clubs, professional and national organizations, and alumnae associations.

140. "Why California Women Should Vote" (1911), pamphlet, Sophia Smith Collection, Smith College.

141. *Woman's Journal,* 15 January 1910.

142. "Jane Addams Wants to Vote" (1911), pamphlet, Sophia Smith Collection, Smith College.

Chapter 5

1. Faludi (1991), Wolf (1993).

2. Skocpol (1992).

3. Gil (1992).

4. Rupp and Taylor (1987).

5. Uhlenberg (1969, 415), Giele (1978, 147).

6. Bianchi and Spain (1986, 122–23, 131). U.S. Department of Labor (1969).

7. Oppenheimer (1970), Corcoran (1978), Schor (1991).

8. Zelizer (1985), Bianchi and Spain (1986, 89), Hayes, Palmer, and Zaslow (1990, 17).

9. About a third of women born between 1900 and 1920 were in the

labor force at age 20; some dropped out during their 30s; and about a third were again employed at age 40. For women born in 1920, the level of early employment changed little, but almost 45 percent were employed by age 40. See Kreps and Leaper (1976).

10. Baker and Sween (1982, 80), Giele, Lachman, and Gilfus (1986), Giele (1987), Giele and Gilfus (1990), Konecko (1982).

11. Schuster (1990).

12. Hulbert and Schuster (1993).

13. Bateson (1989).

14. Hole and Levine (1971) describe the new feminist movement and its two major strands. See also Carden (1974, 1977) and Hess and Ferree (1985). In *Women and the Future* I summarize some of the major policies that resulted; see Giele (1978, 68–69).

15. Friedan (1963), Rossi (1964).

16. Biographical details on Friedan and Rossi come from *Who's Who in America*. I have compared them with broad historical accounts for women's lives in each decade since 1920. For the 1920s, see Brown (1987); for the 1930s, Scharf (1980) and Ware (1982); for the 1940s, Hartmann (1982); for the 1950s, Kaledin (1984); for the 1970s, Wandersee (1988). Scharf and Jensen (1983) cover the women's movement between 1920 and 1940. Rupp and Taylor (1987) describe the women's movement between 1945 and the 1960s.

17. Significantly, Rossi (1982, 341), in her study of feminist delegates to the 1977 Houston convention, found that a delegate's self-rating on political competence was more strongly correlated with the size of her paycheck than with any other variable except her actual political experience; the higher her paycheck, the higher she rated her political competence. In a similar vein, Ethel Klein (1984, appendix A) discovered links between feminist attitudes and a woman's having had "innovative" work, marital, or educational roles.

18. Parsons (1966), M. Johnson (1989).

19. Carden (1977, 40–43). Gelb and Palley (1987) use Carden's framework for assessing feminists' relative progress in shaping public policy.

20. Mead and Kaplan (1965).

21. Conway (1982, 198–200).

22. Bordin (1981, xiv–xviii).

23. O'Neill (1969, 47–48).

24. The list includes Giele (1961), Kraditor (1965, 43–74), Sinclair (1965), O'Neill (1969), DuBois (1975), Buechler (1986, 8), and Gordon (1986, 19).

25. DuBois (1975, 63).

26. Leach (1980, 9).

27. O'Neill (1969, 3–48) argues that marriage and the family were more fundamental objects of reform by the feminists than the focus on the vote. But Degler (1980, 341) shows that suffrage was really more radical than it

sounded.

28. This is a process known as "value generalization," explained above in connection with Parsons's and Johnson's description of adaptive upgrading.

29. Kraditor (1965, 73).

30. Kraditor (1965, 63).

31. Mueller (1988, 22).

32. Kraditor (1965, 63), Degler (1980, 341, 328 quote).

33. Ferree and Hess (1985, 141–66) describe these two types of feminist thought as "career feminism" (focus on equality) and "liberal feminism" (focus on the difference between the sexes).

34. Cott (1987, 227) gives an extensive summary of various historians' critique of the suffrage victory and its aftermath.

35. Andersen (1990, 193), Baxter and Lansing (1983, 21, 181).

36. Poole and Zeigler (1985, 147). *Information Please Almanac* (1993, 37).

37. Andersen (1990, 184); Ferree and Hess (1985, 119).

38. Baxter and Lansing (1983, 13).

39. Mueller (1981).

40. *Information Please Almanac* (1993, 34, 41).

41. National Women's Political Caucus (1985, 10), Clark (1991).

42. Ferree and Hess (1985, 116).

43. Ferree and Hess (1985, 118), Boles (1991, 42).

44. Gelb and Palley (1987, 215).

45. Baxter and Lansing (1983, 179–80), Mueller (1991, 35–36).

46. Snow, Rochford, Worden, and Benford (1986).

47. Cott (1987, 279).

48. Poole and Zeigler (1985, 21–22).

49. Sapiro (1991).

50. Sapiro (1991).

51. Lemons (1973, 189–90).

52. Freeman (1990, 461).

53. Ware (1982, 28).

54. Gelb and Palley (1987, 199–202).

55. Ware (1982, 104).

56. Glendon (1987, 112).

57. Kamerman and Kahn (1989).

58. DeHart-Mathews and Mathews (1986), Hoff-Wilson (1986), Mansbridge (1986, 98–104), E. Pleck (1986).

59. Smelser (1963, 95) introduced the concept of "short-circuiting" to describe the direct conversion of any abstract belief into a concrete action without its having gone through the appropriate steps required for institutionalization.

60. Degler (1989, 208–9), Elshtain (1981, 333–43), Hewlett (1986a).

61. E. Pleck (1986).
62. Mueller (1991, 37).
63. Boles (1991, 44–45). Freeman (1975, 226–29) was the first student of the modern feminist movement to use the term "policy system" to describe the network of women's organizations and pressure groups that engaged in political action.
64. Boles (1991), Gelb and Palley (1987).
65. Boles (1991, 48–49).
66. Gelb and Palley (1987, 213).
67. National Organization for Women, "Official Political Initiatives Action Ballot" (Washington, D.C.: NOW, 1991).
68. Wandersee (1981, 4–5).
69. Conway (1982, 198–202).
70. Lemons (1973, 154).
71. Stetson (1990) brilliantly analyzes the reframing of disability and parental leave issues that eventually made these measures acceptable to equal rights feminists.
72. Cott (1987, 39).
73. DuBois (1975, 63).
74. Leach (1980, 12, 14, 15).
75. Cott (1987, 3–7).
76. This omission has recently been rectified by Theda Skocpol's *Protecting Soldiers and Mothers* (1992), which shows the striking importance of women's clubs to maternal and child health and welfare policy after 1900. Anne Firor Scott's documentation (1991) of the many facets of nineteenth-century women's volunteer associations also links them to civic and cultural contributions.
77. Lemons (1973), Skocpol (1992).
78. Sklar (1981), Scott (1984a).
79. Gil (1992), Sklar (1981), Scott (1991), Skocpol (1992).
80. Gordon (1986, 19) in a study of New Jersey suffragists found that many of these middle-class women, although not themselves members of the paid labor force, were sympathetic with working women, supporting the eight-hour day, prohibition of industrial homework, and appointment of enlightened factory inspectors and labor commissioners.
81. Weiss (1976).
82. M. L. Taylor (1987).
83. McCallum, "Activities of Women in Texas Politics, II," in A. Elizabeth Taylor (1987, 221–30).
84. Gordon (1986, 43).
85. Gordon (1986, 41).
86. Scott (1984b).
87. Gordon (1986, 39).

88. Hewlett (1986).

89. For other efforts to demonstrate crossovers between the public and private spheres, see Dietz (1989), Elshtain (1981, 347), Hewlett (1986b), and Shanley (1983, 360).

90. Stetson (1990, 413).

91. Stetson (1990, 414).

92. Stetson (1990, 416).

93. Rothman (1978, 187–90), Joffe (1983).

94. Chafe (1972, 186–87).

95. Keyserling (1972).

96. Joffe (1983, 117).

97. Joffe (1983, 176).

98. Rothman (1978, 272–74).

99. National Academy of Sciences (1976, 68).

100. Adams and Winston (1980, 66).

101. Hayes, Palmer, Zaslow (1990, 32).

102. Ellwood (1988).

103. The Lexington, Massachusetts chapter of NOW, for example, discussed the economic plight and options of poor women in its January 1994 meeting.

104. Kahne (1994), Wexler (1993).

105. *Information Please Almanac* (1993, 842). The figures are $19,547 for white families headed by women and $11,414 for black; and $41,506 for white and $33,307 for black married-couple families.

106. *Information Please Almanac* (1993, 446).

107. Weitzman (1986).

108. Blankenhorn (1990), Elshtain (1982), Popenoe (1988), Whitehead (1993). Many of these ideas were outlined by William A. Galston in a speech entitled "National Family Policy: Three Good Ideas," delivered to the 10 December 1993 annual meeting of the Institute of American Values held in New York City. The institute is a centrist organization supporting academic research and interchange on the development of a more comprehensive policy to support and strengthen American families. Galston is deputy assistant to President Bill Clinton for Domestic Policy and a member of the White House Domestic Policy Council.

109. The effort is to normalize or mainstream these new family forms. See, for example, Suzanne Slater, *The Lesbian Family Life Cycle* (1994).

110. On child allowances see Kamerman and Kahn (1989). For other causes of teenage pregnancy, Williams (1991).

111. See Fuchs (1990), Folbre (1994).

112. Gill and Gill (1994), Galston (1993).

113. Holmes (1991).

114. Okin (1989) gives a critique of classic and new theories of justice,

especially of the Rawlsian kind. She then uses feminist theories and research to construct her alternative model. See Pateman (1988) for an example of one such feminist theory.

115. J. Pleck (1992).

116. Cott (1987, 278). On the general problem of dealing with difference, see Minow (1984), Scott (1988:167–77), Sapiro (1990:51), and Costain (1988). There is also within each of the social science disciplines an ongoing debate over the question of sex difference. In psychology the work of Carol Gilligan (1982) on sex differences in moral development and in sociology the work of Alice Rossi (1977) on sex differences in parenting have both stimulated an enormous literature both laudatory and critical. For one of the critical statements, see Epstein (1988).

117. Ramsoy (1963) elaborates the possible relationships between system and subsystem. Focus on the interests of subsystems tends to be associated with conflict, whereas identification with the system as a whole is associated with consensus. I have adapted this distinction for dealing with the focus on sex difference as compared with sex equality. In addition, in earlier work I have developed the idea of "crossover" as sharing across the boundaries of formerly differentiated realms, such as when men take on family duties that used to be the province of women or when women enter jobs that used to be reserved for men (Giele 1978, 45–46 and passim). Crossover is another way of describing what happens as a result of inclusion and value generalization in the process of adaptive upgrading.

118. Minow (1990, 275).

119. Glendon (1991), Etzioni (1993, 362).

120. Rebecca Klatch (1987, 206–7), in her study of women of the New Right, shows how the socially conservative are trying to preserve the traditional female role as "the last pocket of common humanity, of the private and personal in an impersonal, mechanized world." As mother and moral gatekeeper, the traditional woman associates her own role with the higher value of self-sacrifice and the role of the career woman with narcissism and self-interest.

121. Rupp and Taylor (1987).

122. There is growing literature on the origins of the maternalist welfare state. See Pedersen (1993) for a comparison of Britain and France, and chapters by Giele and others in Kauppinen and Gordon (forthcoming).

123. Using data from the nationally representative German Socio-Economic Panel Study in 1993, I discovered the increasing incidence of multiple roles among younger cohorts of women in both East and West Germany. Women's multiple roles are emerging not just in the United States but in such countries as Germany. See Giele and Pischner (1994).

Appendix A

1. Computer programs such as Ethnograph and Hyper Research, which are used today for the grouping and counting of themes, were then many years in the future. Today, however, it should be possible to adapt this scheme to any one of the available current methods.

Appendix B

1. Inclusion in the general file of names in itself signified a general level of prominence. The file was constructed from names of all those women who were listed in a variety of biographical reference volumes and books on American women. The major sources from which these names were drawn are: Frances E. Willard and Mary A. Livermore, *A Woman of the Century* (Buffalo: Charles Wells Moulton, 1893); Annie Nathan Meyer, *Woman's Work in America* (New York: Holt, 1891); Mrs. John A. Logan, *The Part Taken by Women in American History* (Wilmington, Del.: Perry-Heale Pub. Co., 1912); *Who Was Who in America,* vol. 1, 1897–1942 (Chicago: A. N. Marquis Co., 1943); Phebe A. Hanaford, *Daughters of America* (Augusta, Me.: True and Co., 1883); Lydia Hoyt Farmer, ed., *National Exposition Souvenir* (Buffalo: Charles Wells Moulton, 1893); *Appleton's Annual Cyclopedia* (New York: D. Appleton and Co., 1862–1903); and the necrology of *The New International Year Book* (New York: Dodd, Mead and Co., 1908–).

2. The suffrage lists were rated by Eleanor Flexner, historian of the suffrage movement; Mary Earhart Dillon, biographer of Frances Willard; Alma Lutz, biographer of Elizabeth Cady Stanton and Susan B. Anthony; and Lawrence Graves, historian of the suffrage movement in Wisconsin. The WCTU lists were rated by Mrs. Dillon; Helen E. Tyler, historian of the WCTU and author of *Where Prayer and Purpose Meet* (Evanston, Ill.: Signal Press, 1949), and Norton Mezvinsky, whose doctoral dissertation, "The White Ribbon Reform, 1874–1910" (Department of History, University of Wisconsin, 1959) was a history of the WCTU.

3. Biographical information was obtained from the following sources: B. F. Austin, ed., *The Temperance Leaders* (St. Thomas, Ont.: n.p., 1896); Gertrude Biddle and Sarah Lowrie, eds., *Notable Women of Pennsylvania* (Philadelphia: University of Pennsylvania Press, 1942); Mabel Ward Cameron, ed., *Biographical Cyclopedia of American Women,* 3 vols. (New York: Halvord Pub. Co., 1924); Clara Chapin, ed., *Thumbnail Sketches of White Ribbon Women* (Chicago: Woman's Temperance Publishing Assoc., 1895); Ernest Cherrington, *Standard Encyclopedia of the Alcohol Problem,* 6 vols. (Westerville, Ohio: American Issue Publishing Co., 1925–30); Clavia Goodman, *Bitter Harvest; Laura Clay's Suffrage Work* (Lexington, Ky.: Bur Press, 1946); Julia Ward Howe, ed., *Representative Women of New England*

(Boston: New England Historical Publishing Co., 1904); Allen Johnson, ed., *Dictionary of American Biography* 22 vols. (New York: Charles Scribner's Sons, 1928); John W. Leonard, *Woman's Who's Who of America, 1914–1915* (New York: American Commonwealth Co., 1914); Mrs. John A. Logan, *Part Taken by Women: National Cyclopedia of American Biography* 13 vols. (Springfield, Ill.: 1939); *Who Was Who in America*, vol. 1, 1897–1942; Willard and Livermore, *A Woman of the Century*.

References

Manuscripts and Collections

New York Public Library: New York Suffrage Campaign Collection.
Schlesinger Library, Radcliffe College: Blackwell Family Papers; College Equal Suffrage League of Northern California; Papers of Catherine Devenney Dunham, 1844–1920; Papers of Ella Harrison, 1892–1898; Papers of Catherine Waugh McCulloch, 1868–1943; Papers of Ella Seass Stewart, 1903–1932.
Sophia Smith Collection, Smith College: Casement Collection; Dreier Papers.

Newspapers

Revolution. New York, 1868.
Union Signal. Chicago, 1885–1915.
Woman's Journal. Boston, 1875–1915.

Woman's Rights

First National Woman's Rights Convention. 1850. *Woman's Rights Tracts,* no. 10. Syracuse, 1853.
Second National Woman's Rights Convention. 1851. *Report of the Woman's Rights Convention.* Held at Worcester, Mass.
Third National Woman's Rights Convention. 1852. *The Proceedings of the Woman's Rights Convention.* Held at Syracuse, 1852. Syracuse: J. E. Masters.
Proceedings of the Woman's Rights Convention. 1853. Held in New York, 1853. New York: Fowler and Wells.

Temperance

Massachusetts Woman's Christian Temperance Union. 1919. *Report of the Forty-Sixth Annual Convention.*

National Woman's Christian Temperance Union. 1888, 1889, 1907. *Annual Address of the President.*

National Woman's Christian Temperance Union. 1976. *Annual Report.*

National Woman's Christian Temperance Union. 1874, 1875, 1877, 1880, 1885, 1890, 1895, 1900, 1910. *Minutes of the Annual Meeting.*

New York Woman's Christian Temperance Union. 1900. *Annual Report.*

Woman's Christian Temperance Union of Wisconsin. 1914. *Forty-First Annual Report.*

Suffrage

National American Woman Suffrage Association. 1893, 1898, 1909, 1910, 1913, 1914. *Proceedings of the Annual Convention.*

New York State Suffrage Association. 1894. *A Record of the Campaign: Woman Suffrage and the Constitutional Convention of 1894. Annual Report of the New York State Suffrage Association.*

New York State Woman Suffrage Party. 1915. *Annual Report of the New York State Woman Suffrage Association.* Forty-Seventh Annual Convention.

New York State Woman Suffrage Party. 1917. *Annual Report for 1917 and Proceedings of the Forty-Ninth Annual Convention.*

Books and Articles

Adams, Carolyn Teich, and Kathryn Teich Winston. 1980. *Mothers at Work: Public Policies in the United States, Sweden, and China.* New York: Longman.

Addams, Jane. 1914. "Why Women Should Vote." Reprint from *Ladies Home Journal.* New York: National Woman Suffrage Publishing.

Allen, Florence E., and Mary Welles. 1950. *The Ohio Woman Suffrage Movement.* Cleveland: Committee for the Preservation of Ohio Woman Suffrage Records.

Andersen, Kristi. 1990. "Women and Citizenship in the 1920s." In *Women, Politics, and Change,* edited by Louise A. Tilly and Patricia Gurin, 177–98. New York: Russell Sage Foundation.

Anthony, Katherine. 1954. *Susan B. Anthony.* Garden City, N.J.: Doubleday.

Antler, Joyce. 1981. "Feminism as Life Process: The Life and Career of Lucy Sprague Mitchell." *Feminist Studies* 7, no. 1:134–57.

———. [1977] 1987. *The Educated Woman and Professionalization: The Struggle for a New Feminine Identity 1890–1920.* New York: Garland.

Bacon, Margaret Hope. 1986. *Mothers of Feminism: The Story of Quaker Women in America.* New York: Harper and Row.

Baker, T. L., and J. A. Sween. 1982. "Synchronizing Post-Graduate Career, Marriage, and Fertility." *Western Sociological Review* 13, no. 1:69–86.

Bales, Robert F. 1953. "The Equilibrium Problem in Small Groups." In *Working Papers in the Theory of Action,* edited by Talcott Parsons, Robert F. Bales, and Edward A. Shils, 111–61. Glencoe, Ill.: Free Press.

Banks, Olive. 1981. *Faces of Feminism.* New York: St. Martin's Press.

Bass, Dorothy C. 1979. "'Their Prodigious Influence': Women, Religion, and Reform in Antebellum America." In *Women of the Spirit: Female Leadership in the Jewish and Christian Traditions,* edited by R. Ruether and E. McLaughlin, 280–300. New York: Simon and Schuster.

Bateson, M. C. *Composing a Life.* New York: Penguin Books, 1989.

Baxter, Sandra, and Marjorie Lansing. 1983. *Women and Politics: The Visible Majority.* Ann Arbor: University of Michigan Press.

Beard, Mary. 1946. *Women as a Force in History: A Study in Tradition and Realities.* New York: Macmillan.

Beaver, R. Pierce. 1980. *American Protestant Women in World Mission: History of the First Feminist Movement.* Grand Rapids, Mich.: William B. Eerdmans Publishing Co.

Beecher, Catherine E. 1835. *An Essay on the Education of Female Teachers.* New York: Van Nostrand.

———. 1841. *A Treatise on Domestic Economy.* With an introduction by Kathryn Kish Sklar. New York: Schocken Books.

Belyea, Marlou. 1976. "The New England Female Moral Reform Society, 1835–1850: 'Put Down the Libertine, Reclaim the Wanderer, Restore the Outcast.'" Paper presented at the Berkshire Conference on the History of Women, Bryn Mawr College, 9–11 June.

Benson, Susan Porter. 1976. "Women, Networks, and Reform: The Providence Employment Society, 1837–1858." Paper presented at the Berkshire Conference on the History of Women, Bryn Mawr College, 9–11 June.

Berelson, Bernard. 1954. "Content Analysis." In *Handbook of Social Psychology,* edited by Gardner Lindzey, 1:488–522. Cambridge, Mass.: Addison-Wesley.

Berg, Barbara J. 1978. *The Remembered Gate: Origins of American Feminism, the Woman, and the City, 1800–1860.* New York: Oxford University Press.

Bianchi, Suzanne M., and Daphne Spain. 1986. *American Women in Transition.* New York: Russell Sage Foundation.

Blair, Karen J. 1980. *The Clubwoman as Feminist: True Womanhood Redefined, 1868–1914.* New York: Holmes and Meier.

Blocker, Jack S., Jr. 1985. *"Give to the Winds Thy Fears": The Women's Temperance Crusade, 1873–1874.* Westport, Conn.: Greenwood Press.

_____. 1989. *American Temperance Movements: Cycles of Reform.* Boston: Twayne Publishers.

Blumberg, Rae Lesser. 1979. "A Paradigm for Predicting the Position of Women: Policy Implications and Problems." In *Sex Roles and Social Policy,* edited by Jean Lipman-Blumen and Jessie Bernard, 113–42. Beverly Hills, Calif.: Sage Publications.

Blumer, Herbert. [1937] 1951. "Collective Behavior." In *Principles of Sociology,* edited by A. M. Lee, 167–222. New York: Barnes and Noble.

Boles, Janet K. 1991. "Form Follows Function: The Evolution of Feminist Strategies." *Annals of the American Academy of Political and Social Science* 515 (May): 38–49.

Bordin, Ruth. 1981. *Woman and Temperance: The Quest for Power and Liberty, 1873–1900.* Philadelphia: Temple University Press.

_____. 1986. *Frances Willard.* Durham: University of North Carolina Press.

Boylan, Anne M. 1981. "Toward a Typology of Women's Organizations: New York and Boston, 1795–1840." Paper delivered at Fifth Berkshire Conference on the History of Women, Vassar College, 16–18 June 1981.

_____. 1984. "Women in Groups: An Analysis of Women's Benevolent Organizations in New York and Boston, 1797–1840." *Journal of American History* 71: 497–523.

Breckenridge, Sophonisba. 1933. *Women in the Twentieth Century.* New York, McGraw-Hill.

Brown, Dorothy M. 1987. *Setting a Course: American Women in the 1920s.* Boston: Twayne Publishers.

Brown, Ira V. 1965. "The Woman's Rights Movement in Pennsylvania, 1848–1973," *Pennsylvania History* 32, no. 2 (April): 153–65.

Brown, Irene Quenzler. 1986. "Friendship and Spiritual Time in the Didactic Enlightenment." In *Autre Temps, Autre Espace (An Other Time, An Other Space)* [sic], edited by E. Marienstras and B. Karsky, 111–27. Nancy, France: Presses Universitaires de Nancy.

Brumberg, Joan Jacobs. 1980. *Mission for Life.* New York: Free Press.

Buechler, Steven M. 1986. *The Transformation of the Woman Suffrage Movement: The Case of Illinois, 1850–1920.* New Brunswick, N.J.: Rutgers University Press.

_____. 1990. *Women's Movements in the United States.* New Brunswick, N.J.: Rutgers University Press.

Buhle, Mari Jo, and Paul Buhle, eds. 1978. *The Concise History of Woman Suffrage: Selections from the Classic Work of Stanton, Anthony, Gage, and Harper.* Urbana: University of Illinois Press.

Calhoun, A. W. 1917–19. *A Social History of the American Family from Colonial Times to the Present.* 3 vols. Cleveland: Arthur W. Clark.

Camhi, Jane Jerome. 1973. "Women against Women: American Antisuffragism 1880–1920." Ph.D. diss., Tufts University, Medford, Mass.

Campbell, Helen. 1900. *Prisoners of Poverty*. Boston: Little, Brown.

Cantril, Hadley. 1941. *The Psychology of Social Movements*. New York: Wiley.

Carden, Maren Lockwood. 1974. *The New Feminist Movement*. New York: Russell Sage Foundation.

_____. 1977. *Feminism in the Mid-1970s: The Non-Establishment, the Establishment, and the Future*. A report to the Ford Foundation. New York: Ford Foundation.

_____. 1978. "The Proliferation of a Social Movement: Ideology and Individual Incentives in the Contemporary Feminist Movement." In *Research in Social Movements, Conflict, and Change*, edited by Louis Kriesberg, 1:179–96. Greenwich, Conn.: JAI Press.

Catt, Carrie Chapman, and Nettie Rogers Shuler. 1926. *Woman Suffrage and Politics: The Inner Story of the Suffrage Movement*. New York: Charles Scribner's Sons.

Chafe, William Henry. 1972. *The American Woman: Her Changing, Social, Economic, and Political Roles, 1920–1970*. New York: Oxford University Press.

Chafetz, Janet Saltzman. 1984. *Sex and Advantage: A Comparative, Macro-Structural Theory of Sex Stratification*. Totowa, N.J.: Rowman and Allanheld.

Cherrington, Ernest H. 1920. *The Evolution of Prohibition in the United States of America*. Westerville, Ohio: American Issue Press.

Chused, Richard H. 1985. "Late Nineteenth Century Married Women's Property Law: Reception of the Early Married Women's Property Acts by Courts and Legislatures." *American Journal of Legal History* 29, no. 3: 3–35.

Clark, Janet. 1991. "Getting There: Women in Political Office." *Annals of the American Academy of Political and Social Science* 515 (May): 63–76.

Clark, Malcolm, Jr. 1951. "The War on the Webfoot Saloons." *Oregon Historical Quarterly* 58 (March): 48–62.

Coffin, Judith C. 1987. "Women, Power, and Politics in France," Paper presented at the Seventh Berkshire Conference of Women Historians, Wellesley College, 20 June.

College Equal Suffrage League of Northern California. 1913. *Winning Equal Suffrage in California: Reports of Committees of the College Equal Suffrage League of Northern California in the Campaign of 1911*. Published by the National College Equal Suffrage League. Schlesinger Library.

Colvin, D. Leigh. 1926. *Prohibition in the United States: A History of the Prohibition Party and the Prohibition Movement*. New York: George H. Doran.

Conway, Jill Ker. 1982. *The Female Experience in Eighteenth- and Nineteenth-Century America: A Guide to the History of American Women*. New York: Garland Press.

Cookingham, Mary Elizabeth. 1980. "The Demographic and Labor Force Behavior of Women College Graduates, 1865 to 1965." Ph.D. diss., University of California, Berkeley. Ann Arbor, Mich.: University Microfilms.

Corcoran, Mary. 1978. "Work Experience, Work Interruption, and Wages." In *Five Thousand American Families—Patterns of Economic Progress,* edited by G. J. Duncan and J. N. Morgan, 6:47–103. Ann Arbor: University of Michigan, Institute for Social Research.

Costain, Anne N. 1988. "Women's Claims as a Special Interest." In *The Politics of the Gender Gap,* edited by Carol M. Mueller, 150–72. Newbury Park, Calif.: Sage Publications.

Cott, Nancy F. 1977. *The Bonds of Womanhood: "Woman's Sphere" in New England, 1780–1835.* New Haven: Yale University Press.

———. 1987. *The Grounding of Modern Feminism.* New Haven: Yale University Press.

Cross, Whitney R. 1950. *The Burned-Over District: The Social and Intellectual History of Enthusiastic Religion in Western New York, 1800–1850.* Ithaca, N.Y.: Cornell University Press.

Dall, Caroline H. 1868. *College, Market, and Court.* Boston: Lee and Shepard.

Dannenbaum, Jed. 1984. *Drink and Disorder: Temperance Reform in Cincinnati from the Washingtonian Revival to the WCTU.* Urbana: University of Illinois Press.

Degler, Carl N. 1980. *At Odds: Women and the Family in America from the Revolution to the Present.* New York: Oxford University Press.

———. 1989. "On Rereading 'The Woman in America'". In *Learning about Women: Gender, Politics, and Power,* edited by Jill K. Conway, Susan C. Bourque, and Joan W. Scott, 199–210. Ann Arbor: University of Michigan Press.

DeHart-Mathews, Jane, and Donald Mathews. 1986. "The Cultural Politics of the ERA's Defeat." In *Rights of Passage: The Past and Future of the ERA,* edited by Joan Hoff-Wilson, 44–53. Bloomington: Indiana University Press.

Dietz, Mary G. 1989. "Context Is All: Feminism and Theories of Citizenship." In *Learning about Women: Gender, Politics, and Power,* edited by Jill K. Conway, Susan C. Bourque, and Joan W. Scott, 1–24. Ann Arbor: University of Michigan Press.

DuBois, Ellen. 1975. "The Radicalism of the Woman Suffrage Movement: Notes toward the Reconstruction of Nineteenth-Century Feminism." *Feminist Studies* 3, no. 1/2:63–71.

———. 1978. *Feminism and Suffrage: The Emergence of an Independent Women's Movement in America, 1848–1869.* Ithaca, N.Y.: Cornell University Press.

_____. 1979. "Woman's Rights and Abolition: The Nature of the Connection." In *Antislavery Reconsidered: New Perspectives on the Abolitionists,* edited by L. Perry and Michael Fellman, 238–51. Baton Rouge: Louisiana State University Press.

_____. 1986. "Class, Politics, and the Revival of Woman's Suffrage in the Progressive Period." Women's Studies lecture, Brandeis University, Waltham, Mass. 6 March.

Duniway, Abigail Scott. 1914. *Path Breaking: An Autobiographical History of the Equal Suffrage Movement in Pacific Coast States.* Portland, Ore.: James, Kerns and Abbott.

Durkheim, Emile. [1893] 1933. *The Division of Labor in Society.* Translated by George Simpson. New York: Free Press, 1960.

Earhart, Mary. 1944. *Frances Willard: From Prayers to Politics.* Chicago: University of Chicago Press.

Edwards, Alba M. 1943. *Comparative Occupation Statistics.* Washington, D.C.: U.S. Government Printing Office.

Ellwood, David. 1988. *Poor Support: Poverty in the American Family.* New York: Basic Books.

Elshtain, Jean Bethke. 1981. *Public Man, Private Woman: Women in Social and Political Thought.* Princeton, N.J.: Princeton University Press.

Engels, Friedrich. [1884] 1972. *Origin of the Family, Private Property and the State.* Edited with an introduction by Eleanor Burke Leacock. New York: International Publishers.

Epstein, Barbara Leslie. 1981. *The Politics of Domesticity: Women, Evangelism, and Temperance in Nineteenth Century America.* Middletown, Conn.: Wesleyan University Press.

Epstein, Cynthia Fuchs. 1988. *Deceptive Distinctions.* New Haven, Conn.: Yale University Press.

Erikson, Erik H. 1950. *Childhood and Society.* New York: Norton.

Etzioni, Amitai. 1993. *The Spirit of Community: Rights, Responsibilities, and the Communitarian Agenda.* New York: Crown Publishers.

Evans, Richard J. 1977. *The Feminists: Women's Emancipation Movements in Europe, America, and Australasia 1840–1920.* New York: Barnes and Noble.

Evans, Sara M. 1989. *Born for Liberty: A History of Women in America.* New York: Free Press.

Faludi, Susan. 1991. *Backlash: The Undeclared War against American Women.* New York: Crown Publishers.

Ferree, Myra Marx, and Beth B. Hess. 1985. *Controversy and Coalition: The New Feminist Movement.* Boston: Twayne Publishers.

Festinger, Leon, Henry W. Riecken, Jr., and S. Schachter. 1956. *When Prophecy Fails.* Minneapolis: University of Minnesota Press.

Flexner, Eleanor. 1959. *Century of Struggle: The Woman's Rights Movement in the United States.* Cambridge: Harvard University Press.

Folbre, Nancy. 1993. *Who Pays for the Kids? Gender and the Structure of Constraint.* New York: Routledge.

Foner, Philip S. 1979. *Women and the American Labor Movement: From Colonial Times to the Eve of World War I.* New York: Free Press.

Fowler, Robert Booth. 1986. *Carrie Catt: Feminist Politician.* Boston: Northeastern University Press.

Fox, Kardena M. 1918. "History of the Equal Suffrage Movement in Michigan." *Michigan History Magazine* 2:90–109.

Freeman. Jo. 1990. "From Protection to Opportunity: The Revolution in Women's Legal Status." In *Women, Politics, and Change,* edited by Louise A. Tilly and Patricia Gurin, 457–81. New York: Russell Sage Foundation.

Friedan, Betty. 1963. *The Feminine Mystique.* New York: W. W. Norton.

Fuchs, Victor. 1990. "Are Americans Underinvesting in Children?" In *Rebuilding the Nest,* edited by D. Blankenhorn, S. Bayme, and J. B. Elshtain, 53–70. Milwaukee: Family Service America.

Furer, Howard B. 1969. "The American City: A Catalyst for the Women's Rights Movement." *Wisconsin Magazine of History* 52 (Summer): 285–305.

Galston, William A. 1993. "National Family Policy: Three Good Ideas." Institute for American Values, Family Policy Symposium, New York City, December 10.

Gamson, William A. 1975. *The Strategy of Social Protest.* Homewood, Ill.: Dorsey Press.

_____. 1989. "Reflections on the Strategy of Social Protest." *Sociological Forum* 4, no. 3:455–67.

Gelb, Joyce, and Marian Lief Palley. 1987. *Women and Public Policies.* Rev. ed. Princeton, N.J.: Princeton University Press.

Giele, Janet Zollinger. 1961. "Social Change in the Feminine Role: A Comparison of Woman's Suffrage and Woman's Temperance, 1870–1920." Ph.D. diss., Harvard University.

_____. 1972. "Centuries of Womanhood: An Evolutionary Perspective on the Feminine Role." *Women's Studies* 1, no. 1:97–110.

_____. 1977. "Introduction: Comparative Perspectives on Women." In *Women: Roles and Status in Eight Countries,* edited by J. Z. Giele and A. C. Smock, 1–31. New York: Wiley.

_____. 1978. *Women and the Future: Changing Sex Roles in Modern America.* New York: Free Press.

_____. 1982. "Cohort Variation in Life Patterns of Educated Women, 1910–1960." *Western Sociological Review* 13:1–24.

_____. 1987. "Coeducation or Women's Education: A Comparison of Findings from Two Colleges." In *Coeducation: Past, Present, and Future,* edited by C. Lasser, 91–109. Urbana: University of Illinois Press.

_____. 1990. "Women's Movements." *World Book Encyclopedia,* 21:385–90.

_____. "Life Patterns of Mature Women in the National Longitudinal Surveys, 1967–82." Final Report to the Radcliffe Research Support Program. Waltham, Mass.: Heller School, Brandeis University.

_____. Forthcoming. "Women's Changing Roles and the Emergence of Family Policy." In *Unresolved Dilemmas: Women, Work and the Family in the United States, Europe, and the Former Soviet Union,* edited by K. Kauppinen and T. Gordon. Aldershot, Hampshire, England: Avebury.

_____, and Mary Gilfus. 1990. "Race and College Differences in Life Patterns of Educated Women." In *Women and Educational Change,* edited by J. Antler and S. Biklen, 179–97. Albany: State University of New York Press.

_____, Lachman, M. E., and Gilfus, M. 1986. "Changing Educational and Occupational Histories of Women College Graduates, 1934–1982." Paper presented at the annual meeting of the American Sociological Association, New York, August.

_____, and Rainer Pischner. 1994. "Emergence of a Multiple Role Pattern among Women Born 1910–1960: A German–U.S. Comparison." *Vierteljahrshefte zur Wirtschaftsforschung,* Heft 1–2:97–103.

Gil, David. 1992. *Unraveling Social Policy.* 5th ed. Cambridge, Mass.: Shenckman Books.

Gilfus, Mary E. 1988. "Seasoned by Violence/Tempered by Love: A Qualitative Study of Women and Crime." Waltham, Mass.: Ph.D. diss., Brandeis University.

Gill, Richard T., and T. Grandon Gill. 1994. "A Parental Bill of Rights." *Family Affairs* 6, no. 1–2 (Winter). New York: Institute of American Values.

Gilligan, Carol. 1982. *In A Different Voice.* Cambridge: Harvard University Press.

Glendon, Mary Ann. 1987. *Abortion and Divorce in Western Law: American Failures, European Challenges.* Cambridge, Harvard University Press.

_____. 1991. *Rights Talk: The Impoverishment of Political Discourse.* New York: Free Press.

Goode, William J. 1963. *World Revolution and Family Patterns.* New York: Free Press.

Gordon, Felice D. 1986. *After Winning: The Legacy of the New Jersey Suffragists, 1920–1947.* New Brunswick, N.J.: Rutgers University Press.

Gordon, Linda, ed. 1990. *Women, the State, and Welfare.* Madison: University of Wisconsin Press.

Grimké, Sarah M. 1838. *Letters on the Equality of the Sexes.* Boston: I. Knapp.

Gurko, Miriam. 1976. *The Ladies of Seneca Falls: The Birth of the Woman's Rights Movement.* New York: Schocken Books.

Gusfield, Joseph R. 1954. "Organizational Change: A Study of the Woman's Christian Temperance Union." Ph.D. diss., University of Chicago.

———. 1955. "Social Structure and Moral Reform: A Study of the Woman's Christian Temperance Union." *American Journal of Sociology* 61: 221–32.

———. 1963. *Symbolic Crusade: Status Politics and the American Temperance Movement.* Urbana: University of Illinois Press.

———. 1981. *The Culture of Public Problems: Drinking-Driving and the Symbolic Order.* Chicago: University of Chicago Press.

Hampel, Robert L. 1982. *Temperance and Prohibition in Massachusetts, 1813–1852.* Ann Arbor, Mich.: University Microfilms Research Press.

Hartmann, Susan M. 1982. *The Home Front and Beyond: American Women in the 1940s.* Boston: Twayne Publishers.

Hause, Steven C., and Anne R. Kenney. 1984. *Women's Suffrage and Social Politics in the French Third Republic.* Princeton, N.J.: Princeton University Press.

Hayes, Cheryl D., John L. Palmer, and Martha J. Zaslow, eds. 1990. *Who Cares for America's Children: Child Care Policy for the 1990s.* Washington, D.C.: National Academy Press.

Herman, Judith L. 1981. *Father-Daughter Incest.* Cambridge: Harvard University Press.

Hewitt, Nancy A. 1984. *Women's Activism and Social Change: Rochester, New York, 1822–1872.* Ithaca, N.Y.: Cornell University Press.

Hewlett, Sylvia Ann. 1986a. *A Lesser Life: The Myth of Women's Liberation in America.* New York: W. Morrow.

———. 1986b. "Conclusions: A Policy Agenda for the United States." In *Family and Work: Bridging the Gap,* edited by Sylvia Ann Hewlett, Alice S. Ilchman, and John J. Sweeney, 187–91. Cambridge, Mass.: Ballinger.

Hill, Joseph A. 1929. *Women in Gainful Occupations,* U.S. Bureau of the Census Monograph 9. Washington, D.C.: U.S. Government Printing Office.

Hill, Patricia R. 1985. *The World Their Household: The American Woman's Foreign Mission Movement and Cultural Transformation, 1870–1920.* Ann Arbor: University of Michigan Press.

History of Woman Suffrage. 6 vols. Unabridged republication of the original editions. 1970. New York: Source Book Press.

[1881]. Vol. 1. Edited by Elizabeth Cady Stanton, Susan B. Anthony, and Matilda Joslyn Gage. New York: Fowler and Wells.

[1882]. Vol. 2. Edited by Elizabeth Cady Stanton, Susan B. Anthony, and Matilda Joslyn Gage. New York: Fowler and Wells.

[1886]. Vol. 3, 1876–1885. Edited by Elizabeth Cady Stanton, Susan B. Anthony, and Matilda Joslyn Gage. Rochester, N.Y.: Susan B. Anthony.

[1902]. Vol. 4, 1883–1900. Edited by Susan B. Anthony and Ida Husted Harper. Rochester, N.Y.: Susan B. Anthony.

[1922]. Vol. 5, 1900–1920. Edited by Ida Husted Harper. New York: National American Woman Suffrage Association.

[1922]. Vol. 6, 1900–1920. Edited by Ida Husted Harper. New York: National American Woman Suffrage Association.

Hoff-Wilson, Joan. 1986. "Introduction." In *Rights of Passage: The Past and Future of the ERA,* edited by Joan Hoff-Wilson, 93–96. Bloomington: Indiana University Press.

Hoffer, Eric. 1951. *The True Believer.* New York: Harper and Row.

Hole, J., and E. Levine. 1971. *Rebirth of Feminism.* New York: Quadrangle.

Holmes, Steven A. 1991. "Unlikely Union Arises to Press Family Issues." *New York Times,* 1 May, A18.

House, James S. 1981. "Social Structure and Personality." In *Social Psychology: Sociological Perspectives,* edited by Morris Rosenberg and Ralph H. Turner, 525–61. New York: Basic Books.

Howe, Julia Ward. 1913. *Julia Ward Howe and the Woman Suffrage Movement.* Speeches and essays edited by Florence Howe Hall. Boston: Dana Estes and Co.

Hulbert, Kathleen Day, and Diane Tickton Schuster, eds. 1993. *Women's Lives through Time: Educated American Women of the Twentieth Century.* San Francisco: Jossey-Bass.

HWS. See *History of Woman Suffrage.*

Information Please Almanac, Atlas and Yearbook, 1994. 47th ed. Boston: Houghton-Mifflin. 1993.

Inkeles, Alex, and Daniel J. Levinson. 1954. "National Character: The Study of Modal Personality and Sociocultural Systems." In *Handbook of Social Psychology,* edited by Gardner Lindzey, 2:977–1020. Reading, Mass.: Addison-Wesley.

James, Edward T., Janet Wilson James, and Paul S. Boyer, eds. 1971. *Notable American Women 1607–1950.* 3 vols. Cambridge: Harvard University Press.

Jenkins, J. Craig. 1983. "Resource Mobilization Theory and the Study of Social Movements." *Annual Review of Sociology* 9: 527–53.

Jensen, Richard. 1973. "Family, Career, and Reform: Woman Leaders in the Progressive Era." In *The American Family in Social-Historical Perspective,* edited by Michael Gordon, 267–80. New York: St. Martin's Press.

Joffe, Carole. 1983. "Why the United States Has No Child-Care Policy." In *Families, Politics, and Public Policy: A Feminist Dialogue on Women and the State,* edited by Irene Diamond, 168–82. New York: Longman.

Johnson, Lorenzo Dow. 1843. *Martha Washingtonianism, or a History of the Ladies' Temperance Benevolent Societies.* New York: Saxton and Miles.

Johnson, Miriam M. 1955. "Instrumental and Expressive Components in the Personalities of Women." Ph.D. diss., Harvard University.

_____. 1989. "Feminism and the Theories of Talcott Parsons." In *Feminism and Sociological Theory,* edited by R. A. Wallace, 101–18. Newbury Park, Calif.: Sage Publications.

Kaledin, Eugenia. 1984. *Mothers and More: American Women in the 1950s.* Boston: Twayne Publishers.

Kahne, Hilda. 1994. "Part-Time Work: A Reassessment for a Changing Economy." *Social Service Review* 68, no. 3:417–36.

Kamerman, Sheila B., and Alfred J. Kahn. 1989. "Single-Parent, Female-Headed Families in Western Europe: Social Change and Response." *International Social Security Review* 42, no. 1:3–34.

Katzenstein, Mary Fainsod. 1984. "Feminism and the Meaning of the Vote." *Signs* 10, no. 1:4–26.

Kenneally, James J. 1967. "Catholicism and Woman Suffrage in Massachusetts." *Catholic Historical Review* 53, no. 1 (April): 43–57.

Kerber, Linda K. 1980. *Women of the Republic: Intellect and Ideology in Revolutionary America.* New York: W. W. Norton.

Kessler-Harris, Alice. 1982. *Out to Work: A History of Wage-Earning Women in the United States.* New York: Oxford University Press.

Keyserling, Mary Dublin. 1972. *Windows on Day Care.* New York: National Council of Jewish Women.

Klandermans, Bert. 1986. "New Social Movements and Resource Mobilization: The European and the American Approach." *Journal of Mass Emergencies and Disasters* 4:13–37.

Klatch, Rebecca E. 1987. *Women of the New Right.* Philadelphia: Temple University Press.

Klein, Ethel. 1984. *Gender Politics: From Consensus to Mass Politics.* Cambridge: Harvard University Press.

Konecko, Cindy. 1982. "One Undergraduate Looks at 'Life'; Coding the Children and Work Questionnaire." *Bryn Mawr Alumnae Bulletin,* Winter, 24–26.

Koonz, Claudia. 1982. "Feminism in the Fatherland: Women's Rights, Gender, and Politics in Wilhelmine Germany." Paper presented at the Seventh Berkshire Conference of Women Historians, Wellesley College, 20 June.

Koyama, Takashi. 1961. *La Femme Japonaise.* Paris: UNESCO.

Kraditor, Aileen S. 1965. *The Ideas of the Woman Suffrage Movement, 1890–1920.* Garden City, N.Y.: Doubleday.

Kreps, J. M., and Leaper, R. J. 1976. "Home Work, Market Work, and the Allocation of Time." In *Women and the American Economy,* edited by J. M. Kreps, 61–81. Englewood Cliffs, N.J.: Prentice-Hall.

Kriesberg, Louis. 1979. "Introduction." In *Research on Social Movements, Conflict and Change,* edited by Louis Kriesberg, 2:vii–xv. Greenwich, Conn.: JAI Press.

Krone, Henrietta. 1946. "Dauntless Women: The Story of the Suffrage Movement in Pennsylvania: 1910–1920." Ph.D. diss., University of Pennsylvania.

Lance, Keith Curry. 1983. "Woman Suffrage and the States: A Resource Mobilization Analysis." Ph.D. diss., North Texas State University, Denton.

Lapidus, Gail Warshofsky. 1978. *Women in Soviet Society: Equality, Development, and Social Change.* Berkeley: University of California Press.

Leach, William. 1980. *True Love and Perfect Union: The Feminist Reform of Sex and Society.* New York: Basic Books.

Lemons, J. Stanley. 1973. *The Woman Citizen: Social Feminism in the 1920s.* Urbana: University of Illinois Press.

Lenski, Gerhard. 1966. *Power and Privilege: A Theory of Social Stratification.* New York: McGraw-Hill.

Library of Congress, Manuscript Division. 1975. *The Blackwell Family, Carrie Chapman Catt and the National American Woman Suffrage Association.* Washington, D.C.: Library of Congress, microfilm.

Linden-Ward, Blanche, and Carol Hurd Green. 1993. *American Women in the 1960s: Changing the Future.* New York: Twayne Publishers.

Lopata, Helena Z. 1971. *Occupation Housewife.* New York: Oxford University Press.

Luker, Kristin. 1984. *Abortion and the Politics of Motherhood.* Berkeley: University of Wisconsin Press.

Lunardini, Christine A. 1986. *From Equal Suffrage to Equal Rights: Alice Paul and the National Woman's Party, 1910–1928.* New York: New York University Press.

Lutz, Alma. 1959. *Susan B. Anthony.* Boston: Beacon Press.

McAdam, Doug, John D. McCarthy, and Mayer N. Zald. 1988. "Social Movements." In *Handbook of Sociology,* edited by N. J. Smelser, 695–737. Newbury Park, Calif.: Sage Publications.

McCarthy, John D. 1986. "Continuities and Discontinuities in Personal Lives and Social Movements." Paper delivered at the Annual Meeting of the American Sociological Association, Washington, D. C.

———, and Mayer N. Zald. 1973. "The Trend of Social Movements in America: Professionalization and Resource Mobilization." Morristown, N.J.: General Learning Press.

———. 1977. "Resource Mobilization and Social Movements: A Partial Theory." *American Journal of Sociology* 82:1212–41.

McDonagh, Eileen L. 1987. "Issues and Constituencies in the Progressive Era: House Roll Call Voting on the Nineteenth Amendment, 1913–1919." Murray Center lecture, Radcliffe College, Cambridge, Mass., 31 March.

274 *References*

_____. 1990. "Women's Right to Vote in a Gendered American State: 'Winning Plan' Politics and Maternalist Reform in the Progressive Era." Boston: Northeastern University, Department of Political Science.

_____. 1992. "Representative Democracy and State Building in the Progressive Era." *American Policital Science Review* 86:938–50.

MacGregor, O. R. 1955. "The Social Position of Women in England, 1850–1914." *British Journal of Sociology* 6:48–60.

MacKinnon, Catharine A. 1987. *Feminism Unmodified: Discourses on Life and Law.* Cambridge: Harvard University Press.

Maine, Henry Sumner. 1888. *Lectures on the Early History of Institutions.* New York: H. Holt.

Mannheim, Karl. [1929] 1936. *Ideology and Utopia: An Introduction to the Sociology of Knowledge.* Translated from the German by Louis Wirth and Edward Shils. New York: Harcourt Brace.

Mansbridge, Jane J. 1986. *Why We Lost the ERA.* Chicago: University of Chicago Press.

Marilley, Suzanne M. 1985. "Why the Vote? Woman Suffrage and the Politics of Democratic Development in the United States, 1820–1893." Ph.D. diss., Harvard University.

_____. 1993a. "Frances Willard and the Feminism of Fear." *Feminist Studies* 19, no. 1:123–46.

_____. 1993b. "From Republican Motherhood to Political Participation." In "Woman Suffrage and the Origins of Liberal Feminism." Notre Dame, Ind.: Department of Government, University of Notre Dame, unpublished manuscript.

Marshall, Susan E. 1986. "In Defense of Separate Spheres: Class and Status Politics in the Antisuffrage Movement." *Social Forces* 65, no. 2 (December): 327–51.

Marshall, T. H. 1963. *Class, Citizenship, and Social Development.* Chicago: University of Chicago Press.

Martin, Jane Roland. 1985. *Reclaiming the Conversation: The Ideal of the Educated Woman.* New Haven: Yale University Press.

Martineau, Harriet. 1837. *Society in America.* 3 vols. London: Sanders and Otley.

Mead, Margaret, and Frances Balgley Kaplan, eds. 1965. *American Women: The Report of the President's Commission on the Status of Women and Other Publications of the Commission, 1963.* New York: Scribners.

Melder, Keith E. 1967. "Ladies Bountiful: Organized Women's Benevolence in Early Nineteenth-Century America." *New York History* 48 (July): 231–54.

_____. 1977. *Beginnings of Sisterhood: The American Woman's Rights Movement, 1800–1850.* New York: Schocken Books.

Merk, Lois. 1948. "The Early Career of Maud Wood Park." *Radcliffe Quarterly* 32 (May): 10–17.

Meyer, Annie Nathan, ed. 1891. *Woman's Work in America*. New York: Henry Holt.

Mezvinsky, Norton. 1959. "The White Ribbon Reform, 1874–1920." Madison: Ph.D. diss., University of Wisconsin.

_____. 1971. "Hunt, Mary Hannah Hanchett." *Notable American Women*, 2:237–39.

Mill, John Stuart. [1869] 1909. *The Subjection of Women*. Edited with introductory analysis by Stanton Coit. London: Longman, Green.

Minow, Martha. 1984. "Learning to Live with the Dilemma of Difference: Bilingual and Special Education." *Law and Contemporary Problems* 48: 157–211.

Morgan, David. [1937] 1972. *Suffragists and Democrats: The Politics of Woman Suffrage in America*. East Lansing: Michigan State University Press.

Morris, Aldon. 1984. *The Origins of the Civil Rights Movement*. New York: Free Press.

Mowry, George E. 1958. *The Era of Theodore Roosevelt and the Birth of Modern America, 1900–1912*. New York: Harper Torchbooks.

Moynihan, Ruth Barnes. 1983. *Rebel for Rights: Abigail Scott Duniway*. New Haven: Yale University Press.

Mueller, Carol M. 1981. "The Rise of Women in Public Office: Alternative Explanations." Working paper no. 89. Wellesley, Mass.: Wellesley College Center for Research on Women.

_____. 1988. *The Politics of the Gender Gap: The Social Construction of Political Influence*. Newbury Park, Calif.: Sage Publications.

_____. 1991. "The Gender Gap and Women's Political Influence." *Annals of American Academy of Political and Social Science* 515 (May): 23–37.

National Academy of Sciences. 1976. *Toward a National Policy for Children and Families*. Washington, D.C.

National Woman's Christian Temperance Union. *Minutes of the Annual Meetings.*

National Women's Political Caucus. 1985. *National Directory of Woman Elected Officials*. Washington, D.C.

NAW. See Notable American Women.

Newcomer, Mabel. 1959. *A Century of Higher Eduction for American Women*. Washington, D. C.: Zenger Publishing Co.

Niebuhr, H. Richard. 1957. *The Social Sources of Denominationalism*. New York: Meridian Books.

Norton, Mary Beth. 1980. *Liberty's Daughters: The Revolutionary Experience of American Women, 1750–1800*. Boston: Little, Brown.

Notable American Women 1607–1950. 3 vols. 1971. Edited by Edward T. James, Janet Wilson James, and Paul S. Boyer. Cambridge: Harvard University Press.

Notestein, Lucy Lilian [1937] 1971. *Wooster of the Middle West*. 2 vols. Kent, Ohio: Kent State University Press.

Noun, Louis R. 1969. *Strong-Minded Women: The Emergence of the Woman-Suffrage Movement in Iowa.* Ames: Iowa State University Press.

Oberschall, Anthony A. 1973. *Social Conflict and Social Movements.* Englewood Cliffs, N.J.: Prentice-Hall.

Okin, Susan Moller. 1989. *Gender, Justice, and the Family.* New York: Basic Books.

Olson, Mancur, Jr. [1965] 1968. *The Logic of Collective Action: Public Goods and the Theory of Groups.* New York: Schocken Books.

O'Neill, William L. 1969. *Everyone Was Brave.* New York: Quadrangle Books.

Oppenheimer, Valerie K. 1970. *The Female Labor Force in the United States.* Population Monograph Series, no. 5. Berkeley: University of California.

Park, Robert E., and Ernest W. Burgess. 1921. *Introduction to the Science of Sociology.* Chicago: University of Chicago Press.

Parsons, Talcott. 1961. "The Hierarchy of Control." In *Talcott Parsons: On Institutions and Evolution,* selected writings edited and introduced by Leon H. Mayhew, 157–72. Chicago: University of Chicago Press, 1982.

――――. 1966. *Societies: Evolutionary and Comparative Perspectives.* Englewood Cliffs, N.J.: Prentice-Hall.

――――, and R. F. Bales. 1955. *Family, Socialization, and Interaction Process.* New York: Free Press.

Pateman, Carole. 1988. *The Sexual Contract.* Stanford, Calif.: Stanford University Press.

Paulson, Ross Evans. 1973. *Women's Suffrage and Prohibition: A Comparative Study of Equality and Social Control.* Glenview, Ill.: Scott, Foresman.

Pedersen, Susan. 1993. *Family, Dependence, and the Origins of the Welfare State: Britain and France, 1914–1945.* Cambridge: Cambridge University Press.

Perun, Pamela J., and Janet Z. Giele. 1982. "Life after College: Historical Links between Women's Education and Women's Work." In *The Undergraduate Woman: Issues in Educational Equality,* edited by P. J. Perun, 375–98. Lexington, Mass.: Lexington Books.

Pharr, Susan J. 1981. *Political Women in Japan: The Search for a Place in Political Life.* Berkeley: University of California Press.

Phillips, Brenda D. 1986a. "The Decade of Origin: Resource Mobilization and Women's Rights in the 1850s." Paper presented at the North Central Sociological Association meetings, Toledo, Ohio, April. [Department of Sociology, University of Tennessee.]

――――. 1986b. "Conceptual Clarification in SMO [Social Movement Organization] Research: The Case of the Women's Rights Movement in the 1850s." Paper presented at the Southern Sociological Society meetings, New Orleans. April. [Department of Sociology, University of Tennessee.]

Pleck, Elizabeth. 1986. "Failed Strategies; Renewed Hope." In *Rights of*

Passage: The Past and Future of the ERA, edited by Joan Hoff-Wilson, 106–20. Bloomington: Indiana University Press.

Pleck, Joseph H. 1992. "Work-Family Policies in the United States." In *Women's Work and Women's Lives: The Continuing Struggle Worldwide,* edited by Hilda Kahne and Janet Z. Giele, 248–75. Boulder, Colo.: Westview Press.

Poole, Keith T., and L. Harmon Zeigler. 1985. *Women, Public Opinion, and Politics: The Changing Political Attitudes of American Women.* New York: Longman.

Popenoe, David. 1988. *Disturbing the Nest: Family Change and Decline in Modern Societies.* New York: A. de Gruyter.

Porter, Kirk H. [1918] 1969. *A History of Suffrage in the United States.* New York: Greenwood Press.

Prelinger, Catherine M. 1987. *Charity, Challenge, and Change: Religious Dimensions of the Mid-Nineteenth-Century Women's Movement in Germany.* New York: Greenwood Press.

Ragin, Charles C. 1987. *The Comparative Method: Moving beyond Qualitative and Quantitative Strategies.* Berkeley: University of California Press.

Ramsoy, Odd. 1963. *Social Groups as System and Subsystem.* New York: Free Press.

Rosenthal, Naomi, Meryl Fingrutd, Michele Ethier, Roberta Karant, and David McDonald. 1985. "Social Movements and Network Analysis: A Case Study of Nineteenth-Century Women's Reform in New York State." *American Journal of Sociology* 90, no. 5:1022–54.

Rossi, Alice S. 1965. "Equality between the Sexes: An Immodest Proposal." In *The Woman in America,* edited by R. J. Lifton, 98–143. New York: Norton.

_____. 1973a. "Women in the Seventies: Problems and Possibilities." In *Discrimination against Women: Congressional Hearings on Equal Rights in Education and Employment,* edited by C. R. Stimpson, 314–29. New York: Bowker.

_____. 1977. "A Biosocial Perspective on Parenting." *Daedalus* 106, no. 2: 1–31.

_____. 1982. *Feminists in Politics: A Panel Analysis of the First National Women's Conference.* New York: Academic Press.

_____, ed. 1973b. *The Feminist Papers: From Adams to De Beauvoir.* Edited and with introductory essays by Alice S. Rossi. New York: Columbia University Press.

Rothman, Sheila M. 1978. *Woman's Proper Place: A History of Changing Ideals and Practices, 1870 to the Present.* New York: Basic Books.

Rupp, Leila J., and Verta Taylor. 1987. *Survival in the Doldrums: The American Women's Rights Movement, 1945 to the 1960s.* New York: Oxford University Press.

Ryan, Mary P. 1981. *The Cradle of the Middle Class: The Family in Oneida County, New York, 1790–1865.* New York: Cambridge University Press.

Salaff, Janet W., and Judith Merkle. 1973. "Women and Revolution: The Lessons of the Soviet Union and China." In *Women in China,* edited by M. B. Young, 145–77. Ann Arbor: Center for Chinese Studies, University of Michigan.

Salmon, Marylynn Salmon. 1986. *Women and the Law of Property in Early America.* Chapel Hill: University of North Carolina Press.

Sapiro, Virginia. 1990. "The Gender Basis of American Social Policy." In *Women, the State, and Welfare,* edited by Linda Gordon, 36–54. Madison: University of Wisconsin Press.

_____. 1991. "The Gender Gap and Women's Political Influence." *Annals of the American Academy of Political and Social Science* 515 (May): 10–22.

Scharf, Lois. 1980. *To Work and to Wed: Female Employment, Feminism, and the Great Depression.* Westport, Conn.: Greenwood Press.

_____, and Joan M. Jensen. 1983. *Decades of Discontent: The Women's Movement, 1920–1940.* Boston: Northeastern University Press.

Schlesinger, Arthur M. 1922. *New Viewpoints in American History.* New York: Macmillan.

_____. 1927–37. *The Rise of the City, 1878–1898.* Vol. 9 of *A History of American Life,* edited by A. Schlesinger and D. R. Fox. New York: Macmillan.

_____. 1950. *The American as Reformer.* Cambridge: Harvard University Press.

Schor, Juliet B. 1991. *The Overworked American.* New York: Basic Books.

Schuster, D. T. 1990. "Work, Relationships, and Balance in the Lives of Gifted Women." In *The Experience and Meaning of Work in Women's Lives,* edited by H. Y. Grossman and N. L. Chester, 189–211. Hillsdale, N.J.: Lawrence Erlbaum.

Scott, Anne Firor. 1970. *The Southern Lady: From Pedestal to Politics, 1830–1930.* Chicago: University of Chicago Press.

_____. 1984a. *Making the Invisible Woman Visible.* Urbana: University of Illinois Press.

_____. 1984b. Seminar, Department of History, Harvard University, 7 March.

_____. 1991. *Natural Allies: Women's Associations in American History.* Urbana: University of Illinois Press.

_____, and Andrew MacKay Scott. 1982. *One Half the People: The Fight for Woman Suffrage.* Urbana: University of Illinois Press.

Scott, Joan W. 1988. *Gender and the Politics of History.* New York: Columbia University Press.

Sewall, May Wright, ed. 1894. *World's Congress of Representative Women.* Chicago: Rand, McNally.

Shanley, Mary Lyndon. 1983. "Afterword: Feminism and Families in a Liberal

Polity." In *Families, Politics, and Public Policy: A Feminist Dialogue on Women and the State*, edited by Irene Diamond, 357–61. New York: Longman.

Shaw, Anna Howard. 1915. *Story of A Pioneer*. New York: Harper.

Sinclair, Andrew. 1965. *The Emancipation of the American Woman*. New York: Harper and Row.

Sklar, Kathryn Kish. 1973. *Catherine Beecher: A Study in American Domesticity*. New Haven: Yale University Press.

_____. 1980. "A Conceptual Framework for the Teaching of U.S. Women's History." *History Teacher*, August, 471–81.

_____. 1981. "Florence Kelley." Paper delivered at the Berkshire Conference of Women Historians, Vassar College, 18 June.

Skocpol, Theda. 1992. *Protecting Soldiers and Mothers: The Political Origins of Social Policy in the United States*. Cambridge: Harvard University Press.

Slater, Suzanne. 1994. *The Lesbian Family Life Cycle*. New York: Free Press.

Smelser, Neil J. 1959. *Social Change in the Industrial Revolution*. Chicago: University of Chicago Press.

_____. 1963. *Theory of Collective Behavior*. New York: Free Press.

Smith, Daniel Scott. 1974. "Family Limitation, Sexual Control and Domestic Feminism in Victorian America." In *Clio's Consciousness Raised: New Perspectives on the History of Women*, edited by M. Hartman and L. Banner, 119-36. New York: Harper Torchbooks.

Smith, Dorothy E. 1979. "A Sociology of Women." In *The Prism of Sex: Essays in the Sociology of Knowledge*, edited by J. A. Sherman and E. T. Beck, 135–87. Madison: University of Wisconsin Press.

Smith-Rosenberg, Carroll. 1971. "Beauty, the Beast, and the Militant Woman: A Case Study in Sex Roles and Social Stress in Jacksonian America." *American Quarterly* 23:562–84.

Smock, Audrey Chapman. 1977. "From Autonomy to Subordination." In *Women: Roles and Status in Eight Countries*, edited by J. Z. Giele and A. C. Smock, 173–216. New York: Wiley.

Smuts, Robert W. 1959. *Women and Work in America*. New York: Columbia University Press.

Snow, David A., E. Burke Rochford, Jr., Steven K. Worden, and Robert D. Benford. 1986. "Frame Alignment Processes, Micromobilization, and Movement Participation." *American Sociological Review* 51:464–81.

Sochen, June. 1973. *Movers and Shakers: American Women Thinkers and Activists*. New York: Quadrangle Books.

Solomon, Barbara Miller. 1985. *In the Company of Educated Women: A History of Women and Higher Education in America*. New Haven: Yale University Press.

Solomon, Hannah. 1946. *Fabric of My Life*. New York: Bloch Publishing Co.

Stanton, Elizabeth Cady, Susan B. Anthony, and Matilda Joslyn Gage. 1881.

Volume 1 of *History of Woman Suffrage,* 1848–1861. 2d ed. Rochester, N.Y.: Charles Mann. 1889. Reissued by Source Book Press, New York, 1970.

Stebbins, Jane E. 1876. *Fifty Years' History of the Temperance Cause.* Hartford: J. P. Fitch.

Stetson, Dorothy McBride. 1990. "The Political History of Parental Leave Policy." In *Parental Leave and Child Care: Setting a Research and Policy Agenda,* edited by Janet Shibley Hyde and Marilyn J. Essex, 406–23. Philadelphia: Temple University Press.

Stewart, Eliza (Daniel). 1888. *Memories of the Crusade: A Thrilling Account of the Great Uprising of the Women of Ohio in 1873 against the Liquor Crime.* Columbus, Ohio: W. G. Hubbard and Co.

Stites, Richard. 1978. *The Women's Liberation Movement in Russia: Feminism, Nihilism, and Bolshevism, 1860–1930.* Princeton, N.J.: Princeton University Press.

Strom, Sharon Hartman. 1975. "Leadership and Tactics in the American Woman Suffrage Movement: A New Perspective from Massachusetts." *Journal of American History* 62, no. 2:296–315.

Tax, Meredith. 1980. *The Rising of the Women.* New York: Monthly Review Press.

Taylor, A. Elizabeth. 1978. *The Woman Suffrage Movement in Tennessee.* New York: Hippocrene Books.

_____. 1987. *Citizens at Last: The Woman Suffrage Movement in Texas.* Austin, Tex.: Ellen C. Temple.

Taylor, Molly Ladd. 1987. "Protecting Mothers and Infants: The Rise and Fall of the Sheppard-Towner Act." Paper given at the Berkshire Conference on the History of Women, Wellesley College, 19 June.

Tilly, Charles. 1978. *From Mobilization to Revolution.* Reading, Mass.: Addison-Wesley.

_____, Louise Tilly, and Richard Tilly. 1975. *The Rebellious Century: 1830–1930.* Cambridge: Harvard University Press.

Tilly, Louise A., and Patricia Gurin, eds. 1990. *Women, Politics, and Change.* New York: Russell Sage Foundation.

_____, and Joan W. Scott. 1978. *Women, Work, and Family.* New York: Holt, Rinehart, and Winston.

Toch, Hans. 1965. *The Social Psychology of Social Movements.* Indianapolis: Bobbs-Merrill.

Toennies, Ferdinand. [1887] 1963. *Community and Society* (Gemeinschaft und Gesellschaft). Translated and edited by Charles P. Loomis. New York: Harper and Row.

Trollope, Mrs. Frances. 1832. *Domestic Manners of the Americans.* London: Whittaker, Treacher.

Turner, Ralph H. 1981. "Collective Behavior and Resource Mobilization as Approaches to Social Movements: Issues and Continuities." In *Research in Social Movements, Conflicts and Change: A Research Annual,* edited by Louis Kriesberg, 4:1–24. Greenwich, Conn.: JAI Press.

———, and Lewis Killian. 1972. *Collective Behavior.* 2d ed. Englewood Cliffs, N.J.: Prentice-Hall.

Tyler, Helen E. 1949. *Where Prayer and Purpose Meet.* Evanston, Ill.: Signal Press.

Uhlenberg, Peter R. 1969. "A Study of Cohort Life Cycles: Cohorts of Native-Born Massachusetts Women, 1830–1920." *Population Studies* 23:407–20.

Unger, Samuel. 1933. "A History of the National Woman's Christian Temperance Union." Ph.D. diss., Ohio State University.

U.S. Bureau of the Census. 1975. *Historical Statistics of the United States: Colonial Times to 1970.* Washington, D.C.: U.S. Government Printing Office.

U.S. Bureau of Education. 1870, 1881, 1889–1890, 1898–1899, 1910. *Report of the Commissioner of Education.* Washington, D.C.: U.S. Government Printing Office.

U.S. Bureau of Labor. 1889. *Fourth Annual Report of the Commissioner of Labor, 1888: Working Women in Large Cities.* Washington, D.C.: U.S. Government Printing Office.

U.S. Department of Interior. 1897. *Compendium of the Eleventh Census, 1890.* Washington, D. C.: U.S. Government Printing Office.

U.S. Department of Labor. 1969. *Trends in Educational Attainment of Women.* Washington, DC: Women's Bureau.

Van Vorhis, Jacqueline. 1987. *Carrie Chapman Catt: A Public Life.* New York: Feminist Press.

Van Vorst, Mrs. John, and Marie Van Vorst. 1903. *The Woman Who Toils.* New York: Doubleday, Page.

Wandersee, Winifred D. 1988. *On the Move: American Women in the 1970s.* Boston: Twayne Publishers.

Warbasse, Elizabeth Bowles. 1960. "The Changing Legal Rights of Married Women, 1800–1861." Ph.D. diss., Harvard University.

Ware, Susan. 1982. *Holding Their Own: American Women in the 1930s.* Boston: Twayne Publishers.

Weber, Max. [1925] 1947. *The Theory of Social and Economic Organization.* Translated by A. M. Henderson and Talcott Parsons. Edited with an introduction by Talcott Parsons. New York: Free Press.

Weir, Margaret, Ann Orloff, and Theda Skocpol, eds. 1988. *Politics of Social Policy in the United States.* Princeton, N.J.: Princeton University Press.

Weiss, Nancy P. 1976. "The Children's Bureau: A Case Study in Women's Voluntary Networks." Paper presented at the Berkshire Conference of Women Historians, Bryn Mawr College, 10 June.

Weitzman, Lenore. J. 1986. *The Divorce Revolution: The Unexpected Social and Economic Consequences for Women and Children in America.* New York: Free Press.

Welter, Barbara. 1976. *Dimity Convictions: The American Woman in the Nineteenth Century.* Athens: Ohio University Press.

_____. 1978. "She Hath Done What She Could: Protestant Women's Missionary Careers in Nineteenth-Century America." In *Women in American Religion,* edited by J. W. James, 111–25. Philadelphia: University of Pennsylvania Press.

Wexler, Sherry. 1993. "To Work and to Mother: The Politics of Family Support and Family Leave." Ph.D. diss. proposal. Brandeis University, Heller School, Waltham, Mass.

Whitehead, Barbara Dafoe. 1993. "Dan Quayle Was Right." *Atlantic* 271 (April): 47–50 ff.

Willard, Frances E. 1889. *Glimpses of Fifty Years.* Evanston, Ill.: National WCTU.

_____. 1895. *Do Everything: A Handbook for the World's White Ribboners.* Chicago: Woman's Temperance Publishing Association.

_____, and Mary Livermore. 1893. *A Woman of the Century.* Buffalo: Charles Wells Moulton.

Williams, Constance W. 1991. *Black Teenage Mothers: Pregnancy and Childrearing from Their Perspective.* Lexington, Mass.: Lexington Books.

Wilson, Margaret Gibbons. 1979. *The American Woman in Transition: The Urban Influence, 1870–1920.* Westport, Conn.: Greenwood Press.

Wittenmyer, Annie E. 1878. *History of the Woman's Temperance Crusade.* Philadelphia: Office of the Christian Woman.

Wolf, Naomi. 1993. *Fire with Fire: The New Female Power and How it Will Change the 21st Century.* New York: Random House.

Wood, Mary I. 1914. "Civic Activities of Women's Clubs." *Annals of American Academy of Political and Social Science* 56:78–87.

Woody, Thomas. 1929. *A History of Women's Education in the United States.* 2 vols. New York: Science Press.

Young, Michael, and Peter Willmott. 1973. *The Symmetrical Family.* New York: Pantheon.

Zelizer, Vivianna A. 1985. *Pricing the Priceless Child: The Changing Social Value of Children.* New York: Basic Books.

Zurcher, Louis A., and David A. Snow. 1981. "Collective Behavior: Social Movements." In *Social Psychology: Sociological Perspectives,* edited by Morris Rosenberg and Ralph H. Turner, 447–82. New York: Basic Books.

Index

Abbott, Agnes, 48

Abbott, Edith, 48

Abbott, Grace, 48

Abolition movement, 54–56, 61, 62; antislavery societies in, 54–55, 132; feminism and, 55–56; woman's rights cause and, 55

Abortion, 164, 178, 182

Adams, Abigail, 29

Adams, John, 29

Addams, Jane, 48, 97, 146, 159

Advocate of Moral Reform (newspaper), 44

African-American women: employment of, 158; suffrage and, 59, 136; temperance unions and, 88; welfare issues and, 195–96

Age of consent reform, 72, 99, 100–101, 111

Aid to Families of Dependent Children (AFDC), 195–96

Alcoholism, and temperance leaders, 81, 239n33

Alcott, Bronson, 34

Allen, Jonathan, 40

American Association of University Women, 177

American Equal Rights Association, 59, 114, 127

American Home Economics Association, 189

American Legion, 189

American Revolution, 7, 10, 28–29, 55, 60–61

American Woman Suffrage Association (AWSA), 60, 86, 105, 107, 109, 114–15, 123, 127, 136–37, 161

Anthony, Susan B., 47, 50, 52, 58, 59, 60, 84, 121, 135; background of, 125–26; suffrage and, 114, 115, 116, 123, 126, 136, 155–56, 161, 173

Antioch College, 48

Antislavery societies, 54–55, 61, 62, 132

Antisuffrage associations, 156

Association of Collegiate Alumnae, 189

Association of Farmer's Clubs, 145

Australia, 3, 5, 10, 27

Autonomy of women, 10–12, 36

Bacon, Margaret, 32

Bailey, Hannah J., 86

Bales, Robert F., 205

Bane, Mary Jo, 195

Banks, Olive, 10

Baptist church, 78, 81, 84, 89, 110, 132, 136, 161

Bateson, Mary Catherine, 169

Beard, Mary, 149

Bebel, August, 11

Beecher, Catherine, 31, 36–37

Belief system, and social movements, 18–20

Benevolent associations, 39–40

Berelson, Bernard, 205

A Better Child Care Act, (ABC), 194

Bible, 33, 40, 58, 65

Birth control, 180–82, 188

Black women. *See* African-American women
Blackwell, Alice Stone, 93, 121–22, 129
Blackwell, Antoinette Brown, 58, 114, 115, 116
Blackwell, Elizabeth, 49
Blackwell, Henry, 53–54, 115, 126
Blair, Karen, 139
Blatch, Harriot Stanton, 153
Blocker, Jack S., Jr., 20, 65, 104
Bloomer, Amelia, 86
Bonner, Neil, 155
Boole, Ella, 106
Bordin, Ruth, 67, 79, 80, 104
Boston Moral Reform Society, 44
Boston Society for Employing the Poor, 44
Boston's Seamen's Society, 44
Boylan, Anne, 40
Brandeis, Louis, 186
Brown, Antoinette. *See* Blackwell, Antoinette Brown
Brown, Irene, 38, 231n27
Brown, Olympia, 115, 129, 155
Brumberg, Joan Jacobs, 42
Bryan, William Jennings, 98
Bryn Mawr College, 146, 158, 168
Buechler, Steven, 15, 16
Bush, George, 178, 192
Bushnell, Kate, 100
Business and Professional Women, 177, 180

Cable Act of 1922, 189
Calvinism, 81
Campbell, Helen, 101
Carden, Maren L., 18, 171
Caregiving, 185–200: feminist goal of equality and, 171–72, 185; woman's rights and, 164
Carnegie-Mellon University, 168
Carse, Matilda, 81
Carter, Jimmy, 178
Catholic church, 72, 81, 96, 101, 145, 148, 149, 154
Catt, Carrie Chapman, 108, 112–13, 127–28, 136, 139, 152, 155–56
Catt, George, 127

Charitable organizations, 27, 28, 37–47; religious beliefs and, 37–38; temperance movement and, 72, 84
Child care, 178, 201, 202; day care in, 192, 198; feminists on, 192–95; men and, 179; nontraditional families and, 196
Child labor, 20, 72, 122
Children: feminist focus on well-being of, 197; nontraditional families and, 196–97; single-parent families and, 167
Children's Bureau, 16, 48, 186, 188, 190
China, 11–12
Christianity: missionary work and, 40–42, 232n36; moral and religious authority of women and, 10, 12; temperance work and, 44–45, 64, 110
Churches. *See* Religion, specific churches
Civil Rights Act of 1964, 169, 180, 201
Civil rights movement, 17
Civil Service merit system, 189
Civil War, 2, 28, 50, 59, 112, 115, 121, 151, 161
Cleveland, Grover, 96
Clinton, Bill, 164, 191, 195
Collective behavior theory, 15, 33
College Equal Suffrage League (CESL), 89–93, 146, 153–54
College of Wooster, 48
College Women's Alumnae Association, 2
Colleges. *See* Higher education
Commission on the Status of Women, 173
Committee on the Causes and Cure of War, 190
Common law, 52
Communal living, 11, 34
Communist tradition, 11
Community experiments, 11
Comprehensive Child Development Act, 194
Congregational church, 34, 51, 84, 132, 146, 161
Congress, women's election to, 176–77
Congressional Union for Woman Suffrage, 137, 161
Congressional Women's Caucus, 184
Consciousness-raising groups, 169
Consumers' League, 179, 189

Continental Congress, 29
Contraception, 180–82
Contracts, 53
Conway, Jill Ker, 172, 186
Cott, Nancy, 7, 8, 34, 178, 187, 199, 225n1
Council of Presidents, 184
Coverture, 52, 53
Cross, Whitney, 33–34
Cultural factors: cult of domesticity and, 36–37; emergence of women's movements related to, 9–10; Republican Motherhood ideal in, 30–37; suffrage movement and, 150–51, 156–60; women's activities outside the home and, 60–61; women's religious activity and, 33, 35

Dall, Caroline, 121
Daughters of Liberty, 29
Daughters of Temperance, 45, 125, 135
Daughters of the American Revolution, 145, 188
Davis, Paulina Wright, 49–50, 52
Day care, 192, 198
Declaration of Independence, 1, 29, 31, 56
Declaration of Sentiments, 1, 56–58, 121, 125
Degler, Carl N., 175, 183
Democratic party, 148, 152, 176, 178, 191, 198
Derr, Albert, 70, 71
Devereux, Lillie, 135
Discrimination in the workplace, 179–80
Divorce, 52, 54, 123, 158, 164, 167, 195, 196
Domestic feminism, 39, 46, 62, 232n29; benevolent associations and, 39–40; maternal associations and, 42–43; missionary societies and, 40–42, 232n36; moral reform societies and, 43–44; temperance and, 63–64; women's temperance groups and, 44–47
Domestic sphere: cult of domesticity and, 36–37; demographic and economic changes affecting, 35–36; education and release from, 31–32; educative

role of women and, 36–37, 231n23; feminist movement and expansion of women's roles in, 9, 27; need for women's equality in, 35–37
DuBois, Ellen, 55, 113, 174, 186
Dukakis, Michael, 178
Duniway, Abigail Scott, 67, 155, 237n12

Earhart, Mary, 99
Earlham College, 48
Economic factors: property rights and, 51–52; suffrage movement and, 120–21; traditional roles of women and, 7–8, 35–36; working women and family income and, 166–67
Education: benevolent and missionary work by women and, 38–39, 40; domestic roles of women and, 31–32; equal rights in, 164; Quaker support for, 32; Republican Motherhood ideal and, 31; role of women in, 36–37, 231n23; scientific temperance instruction in, 72, 101–3; of suffrage and temperance leaders, 80; women's demands for, 48, 120, 121, 158; working women and, 166
Educational Amendments of 1972, 180
Eighteenth Amendment, 97
Elections: gender gap in, 177–78; voting turnout of women in, 175–76; women in public office and, 164, 175, 176–77
Ellwood, David, 195
Emerson, Ralph Waldo, 34
Employment: discrimination in the workplace and, 179–80; equal rights in, 164; industrial jobs for women and, 49–50; parental leave and, 191–92; rights to education and, 48; suffrage movement and, 121, 158; women's admission to professions and, 48–49, 62, 123
Engels, Friedrich, 11
Enlightenment, 4, 10–11, 12, 37, 47
Episcopal church, 67, 81, 132
Epstein, Barbara, 61
Equal Credit Opportunity Act of 1974, 180
Equal Pay Act of 1963, 169, 180, 201

Equal Rights Amendment (ERA), 164, 170, 172, 176, 178–85; changes in public opinion on, 178–79, 180; lessons learned from defeat of, 182–84, 198; social concerns and, 184–85; women's reproductive and family roles and, 180–82

Equal Rights Association, 50, 136, 145

Equal rights feminism, 47–60, 62, 164, 200; abolition movement and, 54–56; accomplishments after 1920 of, 175–78; education and, 48; extension of equal rights and, 172–85; future directions for, 200–203; marriage and, 53–54; political involvement and, 177; professions and employment and, 48–50; property rights and, 51–53; protective legislation for women and, 185–87; public roles of women and, 165; public speaking and, 50–51; sense of own history in, 47–48; suffrage movement and, 56–60, 172–75; women's reproductive and family roles and, 180–82

Equal Rights party, 128

ERA. *See* Equal Rights Amendment (ERA)

Evangelical Christianity, 10, 12, 33, 34, 35, 47

Faludi, Susan, 164

Family: changes in women's reproductive and family roles in, 180–82; child care issues and, 179, 192–95; children's welfare and, 197; combining work with, 166–69; demographic and economic changes affecting, 35–36; equal rights feminism and, 173, 183–84; feminist goal of equality and, 171–72, 190–91; maternal associations and, 42–43; nontraditional approaches to, 196–97; parental leave and, 191–92; property rights and, 52–53; single-parent, 167, 195–96; socialist thought on, 12; of suffrage and temperance leaders, 128, 135; traditional roles of women within, 7, 227n8

Family and Medical Leave Act, 164, 192, 195

Family Support Act of 1988, 195

Federal Prison for Women Act of 1924, 189

Female Anti-Slavery Society, 54–55

Feminism and feminist movements: agenda of, 46–47; antislavery movement and, 55–56; benevolent associations and, 40; caregiving and, 185–200; discourse on sex roles in, 23–26; dynamic of specialization and "adaptive upgrading" in, 171; emergence (1830–70) of, 27–62; equal rights and, 47–50; expansion of women's roles into public sphere as part of, 9; future directions for, 200–203; grassroots support for, 16–17, 184, 198; major branches of, 27–28; origins of thought in, 9–13; in other countries, 4–7, 8–9, 201–2; patterns of conflict or integration in, 199–200; rights in relationships and, 185; social problems and, 184–85; temperance and suffrage leaders and, 135–36; temperance and suffrage movements and, 2–3, 107; temperance as vehicle for, 97–99, 240n54; terminology used in, 225n1; urbanization and, 7–8. *See also* Domestic feminism; Equal rights feminism; Women's movement

Ferraro, Geraldine, 191

Ferree, Myra M., 18, 177

Fifteenth Amendment, 59–60, 112, 114, 115

Finney, Charles, 33, 44

Finney, Joan, 177

Flexner, Eleanor, 13

Foster, Abby Kelly, 81

Foster, Jane Ellen, 86, 107

Foster, Stephen, 81

Fourier, Charles, 11

Fourteenth Amendment, 59, 112, 114, 182, 236n102

Fowler, Charles, 76, 238n28

Frame alignment, 150

France, 11, 12, 13, 27, 202, 228n21

French Revolution, 10, 27
Friedan, Betty, 169, 170, 171, 192
Friendship, 38, 231n27
Fuller, Margaret, 34, 35, 132
Functionalism, 229n34

Gamson, William A., 152
Garrison, William Lloyd, 54, 55
Gender ideology, comparisons for, 70–71, 117–19
Gender roles. *See* Roles of women
General Federation of Women's Clubs, 106, 146, 186, 189, 190
Germany, 13, 27
Gil, David, 187
Gilligan, Carol, 24–25
Glendon, Mary Ann, 182, 200
Graduate school: working women and, 166, 168–69. *See also* Higher education
Graham, Isabella Marshall, 39
Grange, 145, 146, 158
Grasso, Ella, 177
Great Britain, 4–5, 10, 13, 27, 202
Griffin, Elizabeth, 48
Grimké, Angelina, 47, 51, 55, 115
Grimké, Sarah, 7, 47, 53, 55–56, 115
Gusfield, Joseph R., 15–16, 79, 80, 87, 151

Harbert, Elizabeth Boynton, 129
Harris, William T., 23–24, 25
Harvard Medical School, 48, 49
Hay, Mary Garrett, 106, 215
Haynes, Inez, 153
Head Start program, 194
Hess, Beth B., 18, 177
Hewlett, Sylvia Ann, 183, 190–91
Higginson, Thomas Wentworth, 123, 248n67
Higher education: Republican Motherhood ideal and, 31; women's demands for, 48, 61–62, 158; working women and, 166, 168–69
Higher Education Acts of 1960 and 1972, 169
Hill, Anita, 163

Hinchey, Maggie, 149
History of Woman Suffrage, 47, 48, 137, 214, 226n1
Home Protection Ballot, 67, 86, 106, 137, 198
Horowitz, Helen Lefkowitz, 205
Howe, Julia Ward, 59, 60, 115, 117
Hughes, Everett, 89
Hunt, Harriot K., 48–49, 58, 115
Hunt, Mary H., 103

Ideology: comparison between temperance and suffrage movements for, 20; content analysis of newspapers for, 20, 68, 205–12, 117–19; ideal society in temperance movement and, 71–72; modern feminist theory and, 183–84; roles of men and women and, 68–71, 117–20, 165; social movements and, 18–20, 183
Immigration, 72, 96, 139, 148–49
Income, and working women, 166–67
Independent Order of Good Templars, 45
Individualism, 2, 12, 27, 33
Industrialization, 7, 36, 158
Industry, women's jobs in, 49–50
International Women's Year, 177, 194

James, Edward T., 214
Japan, feminism in, 5, 8–9
Jewish women, 148
Johnson, Miriam, 150
Jubilee Convention, 190
Judson, Ann Hazeltine, 40, 42

Kahne, Hilda, 195
Kansas Campaign of 1867, 114, 116
Kearney, Belle, 109
Kelley, Florence, 146, 187
Kennedy, John F., 173
Kerber, Linda, 30
Kilgore, Caroline Burnham, 115
Kinship systems, and traditional roles of women, 7
Knights of Labor, 3, 79, 242n75
Kraditor, Aileen, 13, 16, 104, 151, 173–74, 174–75

Labor force. *See* Employment, Working women
Lance, Keith, 16
Larcom, Lucy, 50
Laws: age of consent reform and, 72, 99, 100–101, 111; child care and, 194; family policy and, 190–97; parental leave and, 191–92; property rights and, 52–53; protective legislation for women and, 185–87; temperance and, 64–65; welfare state and, 187–90; workplace discrimination and, 179–80. *See also* specific laws
Leach, William, 174, 186–87
Leadership: abolition movement and, 55; barriers and innovations of, 133–35; charitable work by women and clashes over, 38–39, 232n29; comparison between temperance and suffrage movements for, 21, 79–87, 213–24; direction of feminist involvement of, 135–36; education of, 80, 128–29; equal rights feminists and, 47; family background of, 128, 135; goal attainment in social movements and, 20–21; intertwining of suffrage and temperance for, 84–87, 239n39; marriage and husbands of, 80–81, 129; new feminist movement and, 170; occupations of, 80, 129–31; personal loss and, 79, 81; public speaking and, 50–51; reform strategies used by, 22, 78–79, 84; regional background of, 132, 133; religious background and, 79, 81–84, 132; of suffrage movement, 113, 123–36, 160–61; of Woman's Christian Temperance Union (WCTU), 73–87, 110, 161
League of Women Voters, 164, 175, 177, 179, 186, 188, 189, 190
Leavitt, Mary Clement, 81
Lehlbach Act of 1923, 189
Lemlich, Clara, 148–49
Lewis, Dio, 65
Liberator (newspaper), 54
Livermore, Mary, 86, 93, 109, 115, 215, 237n12
Lockwood, Belva, 128–29

Longshore, Hannah E. Myers, 54
Longshore, Thomas, 54
Lowell Offering, 50
Loyal Temperance Legions, 72, 88
Lutheran church, 81
Lyon, Mary, 31

McCarthy, John D., 15
McCulloch, Catherine Waugh, 87, 129
"Maine law," 64–65
Mao Tse Tung, 11–12
Marilley, Suzanne M., 18, 109
Marriage: common law on rights of women in, 52; reform movement for changes in, 53–54; of suffrage and temperance leaders, 80–81, 126, 129; working women and, 167, 168
Martha Washingtonians, 45–46, 72
Martineau, Harriet, 34, 45
Marxism, 11
Maternal associations, 10, 42–43
Medicine, women's admission to, 48–49, 62, 166
Men: child care and, 179; discourse about sex roles and, 23–24; feminist goal of equality and, 171–72; gender ideology regarding roles of, 68–71, 117–20; leadership by women and, 38–39, 61–62, 232n29; moral reform societies and, 43–44; temperance societies and behavior of, 45
Meriwether, Lide, 86, 93
Merrick, Caroline, 86, 109
Methodist church, 44, 81, 84, 89, 110, 129, 132, 136, 161
Mezvinsky, Norton, 79
Middle-class women: appeals of feminist thought to, 10–11; marriage and, 53; suffrage movement and, 3, 16, 128, 145–46, 148, 149, 154; temperance movement and, 3, 72
Mill, John Stuart, 10–11
Mills College, 168
Minow, Martha, 199, 200
Missionary societies, 14, 40–42, 63, 145, 232n36: criticism of, 51; education and, 38; membership of, 158; moral authority of women and, 10; temper-

ance and, 3, 69–70, 89, 98, 100; temperance and suffrage leaders and, 132
Moody, Dwight L., 78
Moral authority of women: cult of domesticity and, 36; religion and, 10; women's rights under law and, 53
Moral reform societies, 38, 39, 43–44, 51, 61, 62, 232n30
Mormons and Mormonism, 33, 72, 99, 100, 145, 241n69
Morris, Aldon, 17
Mothers against Drunk Driving (MADD), 20
Mott, James, 51, 54
Mott, Lucretia, 47, 51, 54, 55, 56, 125
Mt. Holyoke College, 31, 146
Mt. Holyoke Female Seminary, 31, 48, 126
Mueller, Carol, 184
Murray, Judith Sargent, 30

National American Woman Suffrage Association (NAWSA), 116–17, 123, 128, 135, 151, 153, 161; internal division in suffrage movement and, 136–37; membership base of, 138, 140–41
National Conference of Charities and Corrections, 97
National Congress of Mothers, 188
National Congress of Mothers and Parent Teacher Associations, 188, 189
National Consumers' League, 146
National Council of Jewish Women, 177, 189, 194
National Economy Act of 1932, 180
National Federation of Business and Professional Women's Clubs, 189
National Federation of Labor, 149
National Federation of Women's Clubs, 106
National Labor Union, 50
National League of Women Voters, 189
National Opinion Research Center, 168
National Organization for Women (NOW), 164, 169, 170, 177, 182, 184, 191, 195, 201

National Temperance Association, 103
National Temperance Hospital, 73
National Trade Union League, 189
National Woman's Loyal League, 113–14, 126
National Woman's Party, 137, 161, 179
National Woman's Suffrage Association (NWSA), 60, 114–16, 126
National Women's Political Caucus (NWPC), 169, 177, 184
New England Woman Suffrage Association, 114
New Harmony, Indiana, community, 11
New Right, 194, 197, 200
New York Moral Reform Society, 44
New York Society for Aid to Widows and Poor Children, 39
New York State Constitutional Convention, 115
New York Woman Suffrage Association, 139
New Zealand, 3, 5, 10
Nichols, Clarinda I., 49, 58
Nightingale, Florence, 27
Nineteenth Amendment, 97, 149, 153
Nixon, Richard, 194
Norton, Mary Beth, 31, 32
Notable American Women, 133, 134

Oberlin College, 48, 51, 126
Okin, Susan Moller, 198–99, 200
Oneida, New York, community, 11, 33
O'Neill, William, 15, 16, 151, 173–74
O'Reilly, Leonora, 149
Organization: benevolent associations and, 40; comparison between temperance and suffrage movements for, 22; integration in social movements and, 21–22; suffrage movement and, 113, 136–49; of Woman's Christian Temperance Union (WCTU), 64, 87–97, 136–37; women's groups and, 62

Packers and Stockyard Act of 1921, 189
Page, Mary Hutchinson, 153–54
Parental leave, 191–92, 202
Parents. *See* Family

Park, Maud Wood, 146, 153–54
Parsons, Talcott, 171, 229n34
Patriarchy, and roles of women, 7, 227n8
Paul, Alice, 137, 139, 152, 161
Pennsylvania Constitutional Convention, 116
Pharr, Susan, 9
Phillips, Brenda, 15
Phillips, Wendell, 115
Pierce, Sarah, 31–32
Planned Parenthood, 182
Political parties: membership of women in, 176. *See also* specific parties
Populist party, 79, 146
Pregnancy Disability Act of 1978, 180, 191
Presbyterian church, 81, 84, 89, 110, 132, 136, 161
President's Commission on the Status of Women, 172, 180
Professions, women's admission to, 48–49, 62, 123, 166
Progressive party, 146, 186
Prohibition, 2, 227n3: as focus of reform movement, 15; moral reform and, 10; social change agenda with, 72; suffragists and, 22–23, 73, 155; temperance and, 107–8
Prohibition party, 79, 107–8, 146, 148
Property rights, 52–53
Prostitution, 38, 43, 44, 100, 120, 121
Protestantism: feminism and, 4, 10, 27, 47; missionary work and, 63; public speaking by women and, 51; temperance and suffrage movements and, 2, 72, 81, 139, 145, 148, 154
Providence Association for Employment of Women, 44
Public office, election of women to, 164, 175, 176–77
Public opinion, and Equal Rights Amendment (ERA), 178–79, 180
Public sphere: charitable work by women and, 38–39; domestic feminism and, 39, 232n29; educative role of women and, 36–37, 231n23; equal rights feminists and, 165; feminist movement and expansion of women's roles in, 9, 27, 61; private feminism and,

197–200; public speaking by women in, 50–51; suffrage movement and, 4, 123, 150; working women and, 12

Quakers and Quakerism, 20, 32–33, 34, 48, 54, 126, 132, 146, 161

Radcliffe College, 158, 168
Reagan, Ronald, 178
Reform strategy: comparison between temperance and suffrage movements for, 22–23; feminist subculture of women's groups and, 28; social movements and adaptation of, 22; suffrage movement and, 113, 149–60; of temperance and suffrage leaders, 22, 78–79, 84; temperance movement and, 64, 97–109, 111
Reformation, 4
Region, and temperance and suffrage leaders, 132, 133, 145
Religion: charitable work and, 37–38; culture and women's activity in, 33, 35; equality of women and principles in, 32–35, 62; missionary work and, 40–42, 232n36; moral and religious authority of women and, 10–12; revivals and, 10, 33, 227n16; social movements and, 33–34; of temperance and suffrage leaders, 79, 81–84, 132; temperance work and, 44–45, 64, 65–67, 87, 97, 240n54
Religious revivals, 10, 33, 227n16
Renaissance, 4
Reproductive rights, 164, 180–82
Republican Motherhood, 30–37, 47, 54, 62
Republican party, 107, 146, 148, 176, 178, 198
Resource mobilization theory, 15, 150
Retirement Equity Act of 1984, 180
Revolution (newspaper), 114, 121, 126
Richards, Ann, 177
Richards, Ellen H., 24, 25, 118
Rights of women. *See* Woman's rights
Roberts, Barbara, 177
Robinson, Joab, 70–71
Rockford Female Seminary, 48
Roe v. Wade, 182

Roles of women: American Revolution and rethinking of, 28–29; belief systems regarding, 20; changes in by 1870, 60–62; changes in during 1920, 90, 165–72; charitable work and, 37–38; combining work and family life in, 166–69; cultural precedents for autonomy in, 9–10; democratic principles and equality in, 29–32; domestic affairs and equality in, 35–37; emergence of women's movements and, 5–7, 9, 227n7; men's reactions to leadership as part of, 38–39, 232n29; missionary work and, 42; new feminist movement on, 169–72; newspaper articles on, 118–20; nuclear family structure and, 7, 227n8; public sphere and expansion of, 9; religious principles and equality in, 32–35; social movement theory on shifts in, 16; suffrage and, 25–26, 113, 174; temperance and suffrage movements and, 3–4, 73; types of feminist discourse on, 23–25; working women and, 180

Roosevelt, Eleanor, 173
Rose, Ernestine, 47, 50, 51, 52, 58
Rosenthal, Naomi, 16
Rossi, Alice S., 169, 170
Russian Revolution, 11
Rutgers Center on Women and Politics, 178
Ryan, Mary, 33, 34, 43

Sabbath observance, 72
Saint-Simon, Claude Henri, 11
Saloons, action against, 45, 63, 65, 233n52
Sanger, Margaret, 182
Schlafly, Phyllis, 182, 198
Schlesinger, Arthur, Sr., 237n12
Schools. *See* Education, Higher education
Schroeder, Patricia, 198
Scientific temperance instruction, 3, 72, 101–3
Scott, Andrew, 156
Scott, Anne Firor, 39–40, 145, 156, 187
Second Great Awakening, 10, 33
Senate Suffrage Committee, 108

Seneca Falls convention, 1, 32–33, 51, 56, 65, 121, 125
Settlement houses, 164, 187–88
Sex discrimination, 169
Sex roles: feminist outlook on, 23–25. *See also* Roles of women
Sexual behavior: moral reform societies and, 43–44; social purity and, 99–100; working women and family life and, 165
Shaw, Anna Howard, 101, 106, 129
Sheppard-Towner Maternity and Infancy Protection Act of 1921, 186, 188–89, 190
Shuler, Nettie, 108
Sill, Anna Peck, 48
Sinclair, Andrew, 13–15, 16
Single-parent family, 167, 195–96
Sklar, Kathryn Kish, 187
Skocpol, Theda, 16, 164, 188
Slavery: abolition movement and, 54–56; suffrage movement and, 112, 113, 132
Social movement theory, 13–15, 17, 150
Social movements, 17–23, 109–10; aspects of development of, 17–18; belief system in, 18–20, 183; leadership of, 20–21; organization of, 21–22; patterns of conflict or integration in, 199–200; religious principles in, 33–34; strategies for reform used in, 22–23
Social reform: expediency argument of feminists and, 173–75; government programs and, 99–103; modern feminist movement and, 184–85; political power and, 121–23; social purity and, 72, 73, 99–100, 111; suffrage movement and, 120–23, 145–46, 160, 174, 186–87; temperance movement and, 71–73, 93–97, 110–11; unionizing activities and, 148–49; welfare state and, 189–90; Woman's Christian Temperance Union (WCTU) and, 190
Social Security system, 178, 188, 194
Socialism, 10, 11–12, 79, 146

Society: cult of domesticity and, 36–37; temperance movement and idealization of, 71–72; traditional women's roles in, 5–7, 20, 227n7; women's movement and feminist subculture in, 28

Society of Friends, 44

Solomon, Barbara, 54

Solomon, Hannah, 135

Sons of Temperance, 45, 46, 72

Soviet Union, 11

Speeches by women, 50–51

Spencer, Anna Garlin, 101

Stanton, Elizabeth Cady, 46, 47, 51, 52, 55, 56, 58, 59, 60, 65, 84; background of, 125; on marriage, 54, 123; suffrage and, 114, 115, 116, 136, 161, 173, 174; temperance work and, 135

Stanton, Henry, 125

State Commissions on the Status of Women (SCSWs), 184

State constitutions: reform movements and, 28; suffrage and, 30, 60, 112, 116–17

State Federation of Colored Women's Clubs, 188–89

State federations of labor, 149

State laws: age of consent reform and, 72, 99, 100–101, 111; property rights and, 52–53; temperance movement and, 103, 110

States: Equal Rights Amendment (ERA) campaign in, 182–83; suffrage organizations in, 138–39; temperance organizations in, 88–93, 105, 110

Stetson, Charlotte Perkins (Gilman), 120–21

Stetson, Margaret, 191

Stevens, Lillian, 80, 97; background of, 76–78; leadership of, 67, 79

Stewart, Ella, 87, 106, 252n123

Stewart, Maria, 54, 55

Stone, Lucy, 47, 48, 51, 53–54, 58, 59, 60, 134; background of, 126–27; suffrage and, 109, 114, 115, 116, 136, 161

Strategies for reform. *See* Reform strategy

Structural-functional theory, 150

Suffrage movement, 27, 56–60, 112–62, 225n1; accomplishments of, 160–62; alliance between other groups and, 139–49; biographical comparison of leaders of, 21, 79–87, 213–24; biographical overview of leaders of, 125–28; content analysis of newspapers and, 20, 68, 205–12; critique by modern feminists of, 172–75; culture and, 156–60; Declaration of Sentiments in, 56–58; democratic principles and, 30; educational and economic opportunities and, 120–21; expediency argument of, 173–75; federal amendment for, 116, 145, 150–53; feminism and, 2–3; historical background to, 113–17; ideology of, 20, 113, 117–23; internal division in, 136–37; leaders of, 123–36, 160–61; length of time of, 112–13; membership base of, 138–39; men and, 112, 115; modern-day feminists and, 163; organization of, 136–49; prohibition and, 22–23, 73; qualifications for voting and, 58–59; reactions against, 156; reform strategies of, 149–60; rival organizations in, 59–60; roles of women and, 25–26, 113, 174; Seneca Falls convention and, 1, 32–33, 51, 56, 65, 121, 125; social change and, 72, 121–23, 174, 186–87; social movement theory on shifts in, 13–15; state constitutions and, 30, 60, 116–17; temperance contrasted with, 2–4; temperance intertwined with, 18, 73, 84–87, 239n39, 239n45; unionizing activities and, 148–49; welfare state and, 187; Woman's Christian Temperance Union (WCTU) and, 89–93, 104–9, 227n3; women's clubs and, 146–48; women's initial reactions to, 4

Supreme Court, 163, 179, 182, 186

Tactics. *See* Reform strategy

Taxation, resistance to, 58, 112, 134

Taylor, Harriet Upton, 137
Temperance movement, 63–111; biographical comparison of leaders of, 21, 79–87, 213–24; collective action against saloons in, 45, 63, 65, 233n52; content analysis of newspapers and, 20, 68, 205–12; emergence and growth of, 63; feminism and, 2–3, 63–64, 97–99, 240n54; historical roots of, 64–67; ideology of, 20, 64, 68–73; leadership of, 64, 73–87; missionary work and, 69–70, 98, 100; modern-day feminists and, 163; moral reform and, 10; publications of, 96, 129; religious beliefs and, 44–45, 64, 65–67, 97, 132, 240n54; roles of women and, 25, 38–39, 68–71; social change agenda of, 72–73, 93–97; social movement theory on shifts in, 13–15; social problems and, 71–72, 164; suffrage contrasted with, 2–4; suffrage intertwined with, 18, 73, 84–87, 89–93, 104–9, 239n39, 239n45; urban society and, 46; welfare state and, 187; women's groups in, 44–47, 61, 62. *See also* Woman's Christian Temperance Union (WCTU)
Thirteenth Amendment, 114
Thomas, Clarence, 163
Thomas, M. Carey, 146, 153
Thomas, Mary Frame Myers, 54
Thomas, Owen, 54
Trade union movement, 3, 89, 148–49, 188
Train, George Francis, 114
Transcendentalism, 34–35
Triangle Shirtwaist factory, 148
Truth, Sojourner, 56

Union movement, 3, 89, 148–49, 158, 188
Union Signal (newspaper), 63, 67, 96, 99, 101, 104, 108, 109, 110, 117, 237n13, 237n14; content analysis of, 20, 68, 205–12; images of women and men in, 69–71, 117–19; reform themes in, 73, 74; social problems portrayed in,

71–72; suffrage themes in, 121, 122–23
Unitarian church, 34, 132, 146, 161
United Methodist Women, 177
Universalist church, 44, 76, 129, 132
Universities. *See* Higher education
University of California at Los Angeles, 168
University of Iowa, 48
University of Michigan, 158, 168, 179
Upper-class women, and suffrage, 16
Urbanization: feminism and, 7–8; maternal associations and, 42–43; suffrage movement and, 158; temperance movement and, 46

Voluntary associations, 42
Voting: as focus of reform movement, 15; gender gap in, 177–78; qualifications for, 58–59; turnout of women for, 175–76; women in public office and, 164, 175, 176–77. *See also* Suffrage

Wald, Lillian, 146
Wallace, Zerelda, 86, 215
Wandersee, Winifred, 185–86
Warren, Mercy Otis, 30
Washington, George, 30
Washington, Martha, 30
Washingtonians, 45–46, 72
WCTU. *See* Woman's Christian Temperance Union (WCTU)
Weitzman, Lenore, 196
Welfare state, 187–90
Welter, Barbara, 36
Wexler, Sherry, 195
Wheaton Female Seminary, 31
White House Conference on Families, 194
White slavery, 72, 99, 111
Whitman, Christine Todd, 177
Willard, Frances, 3, 31, 67, 80, 87, 100, 101, 198, 238n28, 242n75; background of, 75–76, 128; leadership of, 79, 86; suffrage and, 105, 107, 108; temperance work with individuals by, 98–99

Willing, Jane Fowler, 96
Wilson, Woodrow, 152, 154
Wittenmyer, Annie, 65, 67, 76, 80, 86, 96, 103; background of, 75; leadership of, 78–79; suffrage and, 105
Wolf, Naomi, 164
Wollstonecraft, 30, 31
Woman's Christian Temperance Union (WCTU), 3, 5, 60, 145, 198; age of consent reform and, 100–101; biographical comparison of leaders of, 21, 79–87, 213–24; biographical overview of three presidents of, 75–78; content analysis of newspaper of, 68, 205–12; cooperation between suffragists and, 18; emergence and growth of, 63, 88–89; equal rights for women and, 103–9; expediency argument of, 173; feminism and, 107; leadership of, 73–87, 161; membership base of, 138, 139, 159; organization of, 64, 87–97, 136–37; Prohibition party and, 107–8; publications of, 96, 129; reform strategy of, 64, 97–109; religion and, 64, 97, 240n54; scientific temperance instruction by, 3, 72, 101–3; significance of, 109–11; social movement theory on shifts in, 15–16; social purity and, 99–100; social reform and, 190; specialized departments for social change in, 93–97, 110–11; state unions in, 88–93; temperance and suffrage themes intertwined in, 104–9, 155, 227n3
Woman's Journal, 24, 86, 104, 127, 129, 137, 155, 238n19, 248n67; accomplishments of women in, 123; content analysis of, 20, 68, 205–12; images of women and men in, 69, 70–71, 117–19; reform themes in, 73, 74, 120, 146; suffrage themes in, 121, 122–23, 146, 148, 153, 159
Woman's Party, 137, 139, 151–52, 164, 178, 179, 186, 198
Woman's rights: abolition movement and, 55; caregiving and, 164; Declaration of Sentiments on, 56–58; pressure in

other countries for, 4–7; public speaking by women concerning, 50–51
Woman's Rights Conventions, 49, 51, 56, 58, 59, 126
Woman's Temperance Convention, 46
Woman's Temperance Crusade, 20–21, 75
Woman's Temperance Publishing Society, 96
Woman's Temperance Union (newspaper), 96
Women's Agenda, 184
Women's Bureau, 179, 186, 190
Women's clubs, groups, and organizations: agenda of, 46–47; antislavery movement and, 54–55; benevolent work by, 39–40; changes in women's roles and, 60–61; contributions made by, 14, 16; maternal associations and, 42–43; men's reactions to women's leadership in, 38–39, 61–62, 232n29; missionary work by, 40–42, 232n36; moral reform and, 43–44; new feminist movement and, 169; social reform and, 99, 145, 146–48, 164; suffrage and, 156; temperance groups and, 44–47, 89; welfare state and, 187, 188, 190; women's movement and feminist subculture of, 28; working for change and, 27, 28. *See also* specific groups
Women's Equity Action League (WEAL), 169, 177
Women's Joint Congressional Committee, 189
Women's movement: feminist subculture and, 28; future directions for, 200–203; modern-day feminists and social reform and, 164; in the 1990s, 164; in other countries, 4–7; structural features of, 13–23; temperance movement and, 84; traditional roles of women and emergence of, 5–7, 227n7. *See also* Feminism and feminist movements
Women's roles. *See* Roles of women

Women's Trade Union League (WTUL), 2, 3, 148–49, 154
Wooley, Mary, 146
Wooster, College of, 48
Work incentive (WIN) program, 194
Working class, and appeals of feminist thought, 11–12
Working women: contributions to family income by, 166–67; discrimination in the workplace against, 179–80; family life and, 166–69; higher education and, 166, 168–69; improvement in conditions for, 101; jobs in industry for, 49–50; maternal associations and, 43; new feminism and, 171; professions and, 48–49; protective legislation for women and, 186; reorganization of typical life of, 167–68; single-parent families and, 167; suffrage and, 121, 145–46, 148–49, 158; temperance and suffrage movements and, 3; unionizing activities and, 148–49
Working women's associations, 50, 114, 121
World War I, 5
World War II, 5, 8, 166, 192, 198
World's Anti-Slavery Convention, 55, 56, 125
World's Congress of Representative Women, 87
Wright, Fanny, 47, 50

Zakrewska, Marie, 48, 49
Zald, Mayer N., 15

The Author

Janet Zollinger Giele is professor and director of the Family and Children's Policy Center at the Heller Graduate School of Social Welfare at Brandeis University. She holds a Ph.D. from Harvard University and has been the recipient of grants and awards from the Woodrow Wilson Foundation, the Bunting Institute of Radcliffe College, the Ford Foundation, the Lilly Endowment, the National Institute on Aging, and the Rockefeller Foundation. She is the author of *Women: Roles and Status in Eight Countries* (1977), *Women and the Future* (1978), and *Women in the Middle Years* (1982) and coeditor with Hilda Kahne of *Women's Work and Women's Lives: The Continuing Struggle Worldwide* (1992).